Weston Reay

Francis Willington

A life for the foreign missions

Weston Reay

Francis Willington
A life for the foreign missions

ISBN/EAN: 9783741143526

Manufactured in Europe, USA, Canada, Australia, Japa

Cover: Foto ©Andreas Hilbeck / pixelio.de

Manufactured and distributed by brebook publishing software (www.brebook.com)

Weston Reay

Francis Willington

Francis Willington;

OR, A

Life for the Foreign Missions.

ST. JOSEPH'S FOREIGN MISSIONARY COLLEGE OF THE SACRED HEART, MILL HILL, LONDON.

Francis Willington;

OR, A

Life for the Foreign Missions;

BY WESTON REAY.

WITH A PREFACE

BY THE REV. ISAAC MOORE, S.J.

THOMAS RICHARDSON AND SON,
LONDON AND DERBY.
1879.

Dedicated

By permission,

With most profound respect,

To the Right Rev. Dr. Herbert Vaughan,

Bishop of Salford,

and

Founder of St. Joseph's College for
Foreign Missions,

Mill Hill, London.

INDEX.

CHAPTER.	PAGE.
I.—THE OLD MANOR.—THE BROTHER AND SISTER.—DREAMS OF CHILDHOOD	1
II.—THE FAMILY AT THE MANOR	13
III.—IS IT A VOCATION?	30
IV.—PREPARATION FOR THE WORK.—OPPOSING VIEWS	51
V.—THE BROTHER AND SISTER ONCE MORE AT HOME.—CAPTAIN WARNFORD.—THE DEPARTURE OF FRANCIS	68
VI.—THREE YEARS LATER.—A DEATH.—THE FIRST DARK CLOUD	92
VII.—OLD SCENES.—" NOW," AND "THEN."—AGNES GROWN UP	109
VIII.—THE ANNOUNCEMENT.—RESULTS	140
IX.—DEPARTURES	184
X.—THE ORDINATION.—THE FIRST MASS	204
XI.—TWO SCENES FROM REAL LIFE, WHICH SEEM TO HAVE NO CONNECTION WITH OUR HISTORY	224

CHAPTER.	PAGE.
XII.—The Departure of Francis for the East	235
XIII.—A new phase in a life's history.—The Apostleship of Suffering.—Father Neville's secret	259
XIV.—Clara Herbert.—The Letter from Agnes	274
XV.—Divers "Views" on the Work of the Foreign Missions	288
XVI.—How Clara Herbert found "something to do"	298
XVII.—A year later.—Apostolic seed.—The approach of the term	311
XVIII.—"Preparations for Departure" once more.—Nunc Dimittis	326
XIX.—Departure of the Missioner.—"Ite Missa est"	340

Preface.

The tales, whether told in prose or verse, in which men take most delight, are those in which the play of those passions most strongly and universally felt, is depicted. Hence, stories of war, and stories of love, and particularly love stories, have been, and ever will be popular. Nor is the very marked liking for such tales, which is so common, the outcome of any of the baser instincts of our nature. Pure human love, ennobled by the teachings of the Christian Faith, is in itself beautiful and admirable. It checks and crushes the grosser impulses, and prompts to much that is unselfish, even heroic: it claims and commands sympathy. When, however, the strong love of a manly heart is fixed, not on any merely human, but on a divine object, we behold a radiant transfiguration. The heart of the man, and the love it gives forth, glow with a light reflected from on high—a light which beautifies all it falls upon. That light, that heat divine, always given in exchange to every human heart that fixes, or even tries to fix, its affections on God; burns up all that is base, all that is selfish in the human heart; and makes man God-like. There are doubtless other men who labour and suffer, nor is their toil or sorrow borne all for self. For there are, in the order of nature, pure affections, noble ambitions. But where the strong love of God has filled the heart, man claims fellowship with Christ. He desires to live only to labour and to suffer, without one thought of self, for others' good; to bring light to "them that sit in darkness;" to be to them as a ministering angel amidst the manifold woes and wants of life; to help them in their distress; to comfort them in misery; to lead their steps into the paths of peace; to make their lives beautiful with the charm of Christian virtue, and their death blissful with the hope of eternal joy. Now, this little story is all about the birth, the growth, the action of this all-divine, all-sacrificing love in a human heart. From those who are not "heirs of the promise" it is vain to expect much sympathy: a story, telling of a life utterly unselfish, utterly unworldly, can have little interest for them. But one cannot help thinking it will stir with emulous impulse many a generous heart. How many such there are in England at this day, let all the noble sacrifices made for conscience sake in the life-time of this generation bear witness. It is to such this story is addressed, to those who are the true followers of Him whose doctrine it is "that we ought to lay down our lives for the brethren." (1 John iii. 16.)

ISAAC MOORE, S.J.

111, Mount Street, W.

FRANCIS WILLINGTON;

OR,

A Life for the Foreign Missions.

"IGNEM VENI MITTERE IN TERRAM: ET QUID VOLO, NISI UT ACCENDATUR?"—S. LUKE, XII. 49.

CHAPTER I.

The old Manor.—The Brother and Sister.—Dreams of Childhood.

A remarkable outpouring of divine charity in our day has wonderfully revived among Catholics in England the most lively interest in the noble work of the Foreign Missions. Many a heart has opened to receive the sweet influences of unbounded brotherly charity for the poor Heathen, as the vast prospect of this God-like enterprise burst in surpassing grandeur upon the eye of the soul.

Often, by the blessing of God, an earnest word of compassion for the millions perishing in heathen darkness has aroused and lit up the spirit of prayer and apostolic zeal in hearts that were slumbering or cold, and the fire by degrees has spread, so that dear England at length has her share, with faithful Ireland, with noble-hearted France, and other Catholic nations, in the glory of sending forth, from a College in her midst, bands of intrepid missioners, bearing the glad message of salvation to the uttermost parts of the earth.

The hardships bravely borne, and, if need be, the blood cheerfully shed by these apostles of the Crucified, will draw down blessings on the land they have so generously forsaken "*for the joy set before them.*" What unspeakable joy shall be theirs when they at last receive their crown from the pierced hands of their Master, from Him Who, seeking the lost, left His throne in heaven, to embrace on earth suffering and shedding of His Blood, that He might bring life and salvation to those sitting in the shadow of death.

May this simple history of a noble English life, consumed with love for the poor Heathen, awaken sympathy in some hearts as yet untouched, and animate them with the holy zeal of promoting, by every means within their reach, so glorious and Christ-like an enterprise as is that of the Foreign Missions.

The golden sun of an August evening, in the year 1849, was declining, and gilding with its gorgeous rays the tall umbrageous trees that ornament the spacious grounds of the old manor of Willington. Here they formed avenues; there, clustered in groups on the greensward, which stretched out in picturesque inequality of hill and dale, until by a gentle slope it met the right bank of a rapid river, traversing the entire domain. This was the living charm of the landscape, sometimes visibly rippling between verdant meadows that bordered it on either side, at others continuing its course through a wood of some extent, where its waters were lost sight of, excepting by those who may be passing along the pathway high up in the wood, and who may thus look down through the shade at the swift stream hurrying onwards to the sea, into which it empties itself at the distance of about a mile beyond the boundary of the manor grounds.

At the entrance of the wood, a little above the pathway alluded to, was a rocky projection, only attainable by climbing some steps roughly cut in the soil, and half hidden by the underwood and wild flowers which grew there in profusion. Having reached what might be termed the summit of the rock, a kind of table land presented itself, upon which some care had been bestowed in order to render it what it was evidently intended to be, a little spot of devotion, or shrine,—chapel it could not be called, for there was no attempt at forming a shelter of any kind from the heat of summer, or from the rain and wind of winter. It was simply a species of altar, such as we read of the missionaries building up in haste, in desert places, in order to offer up the Holy Sacrifice, when journeying to their destined missions.

On the evening we speak of, fresh and beautiful flowers were carefully arranged on either side of the large rough stone crucifix which stood on the slab which was intended to represent an altar; and amid the wild herbage fringing the rock, and forming as it were a natural reredos, were entwined some magnificent flowering shrubs of South American and Eastern origin, conveyed from the hothouses by the busy hands of the two children who stand together engaged in conversation of a more serious character than the youth of the speakers would lead us to expect.

Let us draw near, and listen to the words which pass between the brother and sister as they stand upon the level of the rock, before the mimic altar, in the golden light of that August evening.

"This, then, is our last walk together for many a long day, my little Agnes," said her brother, as he fondly smoothed the long golden hair of the little girl, who was gazing with her large earnest blue eyes upon the vast expanse of sea which stretched out before them in the distance. "I could not help thinking of it to-day, when the Bishop said we were now *soldiers of the Cross*, and then spoke so beautifully of the Sacred Heart of Jesus, and how the Spirit of Love we have received to-day will sweeten whatever is hard to bear."

"Yes; so very hard," replied Agnes, echoing her brother's last words, while tears, which she bravely strove to suppress, suffused her eyes.

"Never mind, darling; we shall come home at Christmas," said Francis, with the tender encouraging air of a brother just two years older than the loving little being he addressed. "And then," he continued, "we shall be able to tell each other all we have learnt, and are going to learn, and we will come and visit my desert altar again, and I will paddle you across to Sancian, and tell you all the new things I have read about the missionaries, as we sit together in the hut of S. Francis."

Agnes's eyes brightened as she listened to the genial tones of Francis, and then, with one of those sighs which the innocent hearts of children alone can give forth, she said, "Oh! what a happy day this has been, after all, Francis, has it not? If it had not been for our separation to-morrow, and the departure of dear Madame this morning, it would have been almost like heaven. I never shall forget how I felt when, coming out from the chapel after holy Confirmation, Father Neville met me, and said: 'Now the beautiful Spirit of Jesus is resting in little Agnes's breast.'"

"Yes," murmured the boy, in a low voice, "that beautiful Spirit, He is ours; He is come to make us strong in doing God's will, and God's will is that 'all men should be saved.' And now *we* are soldiers, Agnes, you and I, to fight God's battles, and help to save men. Oh, if ever I wished to be good, I wish it a thousand thousand times more to-day; do not you feel the same, Agnes?"

"Oh, yes," replied Agnes, softly, we had almost said prayerfully; and then she was silent. Perhaps she felt instinctively there was something in her brother's words a little above her comprehension.

They had scarcely ceased speaking, when three figures appeared coming towards them. The faces of both brother and sister were instantly beaming, and whatever traces of pensiveness their previous conversation had left upon them immediately vanished as they darted forward to meet the three gentlemen, who were advancing slowly, and with measured steps, in the direction of the children.

"Oh, my lord," both exclaimed together, as they knelt for an instant before the venerable figure whose purple bordered soutane, and whose pectoral cross announced to be a Bishop; "Oh, my lord, how glad we are you are come out." And then they continued talking to him in a strain of frank simplicity, mingled with reverence, which testified that the affectionate confidence of childhood was not prejudicial to the respect due to the ecclesiastical dignity of him whom they addressed. It was the Bishop of the diocese, who had come on the present occasion to give Confirmation in the domestic chapel of his old friend Colonel Willington, not only to the son and daughter of the latter, but also to the children of the few Catholics, who, in that remote part of the West of England were found scattered here and there in the neighbourhood. It had been his custom to pay a visit to the Manor whenever he passed through that part of his diocese; thus Colonel Willington's children were no strangers to him, whilst his amiability of character, and his love of "*the little ones*," had won the confidence of their young hearts, no less than their veneration.

"Ah! here is Francis's altar; it wears to-day quite a festive appearance," said the Colonel, pointing with his stick to the rock at a little elevation from where they stood.

"It is our Confirmation day, you know, papa," said Francis; "besides, to-morrow"—he paused a moment, and then added bravely—"to-morrow I bid adieu to my desert altar, and go to St. Edgar's for hard work."

"And Agnes also leaves at the same time, does she not?" said the Bishop.

"Yes," replied the Colonel, smiling fondly at the bright little girl who held his hand; "she goes to the good nuns at Torrington, so we shall be only three at the old place, Father Neville, Mrs. Willington, and myself."

Father Neville was in lively conversation with his young friend and pupil, Francis, when the latter suddenly broke away from him, and running up to his father, said gaily: "Papa, Father Neville will not be persuaded that his lordship will let me paddle him across to Sancian, and I am sure he will. Will you not, my lord?" he added, turning with his bright animated countenance to the Bishop, who was not a little at a loss to conjecture what amount of courage he was thus suddenly called upon to display.

"You must first let me know," he replied, laughing, "where is your 'Sancian,' and what is your means of transport thither; then I will see what courage I can muster for confiding myself to your guidance."

"Oh, yes; come, come this way," cried both the children, delightedly, as they proceeded to enter on a winding narrow pathway, hedged on either side by luxuriant shrubs, and which gradually conducted to the banks of the river.

Immediately in front of the spot on which they found themselves, the banks suddenly receded, so as to form a broad space of water, in the centre of which was a small but complete island, covered with underwood and thickets, and a few trees. This was the "Sancian" of Francis's youthful imagination, and in order to reach it he had, with the aid of Philip, the faithful follower of the Colonel in his former military career, and now a domestic at the Manor, made a rough but tolerably substantial raft, by means of which the island could be reached in safety.

"Now, my lord, see my raft, by which I can conduct you to the hut of St. Francis Xavier," cried Francis, as he stooped down to unfasten the cord which attached the raft to the bank, and then, jumping upon it, bowed playfully to those who were standing on the shore, inviting them to follow him.

"She's quite safe, if your lordship will please to step on," said a familiar voice behind them; and turning round they beheld a bright eyed, sunburnt, intelligent looking man, his hat in his hand, as he inclined profoundly before the Bishop to receive his blessing, for the difficulty of kneeling upon that uneven ground, with the inconvenience of a wooden leg, was evident.

"Ah, Philip, is that you?" said the Colonel. "You are just the man we want. Master Francis is bent upon paddling us over to his "Sancian," and I think the voyage, short though it is, will be made more prosperously if you give a hand."

And accordingly Philip hopped on to the raft, and all having stepped on it, it was launched, Francis paddling on one side and Philip on the other, until, partly by their efforts, and partly by the drift of the current, they reached the island, in that part where a few roughly cut steps afforded a landing, and from thence, by a narrow pathway from which the underwood and briars had been cleared, they followed Francis, who led the procession exultingly to what he called the *Hut of St. Francis Xavier*, an open shed, with a stone for a seat, and whose only ornaments were a large wooden cross, and a small framed engraving of the well known representation of St. Francis, the apostle of the Indies, dying.

"There," said Father Neville, "our future little missionary has done all this; built up the hut, and cleared away the briars and thickets, and made the raft, and"—

"With the assistance of Philip, in good measure, I fancy," said the Colonel, laughing.

"Oh, yes," cried Francis, "Philip has helped me to do it all, and also to cut the steps which lead to my altar, which you saw just now, my lord;" for it was the Bishop whom he was initiating into the exploits of his youthful devotion—"and to fill up the hollow places in the rock, so as to form a flat place for an altar; and on feasts, Philip brings flowers from the hothouses of which he has the care, and puts some on my desert altar, and some here under the picture of St. Francis."

The boy turned as he spoke, and looked affectionately towards the sunburnt soldier of former days, who stood respectfully apart, but whose eyes, moistened with tears, regarded his master's son with pride mingled with tenderness, reading in that sparkling animated countenance, as he believed, the promise of a future soldier, brave as had been his father.

"What are you doing, Father Neville?" cried out Agnes, as she perceived the good Priest busily engaged in cutting some letters on the trunk of a tree which grew at the entrance of the hut, and indeed formed one of the posts supporting it.

"Read;" he answered, smiling. Agnes looked at the characters, and then, calling to her brother, exclaimed delightedly, "Oh, Francis, come and see what Father Neville has written. 'Francis John de Britto, ...Agnes Teresa. Aug. 20th, 1849.'"

At the sound of that second name he had received that day in Confirmation, the whole conntenance of

Francis seemed for a moment transformed. Instead of a boy of twelve years only, he appeared to be suddenly gifted with the thoughtfulness, the mental strength of manhood. The expression which passed over his face was but momentary, but it told of capacities of heart and mind which at so early an age can rarely be discerned.

"Francis John de Britto," said the Bishop, smiling, "I congratulate you on your attempts to learn arts useful for missionary life, as it is evident you have done here, and I hope one day you will"—

"Say, 'Be a missionary,' do say it, my lord," whispered the boy, as he clung to the Bishop's arm, and looked up with his dark earnest eyes into his face.

"Well, I hope you may be a missionary, my child, if it is God's holy will: time must prove that."

"And little Agnes Teresa a Carmelite, my lord, of course," said Father Neville, with a playful glance at Agnes.

"Ah, possibly; time also must prove that. It needs more than the name to give a vocation," answered the Bishop, half playfully, half seriously. "What does the Teresa of to-day say to it? Did you wish to be a daughter of St. Teresa when you chose her name in Confirmation, my child?"

"Oh, no, no," answered Agnes, laughing; and with entire ingenuousness she added, "I should not like to be shut up behind a *grille*, like those nuns in France that Madame de Musillon has told me so much of. I chose the name of St. Teresa because, since I have read her life, I love her so much, and because she had such hard work to be as good as God wished her to be, and because she loved her brother Rodriguez so much, and was so loving for all the world."

"And so you are going to try and imitate her, by loving all the world in the way she did, eh, little one?" said Father Neville, smiling.

"I am going to pray to her very much, Father, and try to know more about her," replied Agnes, as she leapt from the island to the raft, for they were now about to return to the house, it being the hour of Benediction.

That evening the brother and sister mingled their voices for the last time, at least for some months, in singing at the sweet Benediction service. It was a fitting close to the day of their Confirmation, a fitting preparation for the separation which was to take place upon the morrow.

CHAPTER II.

The Family at the Manor.

Whilst the carriage is swiftly bearing away from the old home, Francis and Agnes Willington, accompanied by the Colonel, to their respective destinations, for the purpose of pursuing their studies with every possible advantage, spiritual as well as intellectual, let us give a brief sketch of the family, one of whose members will form the principal object of interest in this little narrative.

Colonel Willington, although the heir to a considerable property, had in early life embraced the profession of arms, and had passed nearly the whole of his military course in different parts of India. His career had been active and brilliant, but short, having received a wound in a sanguinary engagement with the Sikhs, whilst he was still in the vigour of manhood, which rendered retirement from actual service absolutely necessary. And thus it was that he returned to his ancestral home just in time to close the dying eyes of his aged father, whose death would, in any case, have required his presence at the

Manor, where it would now be incumbent on him chiefly to reside.

During a year's leave of absence from his regiment, which had been granted to him a few years after his first arrival in India, when he had returned to England for the purpose of recruiting his health, which had become impaired by the climate of the East, he had married a young lady of qualities both of mind and heart which rendered her in every way desirable for the wife of one whose birth and position in society enabled him to co-operate in an influential manner with all Catholic interests. Several children had been born to them, of whom, however, Stanislaus the eldest son, and Francis and Agnes the two youngest children, alone survived. With the exception of the two latter, all had been born in India, whither Mrs. Willington had accompanied her husband shortly after their marriage, but from whence some years after she had been obliged to return in consequence of extreme delicacy of health, bringing with her her children then surviving. Francis was born a year after the final return of Colonel Willington from India, which we have already referred to, and Agnes was scarcely two years his junior.

Until the period at which our narrative opens, Agnes had been exclusively under the tutelage of a French lady of high birth and of more than ordinary mental endowments, but whom reverse of fortune, and the caprice of a rich and aged relative had compelled to seek some remunerative occupation. Colonel and Mrs.

Willington had made the acquaintance of Madame de Masillon in one of their not unfrequent visits to the French capital, and had recognized in her a person in every way fitting for the charge of governess to their little Agnes. Madame de Masillon had moreover been the instructress of Francis in several languages, and had also, by her skill and attention, developed in him, as well as in his sister, the musical talents which both possessed in a remarkable degree.

The departure of Madame de Masillon from the Manor, which we have mentioned in the preceding chapter as having taken place on the Confirmation day of the brother and sister, was occasioned by the approaching death of the aged relative whose caprice had driven her to seek a home on a foreign shore, but who now recalled her in order to obtain her forgiveness for the past and a reconciliation before his supreme hour should have arrived. The parting was felt by both her young pupils as a severe trial, for they loved her tenderly; nor was she less regretted by all at the Manor, for all esteemed her highly, whilst Mrs. Willington, whom habitual ill-health obliged frequently to many hours of solitude, had found in her a true friend, whose companionship had been a solace in many seasons of sharp suffering, and the weary languor resulting from it.

There was another inmate of the Manor regarding whom we must say a few words, inasmuch as he will frequently appear during the course of this narrative.

Father Neville had formed the acquaintance of Colonel Willington before the latter had entered on his military career, but it was only after many years of separation that ordinary acquaintanceship was to ripen into intimate friendship. They met again for the first time at the house of a mutual friend, where Colonel Willington was paying a short visit as he was journeying homewards. They spoke of their former acquaintanceship, and of the many changes that had occurred in the lives of each during the intervening years.

It was at the conclusion of a long and earnest conversation that the Colonel had thus addressed his companion : " Father Neville, I have a proposition to make to you. Will you come and live at the Manor with us ? The good priest who for some years was my father's chaplain wanted, he said, more work to do, and could not rest until he went off to some very busy mission. Since his departure last year my father has been unable to meet with a suitable priest to replace him. You know, moreover, that my dear father is drawing near his last hour, and I wish you to be near him. I am returning home a maimed old soldier," he added, with a half sad smile, as he moved his wounded arm, still supported in a sling, " and you— you have also"— He paused, for at that instant an expression swept over the countenance of the priest which stayed the words which were about to follow.

Father Neville's hands were clasped, and his head bent down upon them: then, raising it, he said, with

or, a Life for the Foreign Missions. 17

one of those smiles which only appear on the faces of persons whose souls have learnt in the school of suffering to sanctify human passion, by bringing it into subjection to the Divine Will: "I know what you would say; but the wound even yet is bleeding, it must not be touched, even by one I value as much as you. Let me hear the rest of your proposition," he added, immediately recovering from his emotion, and resuming his accustomed serene cheerfulness, with that ease which those long practised in interior mortification acquire.

"Well," continued the Colonel, in a tone which was rendered gentler and more genial even than was its wont by the passing struggle he had just witnessed in his friend, "if you like the idea of coming to be our chaplain at the old place, I can promise you a sincere welcome; as much society as you will care for; abundant time for your literary labours, for the quiet pursuit of which every facility shall be afforded you; a devotional old chapel in which to say your daily Mass, and more souls to look after than you might imagine in a rural district. What do you say, will you come with me?"

"I will say holy Mass to-morrow for the intention of knowing God's will in the matter," replied Father Neville.

When Colonel Willington returned to his home he was accompanied by the good priest he esteemed so much, and who became the resident chaplain, the sincere friend and spiritual father and guide of the whole family.

Such was the tutor of Francis Willington's early years. Naturally inclined for study, the boy had found in Father Neville a master well skilled in awakening his desire of knowledge, and in exciting his thirst for all that might enable him to glorify God by the cultivation of his intellect. The experienced eye of the man of letters had discerned in the young Francis, even at a very early age, not only a more than ordinary aptitude for study, but also a breadth and depth of thought, and a latent power which augured that his career in life, whatever it was destined to be, would in all probability be one of more than common interest and usefulness.

Although he had, as yet, been thrown but little amongst other youths, and that moreover he was possessed of a temper naturally amiable, nevertheless there was not a vestige of effeminacy in his character or in his bearing; on the contrary, there was a certain vigour which was something different to the mere buoyancy of early youth, mingled with an earnestness, a reflectiveness discernible to all.

The character of his father had moreover, in all probability, a beneficial influence upon the young Francis. Colonel Willington, although possessing in an eminent degree a genuine practical piety, was nevertheless a thorough soldier, in the true sense of the word. He had embraced, as we have already said, the profession of arms from choice, and Providence had favoured him in contriving for him a career which was in accordance with his inclinations; that is to say, active service in a foreign land. The associations connected with a military life, above all in India, had been in no way prejudicial to his religious principles, or to his practical piety; on the contrary, all that he saw around him did but deepen the roots of faith in his soul, and render his sentiments of gratitude more profound for the knowledge of that truth which he possessed in all its fulness. He had become, moreover, deeply interested in the people amongst whom he lived, in the men, above all, who were the native defenders of the British possessions, the poor despised Sepoys. The Colonel was a devoted patriot, as every true soldier must be; and as he studied the character of those men, so passionately devoted to what they believed worthy of their confidence and esteem, he saw the source of those terrible mutinies which from time to time send a panic across the ocean to English shores, and strike terror to English hearts; he saw at the same time how their conversion to a religion wherein they would find all the antiquity and grandeur, all the self-denial and purity their noble natures loved, would render them faithful allies, strong in their devotedness, to which their very pride would be subservient.

Colonel Willington, moreover, regarded the race amongst whom it was his lot for many years to live, not only with the eye of a patriot, but also with the heart of a Catholic. He discerned the faint traces of a long lost faith, which centuries of error had perverted into horrible idolatry. He discovered it in the preeminent place which the idea of sacrifice holds in the mind of the Hindoo, in the self-imposed penance, in the dedication of children to lives of public expiation, and in many other practices existing amongst the Brahmins, which, although distorted, are manifestly the glimmering embers of an ancient faith, and as he saw in that people the capacity for appreciating and grasping the breadth and length and height and depth of the religion of Christ, his Catholic heart ached for their misfortune in being alien to that faith which would sanctify their passionate natures, and direct all that devotedness which they testify in the worship of their false deities, into its legitimate channel—the glory of the Living God.

But although the Colonel was a true-hearted Catholic, he was not a *Catholic Missioner*. He beheld the miseries of that people, and he mourned for them; he saw the material difficulties that are stumbling-blocks to their conversion; he comprehended in all its extent the formidable obstacle opposed to the Hindoo's conversion in his horror of *loss of caste*, the inevitable result of his reception of Christianity; but had he had the vocation of a missioner, the memory of the Heart of Jesus, with its quenchless thirst for the salvation of *all* men, would have risen up before him to inspire him with more hopeful thoughts. He would have recalled to himself how the burning words of those sent to preach "the glad tidings of the Gospel," telling the poor Heathen of a love they had never imagined in their wildest dreams, had awakened their benighted intellect, and opened the well-springs in their poor hearts, which until then had been closed. But the soldier and the patriot, with his true Catholic heart, did what he could, what we all can do, he prayed for that unhappy race for whose conversion so many martyrs have shed their blood, and until his death he failed not daily to put up the well known prayer of S. Francis Xavier for the conversion of infidels, of whose misery he had been so long the witness.

The life which Colonel Willington had led after his final return to England had been quiet without being isolated. There was but little society, it was true, in the immediate vicinity of the Manor, but the Willington family was well and widely known amongst the higher circles of Catholic society, whilst the Colonel's military connection brought many a visit from old friends and former companions in arms, to whom his house was ever hospitably open.

The Manor was celebrated amongst those who knew it, for its genial cordiality and intellectual cheerfulness, which formed, as it were, its distinguishing character. Even men of learning, as well as accomplished politicians, found in the extensive fund of general knowledge which the Colonel possessed, a fertile source from whence to draw useful information for themselves, whilst the charm and variety of his conversation were such that his society was regarded as a rare and valued pleasure by all who were admitted to its enjoyment.

Ecclesiastics found in this true type of an English gentleman, a faithful friend and sincere helper in every good work, whilst a cordial welcome at all times awaited them at his house. But there was one class amongst those invested with the sacerdotal dignity for whom the Colonel had throughout his life entertained a very special predilection. At home or abroad, he had ever found particular satisfaction in the company of the Fathers of the Society of Jesus, amongst whom he felt himself as much at ease as with members of his own family, or with the most esteemed of the companions to whom his military career had associated him, and having met many of these Fathers at various epochs of his life, he was enabled, from time to time, to contrive for himself and for his family the privilege of a visit from one or more of them at the Manor.

It will be evident that such a man as Colonel Willington would be utterly opposed to anything like empty sentimentality in his children. It was a subject of secret satisfaction to him when he perceived in the little Francis the promise and the marks of a man vigorous in thought and earnest in purpose, although he suspected not the source from whence that vigour and that earnestness were derived.

Francis had scarcely attained his eighth year when he began to be familiarly called by those who knew him, and were the witnesses of the evident bent of his inclinations, the *Little Missioner:* nevertheless, neither his father nor any of those who thus addressed him—save one, which was Father Neville—attached any serious importance to his childish predilections, or regarded them as real manifestations of a future vocation.

Once he had been surprised in the little sacristy where Father Neville was accustomed to vest for Mass, standing before the crucifix, and fully vested in the sacerdotal vestments which were awaiting the arrival of the priest at the appointed hour, his arms extended after the manner of the celebrant during the Canon of the Mass, his eyes uplifted and rivetted on the crucifix, whilst upon the child's face shone forth that radiance which is rarely to be seen, but which sometimes accompanies intense prayer. The man who served as senior acolyte, on looking through the glass door of the sacristy, started at the strange scene before him, but discerning in it nothing more than the playful action of a child, was about to proffer some words of reproof for the disarrangement of the vestments. At the same moment Father Neville appeared. His quick eye saw all in a glance.

"Hush!" he said, almost sternly, to the acolyte,

who was regarding with ruffled countenance the alb and chasuble, which, as may be supposed, lay on the ground from the little shoulders of the mimic priest; then, approaching the child, he kindly laid his hand upon his head, and said in a low voice: "My child, what are you doing?"

Francis was slightly confused at being thus surprised, but on seeing who was his inquirer, he looked up confidently into the old Priest's face, and without seeming to interrupt the interior thought which absorbed him, he replied: "Oh, my Father, I pray for the poor Heathen. Oh, how I wish I could say Mass for them."

The hand of Father Neville still rested on the child's head, and stooping down, he whispered: "Wait, my child, a few years; try to be very good, very patient, above all," he added, with marked emphasis; "and perhaps God will give you your desire. But you must not yet put on the sacred vestments. Why did you do so?"

"I thought perhaps God would attend to my prayer more quickly," he answered, "because when I clothed myself as a Priest, and stood as you do, Father, when you say Mass, I meant our Lord to understand by it my wish to be a Priest in reality. But when you came in, Father, I had forgotten everything but the poor Heathen. Tell me something I can do for them, even to-day, besides praying for them, you know."

Father Neville paused a moment, and then said

gently, "When you feel inclined to do something, even if it should be a good thing, and are restrained from doing it by some one set over you, be very patient in that little trial."

No more words passed, but the glance which was exchanged between the Priest and the child showed that they understood each other.

The little scene we have described was but one episode out of many, in the early childhood of Francis Willington, which seemed indicative of a future vocation. He had, with his own hands, and as far as his strength permitted, cut the steps in the wood which conducted to the little altar on the rock we have described in the preceding chapter, handling the briars which grew and were thickly entangled across the rugged path which it was necessary to clear, and toiling in the heat of summer till for very exhaustion he was obliged to desist. He had himself, with but the aid of the faithful Philip, the privileged fellow labourer in his childish toil, erected the shed upon the island, which he called S. Francis Xavier's hut, and helped to form the raft by which to cross the stream. There he had sat in the long summer days, and read the works which his pure young fancy lead him to demand, and which he devoured with the interest and enthusiasm with which children in general read tales. The "Annals of the Propagation of the Faith," of the "Holy Childhood," the "History of Japan," the "Christian Missions," and other books of a similar class, were to him, even at a very early age, as it were nourishment, recreation, and life. Sometimes Agnes was his companion, and she would sit quietly watching the river roll towards the sea, whilst he read to her aloud, and perhaps thus unconsciously cast the first seed, humanly speaking, which was to fructify in that innocent soul, and hereafter bring forth a golden harvest.

Of his elder brother Stanislaus, of whom as yet we have but just made mention, Francis had known but very little. He had already left home for college when Francis was born, being twelve years his senior, and had but returned in the vacations until he had finished his studies, when he too, like his father, entered the army, and singularly enough the regiment to which he was appointed was, almost immediately after his entrance into it, sent to India, so that the son passed the few years which he was destined to spend in a military life in the same country, although not in the same part, as his father had done.

Stanislaus was in many respects the counterpart of the Colonel: the same upright generous nature; the same amiability of character and manly earnestness; and if there was in him a certain element which savoured too much of the man of the world and the *militaire* in his less favourable aspect, the evil in Stanislaus Willington was counteracted by his Catholic education, by his high sense of honour, by the superiority of his mental endowments, which soon caused him to grow weary of the frivolity of a mere worldly life, and finally, by the beneficial influence of an attachment which he formed some years later to her who ultimately became his wife.

There remain but two other members of the Willington family to be mentioned before proceeding with our narrative; namely, the two sisters of the Colonel, ladies of middle age, who resided at the Grange, which was the "jointure house" of Willington Manor, and where the Miss Willingtons had taken up their abode upon the arrival of their sister-in-law with her children from India.

Although both sisters were possessed to a great degree of those advantages of mind and heart with which their family seemed singularly gifted by heaven, nevertheless their characters and their perceptions of things were widely different.

With the exception of an annual journey during childhood to the *pensionnat* in a convent in the north of France, where for the most part they had been educated, and a tolerably extensive continental tour during a later period of their youth, neither of these ladies had travelled much beyond the neighbourhood of their quiet home.

Upon the elder sister, Cecilia, the somewhat limited circle of their acquaintance, and the absence of aught that could thwart their inclinations and views, had been in no way prejudicial, owing to the large-heartedness with which, in common with her brother, nature had endowed her. The superiority, besides, of her mental capacities, enabled her to widen the horizon of her field of thought, to go out of self, out of the limits into which a monotonous and uncontradicted life generally tends to concentrate the minds of women. There was in Miss Willington an inward force which enabled her to expand to other influences than those which were connected with native land, and early home, and family links, and all those, as it were, private and personal associations, which, although good in themselves, nevertheless, if not purified from what is simply natural by higher and more spiritual influences, which are more remote and of wider compass, often render the heart unconsciously selfish, and the mind narrow and self-sufficient.

With Margaret Willington it was not the same. Without being unamiable she was *concentrated;* although possessed of a fund of solid virtue, or rather of virtuous dispositions, and endowed with a spirit of deep piety, nevertheless there was a boundary to her soul's eye, beyond which it seemed impossible for her to pass, and which she appeared to think it right and proper that she should not pass; a certain quiet adherence to her views, and a calm though perhaps unconscious idea of their infallibility; a complacency in her own "solidity," which would have rendered this otherwise good and estimable woman almost unamiable in her intercourse with others, had not the cultivation of her tastes, her refined education, and a certain natural reserve, which made her complacently regard her own views of things in secret, rather than seek to discuss them, prevented her from being obtrusive, and so far counteracted that which was displeasing in her character as to enable her to be simply *unattractive*.

The gate conducting to the Grange, where the Miss Willingtons resided, was immediately opposite one of the lodge gates of the Manor, the broad turnpike road alone seperating the grounds of the two residences. It was a charming abode, was that low, grey, old-fashioned house, with its gable windows looking far out to the sea, and surrounded by its luxuriant shrubbery, and its quaint, old, well kept gardens. The Colonel's children had ever loved to visit at the Grange, for the features we have remarked in Miss Margaret's character were not such as to render her unattractive to the young, and her gentle though not cordial manners, and her really kind heart, caused her to share with her sister the affection of her youthful relatives, even although their elder aunt, as would be natural from her more genial nature, was, it must be avowed, the companion of their choice, whenever there was question of a walking or driving party, as was frequently the case.

We have now given an outline of the earliest associations of him whose history will form the chief point of interest in the following pages, and we will proceed at once with the relation of that after life whose spring tide was so full of promise.

CHAPTER III.

Is it a Vocation?

Five years have passed away since the day on which our tale opened,' that day on which the Holy Spirit had descended upon Francis Willington in the Sacrament of Confirmation, and when he had received, in accordance with his earnest desire, the additional name of John de Britto.

He has just entered his eighteenth year, and as he walks in a retired part of the college garden, engaged in conversation with a Priest of dignified bearing and thoughtful countenance, few could have failed to remark the student as well as his venerable companion. The inward vigour of which his childhood had given promise had year by year developed itself. It was stamped upon his countenance; it shone in his quick dark eye; it revealed itself in the firm and measured step, and in the very gestures he involuntarily used as he pursued his conversation, which was apparently one of all-absorbing interest. There was something in the subdued voice, in the calm earnestness which accompanied his words, the air of respectful attention with which he listened to the replies of his reverend companion, and in the deliberate firm response which seemed ever ready to meet each proposition, which revealed that the youth of seventeen possessed within him not only a latent power, but also a maturity of judgment beyond his years, and which had little in common with the ordinary impetuosity of early youth.

"May I feel assured, sir, then, that my father will receive a letter from you before my arrival at home?"

"Certainly," was the reply. "But you must clearly understand that I am not intending to tell your father that I am certain you have a vocation for the Foreign Missions." A shade of disappointment passed over the youth's face, which the penetrating eye of Doctor Wainwright, the Rector of the College, was not slow to observe. "You expected I was going to decide the matter at once, then?" continued the Rector, smiling kindly at his young companion as he spoke.

"Well, yes, sir, I did," replied Francis ingenuously. "I thought that your intimate knowledge of me for the last five years would have enabled you to form a judgment, so that my father could have been at once prepared for that which I wish him to know appears *inevitable.*"

"Well," replied the Rector, "but do you apprehend so lively an opposition on the part of your father, should it be in the designs of God to call you to the work of the Foreign Missions?"

"No," answered Francis, "certainly not if he can

but be brought to believe that I have a vocation. There is the difficulty. There are hundreds of people who would not think of doubting the attraction and desire their sons have for the priesthood generally, but when there is question of their desire to become *Missioners* to the Heathen, they seem to take alarm immediately. Moreover, I do not believe my father ever suspected I had a vocation of this kind, though I should have thought the bent of my inclinations was manifest enough long before I came to college. I did not reflect upon it at the time, but I see it now: and I know what I felt in childhood was but the germ of what I feel day by day strengthening within me now."

His face glowed as he spoke, and the experienced eye of him with whom he conversed saw clearly that it was not an unformed boy who addressed him, but one whose faculties had been matured by some interior pre-occupation, some intense desire which he was necessitated to restrain, and which desire restraint did but intensify the more. Francis had spoken truly when he said that he believed the Rector knew him sufficiently to be enabled to form a tolerably safe judgment as to his vocation. Five years of constant watchfulness, of careful training, of attention to his disposition amidst his studies, his companions, and in the daily *rubs* of college life, had placed Doctor Wainwright in a position to pronounce as accurate a decision as to the *probability* of Francis's vocation as is possible at his early age; nevertheless, *because* he was experienced, he hesitated to pronounce too promptly. He believed it necessary to "*prove the will of God*," and to try still longer the ardent aspirations of the generous youth who walked at his side.

"I am not, remember, doubting in any way the truth of what you tell me," he continued, in answer to Francis's last words; "I am only pointing out to you that it would be unreasonable on my part to write and tell your father, without hesitation, that you have a vocation to the Foreign Missions. It is only in the course of training for that work that your vocation will fully develop itself. You know it, Francis; here there is no constraint. I will have full liberty left to each student to discover his *attrait;* and never would I permit influence of any kind to be exercised which might thwart the designs of Providence. Nevertheless, we must be prudent. Many youths are borne on by the pious impressions and impulses natural to their age, and afterwards they discover their mistake. This happens if they are not watched, if they are not tried: but this I can promise you conscientiously, Francis—I can, in my letter to your father, assure him of my conviction of your *probable* vocation for the Foreign Missions, which I believe needs but regular training in order to be fully developed. Are you satisfied now?"

Francis had grasped Doctor Wainwright's hand.

"Oh, yes, it is all I ask," he answered; "thank you, thank you."

They continued conversing some little while longer, on the plans to be formed should the Colonel give his consent; of the return of Francis after the vacations—which were just about to commence—to S. Edgar's College for another year, in order to await the age necessary to be attained before admission to the College *des Missions Étrangères* at Paris; and when they separated, the student's countenance reflected the joy of his heart, and the hope which during that conversation had become strengthened within him.

"What news? Nothing painful, I hope," said Father Neville, as he met Colonel Willington on the broad terrace in front of the house, a few days after the conversation related above had taken place.

"Nothing precisely *painful*," replied the Colonel, continuing to regard an open letter which he held in his hand, with his countenance somewhat troubled; then, holding out the letter to Father Neville, he added: "Read it yourself, and tell me what you think of it."

As the old Priest perused Doctor Wainwright's letter regarding the vocation of Francis, his face each moment revealed more clearly the deep interest he felt in the subject before him; and returning the letter to the

Colonel, he said, after a minute's pause: "Well, are you astonished? Were you not prepared for this?".

"Not in the least. I had no idea that Francis had such a project in his head. That he would eventually enter Holy Orders I believed probable; but the Foreign Missions, oh, certainly not."

"But, certainly, indications of his inclination that way were very palpable, even in his childhood," replied Father Neville.

"Bah!" retorted the Colonel, almost with impatience, "all that goes for nothing. It is as likely as not the fancy of a childish imagination, mingled with pious sentiments drawn from the class of reading for which he had a natural taste. Many boys, many youths, are pleased for a time with the idea of missionary life: it is something exciting. Why, I knew a youth in whom I interested myself to contrive his admission to the College for Foreign Missions in Paris —for his parents were in a somewhat humble sphere of life—he had the same idea of going abroad for missionary labour, and gave, so they said amongst his friends, every indication of a vocation. When I had made arrangements in his favour, and communicated to him what I supposed he would be transported with joy to hear, I thought my young friend took it very coolly; and at length it turned out that his supposed vocation had disappeared, and that he preferred going to another college, where he might study for the Priesthood in England. Have I not then cause to be suspicious of these boyish predilections, which in a few years vanish like the dew?"

Father Neville had awaited patiently the conclusion of the Colonel's speech, and then, with a quiet smile, and the familiar tone of an old and intimate friend, he said :

"You have, I am well aware, long and wide experience in many things; but there is one kind of experience in which I presume you will acknowledge I have the advantage of you. I mean the experience of the human heart, of all that regards the secret intercourse of souls with their God, of the operations of grace in souls, and the various indications by which we are enabled, by God's help, to judge when it is really grace that is acting, or when it is simply mere human feelings acting on pious dispositions."

The Colonel smiled. It was the first time he had done so since he had perused Doctor Wainwright's letter; but mature years had not destroyed in him the sense of the ridiculous, which was an element in his character—that element, we may say in passing, which is so valuable an aid in supporting the pains and wearinesses of life—and Father Neville's words on the present occasion seeming to represent him to himself as a master in spiritual matters, so touched the vein of mirth in the veteran Colonel, that the cloud which had hung over him in great measure disappeared, and he answered, laughingly,

"Well, yes, certainly I do not pretend to be a

discerner of spirits; that would be rather out of my sphere. But what, then, is your opinion of Francis?" he added, more gravely. "Do you believe in the apparent inclinations of his childhood as probable indications of a vocation for the Missions?"

"Candidly I do," was the reply; "and for this reason, or rather for many reasons. First, those inclinations were continuous, always going on steadily, manifesting themselves more clearly in proportion as the child advanced in age; there was no change in the *kind* of attraction which prompted him to those exterior manifestations; only its intensity and its manner of manifesting itself became each year, I may say, more in accordance with his advancing age. Thus, when I used to check his natural ardour, and restrain him from doing things—good in themselves very often, and which in ordinary children we should have had rather to encourage, and even to suggest to them—and when I asked him afterwards how he had felt disposed in receiving those restraints, his answer was invariably: 'O, Father, I offered it to God for the poor Heathen;' or, 'for an increase in the number of Missionaries;' or for such and such a mission, regarding which he had been lately reading in the 'Annals of the Propagation of the Faith,' or in the 'Holy Childhood.' Moreover," continued Father Neville, taking advantage of his companion's attentive silence to pursue the enumeration of his arguments in favour of the probable vocation of Francis, "those attractions of childhood displayed by Francis in his altar in the wood, for example, and his hut of S. Francis, and the rest, were not mere child's play ; he did not *rest* in those things ; they were with him, but, so to speak, the exuberance of the absorbing thought of his young mind, the overflowing expression of what was filling his young heart. They were with him, I dare to say it, the involuntary and unconscious manifestation of an inward reality. His quick eye often revealed to me, without his knowing it, the impatient yearning of his soul for the day when he might satisfy the burning desire which, even whilst he was so young, had been enkindled within him. How wonderful is the operation of divine grace in some pure souls!"

The old Priest paused, and for a moment appeared to be holding some secret communication with that Divine Spirit whose action it had been his life-long study to follow with fidelity, and to discern in others, in order that he might guide them rightly.

"You have spoken eloquently, my dear friend, in behalf of Francis and his probable vocation," said the Colonel, smiling, "but you have yourself introduced a word which forcibly reminds me of the predominant defect in his character. Of course, you at once comprehend that I allude to his tendency to impatience—impetuosity. This is, I believe, a very great obstacle in the way of his success as a Missioner, where for years they have to toil, and *seem* to do nothing but toil fruitlessly ; where, too, after some little advantage gained, some unforeseen grievous circumstances occur which ruin all they have done, and they have to begin again as from the first building up of the edifice."

A bright smile played over the old Priest's features as he listened, and then he replied: "You know, you remember, my dear friend, as well as I do, those consoling words of S. Paul: '*Scimus autem quoniam diligentibus Deum omnia cooperantur in bonum, iis qui secundum propositum vocati sunt sancti.*'* Now I believe, in the purposes of God, Francis is called to be a saint, and a great saint; and that very quickness or impatience of restraint, in the good desires implanted in him, will be probably instrumental in his sanctification, by the struggles it already has, and will still more compel him to suffer. Besides this, I must tell you, the ardour of that dear boy is not the mere impetuosity of youth, which is but as the foam upon the sea; neither is his impatience—let us call it by the harsher word—the effect of an *irritable* temper, or of a selfish unmortified nature, unwilling to suffer, or to be guided: it is rather the result of that fire in his heart, not of human or earthly origin, which from earliest childhood has been prompting him on to actions compatible with the vocation I believe God has given him, which has very often rendered irksome to him occupations and things which were not compatible with it, and with the desires it called forth within him. He did not wish to be premature, his

* Rom. viii. 28.

understanding is too good for that, but he *did* pant for the time when the restraints placed upon his legitimate attractions would be removed, and that he might give full scope to his aspirations. You remember there was One who said long ago that there was a martyrdom which He had to accomplish, and '*how He was straitened*' until the hour of its accomplishment should arrive, and that '*He desired with desire*' to give His friends testimony of His love '*before He suffered.*' Tell me, do you not believe there are pure souls in whom the good Jesus plants the germ of that same desire, that divine impatience which He possessed Himself,—that His Heart is capable of imparting to those who have a special devotion to it, as Francis has, and who thirst,—as he has from childhood, to make It known and loved; of imparting, I say, some sparks of that fire which consumed the Sacred Heart, so that they too are consumed with desire for Its glory, and for the salvation of souls? Oh, yes, believe me it is so."

The old Priest paused, and the Colonel regarded him with secret admiration as he watched the eye glowing with the very fire of which he spoke so eloquently. He was almost conquered, but there was still one argument which, it must be owned, seemed legitimate enough, and which he opposed to Father Neville's words.

"But," he said, "the impatience of Francis, which was his predominant fault in childhood, was in itself a fault, and productive of many others."

"I deny," was the bold answer, "that the *first*

cause of that which you call impatience in Francis was in itself a fault: far, very far from it; but that human feelings and human passion came to *mingle* with it I certainly allow; as also that imperfections and faults are found where grace should reign supreme. We have human hearts: and alas! it is the property of poor fallen nature to spoil what is divine. Our Lord looked for good grapes, and He tells us He found but wild ones. Francis has been, and is, like all of us, human, and therefore full of imperfections; he has had, however, five years of pruning since the day he left here for college. There has been, you have seen it each vacation, a wonderful development of his good qualities, and in proportion a decrease of his faulty tendencies. He will have much more pruning still when he goes to the college at Paris, as I am convinced you will see it is God's will he should."

"If it is God's will, let God's will be done," replied the Colonel, expanding his generous heart to the influence of grace; "for God forbid that I should oppose it, above all in so grave an affair as my child's vocation to that which I know I esteem to be a glorious mission."

"God bless you!" broke from the old Priest's lips, in a tone subdued by suppressed emotion, and after some short conversation on the same subject they entered the house.

To what shall we compare the first defined hope of the approaching realization of a long and ardently desired project? We are at a loss to know, for whatever poetical thought might suggest, it would be very far off from expressing that thrill of joy deep down in the heart, and known only to God, which makes itself felt when the object towards which our every thought has tended, perhaps for years, which has been the day dream beneath whose influence we have lived and acted, seems approaching so near as to be almost within our grasp.

It was this first definite assurance, humanly speaking, of seeing the dream of his young life believed in by one who would, because he had been brought to believe in it, assist in realizing it, that made the heart of Francis Willington throb with a tranquil joy it had never known before, as he stood in the presence of his father and Father Neville, in the old library at the Manor, on the first evening of his arrival for the vacations.

Who shall describe the calm deep happiness of that generous youth, as he walked, during the few weeks of his sojourn there, amidst the scenes of his childhood? As he looked on the rough objects of devotion, contrived by his own childish hands, he inwardly praised God, who had developed in him what His grace had begun, and of which those simple objects were the outward manifestation. He could, moreover, speak out boldly now, of the reality of his sentiments of childhood, and explain to himself that inward craving of which years before he had been conscious, but which he had but understood in part.

There was but one cloud to cast its shadow across the golden sunlight which rested full upon him in those halcyon days of promise. It was not the absence of the sister whose childhood had been so bound up with his, and with whom it would have been now so sweet to converse of his future prospects. No; Francis was too absorbed in the one great thought of his life to permit a mere sentiment to obscure the light that was shining on his soul, and filling it with an all-holy joy. He had exchanged letters with Agnes, in which he had informed her of his happiness, and had received in return her loving, ardent, sympathetic congratulations, and that sufficed him. But there was in that strong heart—so manly and so pure—another and a deeper love than even that which bound him to his fair young sister; deeper, moreover, than the devoted and reverential affection he bore his noble-hearted father. It was the purest, and—may we not say it?—the strongest and most enduring of any love of which the human heart is capable,—the love of a child for his mother.

We have not had occasion, as yet, to make frequent mention of Mrs. Willington; nevertheless the link uniting the mother and the youngest of her sons formed no little element in the sanctification of the latter, whose history we are relating. His character, as we have remarked, was pre-eminently manly, firm, energetic, and generous: but, as is ordinary with such, his heart was tender, compassionate, and affectionate, such as must be those who are destined to suffer, and to sacrifice themselves for God's love and glory.

Now Mrs. Willington, as we have already stated, possessed a singularly amiable disposition, united to mental endowments far above the ordinary measure. Her love for her children, moreover, ardent, intense, and tender as it was, made her not forget the responsibility which devolved upon her as a Christian mother, of guiding them in the way of virtue; but much of the duty in this respect, which she would have taken more exclusively upon herself, had, in consequence of her habitual suffering state of health, fallen to the share of the Colonel, of Father Neville, and of Madame de Masillon. Loving all her children devotedly, it cannot, however, be denied that Francis was the object of a special predilection, which was reciprocated by her son with a love which was in its intensity unequalled by any other sentiment in his young heart, save one,—that of his deep strong love of the Sacred Heart, and the desire to make It known and loved by the nations who as yet were ignorant of Its boundless charity.

The physical suffering of his mother had served to intensify the affection which from earliest childhood had gone on increasing in the breast of Francis, in proportion as with advancing age he had been rendered more and more capable of appreciating the strength and tenderness of that maternal love of which he was the object, inasmuch as gentleness and compassion are ever found allied with that ardent generous manly zeal which marks the vocation of a missionary and a martyr.

Now it was, however, that that love, which had hitherto been but a source of pure happiness to him, even though compassion for his mother's sufferings formed so large an element in it, was to become a two edged sword. Now, for the first time he was to learn the jealousy of that Divine Heart to which he had consecrated himself, and to know by practical experience the truth of those words spoken by our Lord Himself, "*I came not to bring peace but the sword.*"

Day after day passed on, during which Francis gave full vent to the deep full joy of his young heart, thrilling with its new-born promise of the realization of his life's one hope. Nevertheless, he could not bear as yet to cast a cloud upon the happiness of the mother whose very physical suffering seemed for a time allayed in the joy she experienced in the society of her son and child of predilection. At length, however, the day arrived when he felt the secret must be imparted to her, for but one week more of his vacation remained, and he desired not to delay the painful duty until the last moment, so as to be compelled to leave her in the midst of the first struggle that she must inevitably submit to before she could bring her will into entire conformity with that of God.

It was a golden evening, such as that on which our narrative commenced. The couch of the invalid was placed in the deep bay window of the drawing room, looking to the west. It was the spot she chose towards evening, because from thence she might watch the sun as it sank down into the deep ocean which lay outstretched as far as the eye could reach. It reminded her of that day, she said, whose sun shall know no setting; that day which constant suffering had rendered so ever present to her soul's eye that it was as its habitual vision.

Francis entered the room, and as he approached his mother he saw her soft dark eyes brighten with pleasure as she answered his greeting in her low gentle tones of endearing welcome. He sat down beside the reclining chair to which the invalid had moved upon his entrance, and after some short conversation upon indifferent subjects, he said very gently, but turning away his face as he began, and looking far out to the sea:

"My mother dear, I have yet another week to spend with you before returning to College, but there is something I must tell you at once." He went on, now he had commenced, speaking rapidly, for he wished to make known all in a moment. "The Sacred Heart, of whose love you, dearest mother, used so frequently to speak to me when I was a child, has called me to go far away from England, to carry the knowledge of Its love to the poor Heathen. Jesus, I feel, wills me not only to be a Priest, but a Foreign Missioner. You will make me happy by giving me your blessing, will you not, dear mother, and by saying you will for me what God wills?"

The little white hand he had held while he had been speaking had grown very cold, and when now for the first time he turned his head again towards her whom he addressed, he started, for the anguish depicted on that suffering but beautiful countenance was never to be forgotten. No words came forth, and he feared she was about to faint.

"Speak to me, my mother," he said, bending over the delicate frame which seemed for the moment crushed beneath the blow but just sustained. Then, after a pause, happy in seeing his mother smile again, he said, "Say, dearest, that you will give me all to the Heart of Jesus for the poor Heathen."

As he spoke, *the sword was piercing his own soul* no less than that of his mother. It was his first real missionary work; it was a drop of the martyr's chalice, and he accepted it manfully, though his heart was bleeding as he did so. The pale lips of Mrs. Willington seemed to move, but the voice was so weak that no words could be recognised. Francis knelt down in order to catch the sound; at length it came.

"If Jesus calls you far away, I have no right to wish it should be otherwise; but, my child, the struggle seems almost more than I can bear. I know that it is weak, it is selfish, for yours is a glorious mission ; but in these years of suffering, in which I have for so many hours thought of you, my dearest child, and figured to myself your future, I have habituated myself to see you as a Priest—indeed, this was my cherished hope—but labouring in the English portion of God's vineyard, so that from time to time I could have you with me, share, in some sort, your cares; and, oh!—God knows how I have fostered the sweetest thought of all—it was to see you at my side, in your sacerdotal vestments, at the last hour, that you might close my dying eyes, and give me, your mother, your blessing as a Priest. Oh, my God, my God! how I have clung to this bright hope, this day dream of years, and now"—

Nature in that moment was gaining the ascendancy. Grace for a little while seemed baffled in the strife. It was not a time for human words; there was no reasoning needed; no moving of the will : for it was established in the will of God. But poor weak nature would assert its claims ere grace should bear away the victory. There was silence for some minutes, during which both the mother and the son had recourse to that Heart for whose glory both were suffering. It was a touching scene : the sorrow-stricken face of that woman, strong in her weakness ; the slightly silvered hair which shaded the pale suffering brow, contrasting with the olive cheek of the youth, which he rested lovingly, soothingly, upon the mother's head, which reposed against his shoulder. His dark quick eye wore an expression of suffering which until now had not characterized it, and the manly countenance denoted the struggle, the anguish, that was going on within. His was the hand that was plunging the sword into his mother's heart: he felt it, he knew it; but it must be done for Jesus' sake, *and for the sake of the poor Heathen;* and the hot tears that sprang to his eyes as he made the first great step in the martyr's career would have done no dishonour to a Xavier or a De Britto.

During the few remaining days of his vacation, Francis passed as much time as possible with his mother, sometimes driving her out in the low carriage which she was accustomed to use, sometimes, when she was less suffering, walking with her on the broad terrace, or enticing her to extend her walk a little into some of the various avenues or laurel-hedged paths with which the Manor grounds abounded, always supporting her with his firm arm, and cheering her with his affectionate cheerful conversation.

He did not avoid the topic which he well knew was casting so deep a shadow over the happiness which his mother felt in his company: on the contrary, he rather encouraged it, hoping, in doing so, to habituate her to the thought of the ultimate and inevitable separation. As the time of his departure, however, approached, he found himself obliged to refer to the period of his return the following year, without any further allusion to the departure which would so soon succeed for the College *des Missions Etrangères* in Paris.

When he left home he felt he had advanced a stage towards the goal; he had commenced to suffer for the poor Heathen; he had, for the love of the Sacred Heart and the souls for whose salvation It thirsted, made his own young heart bleed, in plunging the sword of sorrow into his mother's soul, that mother for whom his filial love was, and ever had been, a passion.

CHAPTER IV.

Preparation for the Work. Opposing Views.

When Francis returned to S. Edgar's, it was as one whose vocation is recognised and regarded as more certain than is that of ordinary youths of his age. He had, from his first entrance at the College, given such continuous and marked testimonies of his call to the Priesthood, so decided an attraction, moreover, for the work of the Foreign Missions, that both the Rector, and all those who knew Francis, believed themselves justified in considering his future career settled, so far at least as human foresight can extend, and thus they were now more definite in their manner of forming him, and in fostering in him the good seed the Lord of the harvest had sown in his pure soul, in order that he might in his turn go forth and increase that harvest for the glory of the Divine Master.

How swiftly fleets the time of actual preparation for the realization of a long-desired project! Study had ever been to Francis congenial to his temperament, but now that the probability of his vocation was acknowledged, and that his superiors judged it expedient to urge him on, if that had been necessary, in the studies compatible with that probable vocation, he not only advanced with rapid strides, but he did so, moreover, with a joyous facility which, as it were, increased his natural capacities, and lent an additional power to all his faculties. He found much consolation and assistance in his labours from the affectionate and wise sympathy testified towards him by the Rector and Masters of the College. As hitherto no influence had been exercised in reference to his vocation, so now that that vocation was regarded as settled, there was not a shadow of attempt to extend other views before him, which possibly might cause his eye to wander a little from the high mark heaven had set before him, to examine, so to speak, the easier and more trodden path which human wisdom and earthly influence should present to him. No; at S. Edgar's there was nothing of this, and Francis felt the immense advantages, both spiritual and intellectual, of the absence of all restraint regarding the God-given *attrait* which possessed his entire soul for the conversion of the Heathen.

In the course of that last year which Francis was destined to pass at S. Edgar's, an event took place which changed a little the face of things at the Manor, and made some addition to its small family circle. Stanislaus, whose ten years of service in India began to warn him of the necessity of demanding leave to return to England for a time, having communicated his intention to his father, had received from him the serious advice, and even request, that he would retire altogether from active service, in order to prepare himself for the responsibilities which would devolve upon him when he should enter into possession of the large property to which he was heir.

After some consideration, the young officer consented, in leaving India, to do so, not for a year or two, as he had originally intended, but permanently; and it must be admitted that if, on the one hand, it was some little sacrifice to quit a profession for which he had, like his father, a natural attraction, there was, however, a counter attraction in old England, which obliges us to own that his sacrifice could in no way be called heroic.

Before reaching the Manor, Stanislaus had paid a visit—the prelude of several succeeding ones—to the house of an old friend of his father's, whose daughter Mary was the magnet which had so easily attracted the young officer homewards from the far East; and before the close of that year a marriage was announced which was to the entire satisfaction of all parties, and to none more so than to the Colonel and his invalid wife. It was finally arranged that the newly married pair should take up their abode at the Manor, instead of at the Grange; and thus, as the Colonel said, the "old ladies"—meaning his two sisters—"might be left in peace to end their days at their beloved Grange."

Before the expiration of Francis's last year at S. Edgar's the marriage of his brother had taken place, the Manor had received its two new inmates, and had opened its hospitable doors to many visitors, invited to welcome the heir and his young bride to their future home.

The guests who usually assembled at the Manor were, for the most part, the families of early friends of the Colonel or of Mrs. Willington, and who thus, being on more intimate relations than those which are ordinarily classed under the head of *acquaintance*, felt more or less genuine interest in the different members of the family. Moreover, as we have before remarked, Colonel Willington liked greatly to see Priests amongst his guests, and above all those of the Society of Jesus, when he could obtain that honour, for such he truly regarded their visit, were it but for a day, in passing.

Now it so happened that on the present occasion many inquiries were made regarding Francis, who was expected to return home whilst even the guests assembled in his brother's honour were present, and thus it was that the probabilities of his future career became known, and various views regarding it expressed. Miss Margaret, on first hearing the news of her young nephew's probable vocation, was aghast with astonishment that her opinion had not been requested; and not even her studiously quiet manner and nervous reserve could disguise the indignation she felt on account of Francis's predilection for the Missions among the Heathen, rather than at home in his own country, where Priests were so much needed. When alone one day with the Colonel and Stanislaus, and that the latter, not knowing the strength of his aunt's sentiments upon the subject, innocently mentioned the fact of Francis's probable vocation, the colour mounted to Miss Margaret's brow, and her virtuous indignation and patriotic zeal could no longer be suppressed. Therefore, in the most measured tone, and most gentle voice, she delivered the following speech, accompanied by certain nervous movements, which revealed how strongly *nature* was working within, despite the efforts to disguise itself under the semblance of zeal and patriotic charity.

"It is no affair of mine, certainly," began the good Miss Margaret, "since you have never even mentioned the subject to me, and that I have heard it from others; but I must say I regret exceedingly to hear of Francis's project, and of your consent, to his going to the College in Paris, with a view of preparing himself for the life of a Foreign Missionary. According to me it is absolutely *wrong* for young men with a vocation for the Priesthood to be leaving England, where Priests are so much needed, and where there is so much work to be done amongst our own poor fellow countrymen. I can scarcely think of it without indignation."

"My dear Margaret," replied the Colonel, half smiling at his sister's warmth, but resolved nevertheless to express his sentiments plainly and without disguise in return, "your indignation might certainly be expended upon something which would more justly call it forth. In the first place, Almighty God is no respecter of either persons, or nations, or peoples. The souls of the poor benighted savages and pagans abounding in the different countries of the world, known or unknown to men, are equally redeemed by the Blood of His only Son, as are those of our fellow countrymen. Hence, whether a man saves the souls of Englishmen, or of North American Indians, or of Japanese idolators, it matters in reality but little in itself; since each soul is bought at the same infinite price. Then you must remember that there is such a thing as *vocation;* that is, a call from God to a particular work. You admit it in the case of vocation to the Priesthood itself, or to Religion, and even to one particular Order of Religion rather than to another. Why not, then, when there is question of a vocation for labouring in the *Foreign* Missions, rather than at home? The principle is the same, and ought to be respected. We have no right to question the ways of God, and to demand of Him reasons for the desires He excites in souls."

"If it *is* from God," replied Miss Margaret, quietly, and with an emphasis which plainly indicated her own doubt upon that head. "Young persons are often led astray by the dreams of their imagination, which they take for inspirations."

"All that has to be proved," replied the Colonel. "If it is simply a dream, the realities of the preparation, during his years of College training, and increasing age, will awaken him, and then—he will not be a Foreign Missioner."

"What can be more noble," continued Miss Margaret, returning to her starting point, which it seemed impossible to her to lose sight or hold of, "than the self-devoted lives of those Priests toiling amongst the squalid poor of London and our other great populous cities; or, again, labouring in newly-opened and struggling country missions, to bring back the faith to a people and a land where so many Catholic associations still exist? Oh," she added, with a shake of the head, and a tone which showed how strongly "*my own views*" agitated the heart hidden under that quiet exterior; "I cannot bear to hear of Priests and Religious leaving their country, where there is so much to be done."

"You cannot bear to hear, that is to say, of Priests and Religious regarding all souls in the light of God, and from His point of view," answered the Colonel, more seriously than he had yet spoken; "for it really comes to this, if you analyse it. Do you not think, nay, you are bound to believe, that God is at this moment looking down with as much compassion on the poor Indian on the banks of the Hooghly, or the savage in the wilds of Africa, as on the man who, although living in a civilized country, cares no more for his soul than if he had never heard the name of God? Do you not think the Saviour's Heart yearns with as much tender compassion for the soul of one as of the other?"

"Of course, no one doubts that," replied Miss Margaret, quietly; "but I cannot understand a zealous young Priest not feeling more desire of converting his own country than"—

"My dear Margaret," said the Colonel, interrupting her, "in the sight of God, that infinite and eternal Being, there is but *one* country. It is true He looks upon some with particular predilection, if we may judge by His dealings with them in spite of their errors, and He does so probably *because* of their constant generosity in giving to Him what they had most precious. Take, for example, France: in all ages, despite the sins of which many of her children have rendered themselves guilty,—she has given, with a generosity that has never waned, her life's blood, so to speak, her sons and her daughters, to carry the name and extend the kingdom of God throughout the world. There is scarcely a corner of the earth which has not been moistened with the blood of martyrs, children of that great nation; great, chiefly on account of its unfailing generosity, in sending forth Missioners of either sex, to save the souls of those poor far-off children of the same Father, who had never heard

His name. The 'Propagation of the Faith,' the 'Holy Childhood,' and every other work which has for its object the salvation of the heathen nations, have originated in France; and I agree with all who believe that it is in memory of her devotedness that the arm of God has been withheld from striking her, in chastisement for her present infidelities. Therefore," continued the noble veteran, bringing himself back to the point in question, "a man who is replenished with a true Catholic missionary spirit, and who is divinely called to go and labour among the Heathen, so far from doing an injury to his own country in obeying that call, will send back, as it were, from afar a double blessing. We all believe in the great apostleship of prayer, and we know from the accounts that reach us from Missionaries amongst the Heathen that the newly converted amongst them grasp that blessed doctrine, as we may call it, with a wonderful facility and delight, and practise it with the utmost fervour. Do you not think that those simple grateful hearts will pray for the country which has sent out to them deliverers, to free them from a bondage the most terrible of all? We know how even the little children in India and China, indeed in every part where French missionaries have been, pray for France, and will never cease to pray for her. Besides, generosity will never go unrewarded by God. '*Give, and it shall be given to you,*' said One whose promise cannot fail. Therefore our patriotism should promote and strengthen missionary action, for it is certain that the sending missionaries abroad will never hinder the progress of Catholicity at home. Why, it would be absolutely a want of faith to think so. If we are poor in Priests, they will become multiplied by our generosity in giving them to those who ask for them, as the poor Heathen do."

"But," persisted Miss Margaret, "when we consider the multitudes, in London alone, who are as ignorant of all that regards their salvation as the very Heathen, does it not seem out of order that we should be sending Priests away, when they are so sadly needed at home?"

The Colonel could not suppress a smile at Miss Margaret's characteristic expression, by which she habitually made known that all must be *disorderly* that did not range itself within the small, square, and altogether *un*-elastic compass of her own particular views.

"Whose fault is it," replied the Colonel, "if the masses of people about us in this little island are ignorant of the truth? Scarcely can a man walk for ten minutes in London without passing a Catholic Church or Chapel, and where that Church or Chapel is, there is certainly a Priest, and perhaps several. Churches, and consequently Priests to supply them, are increasing rapidly each year. It is the same with Congregations of Religious devoted to instruction and to other active works of charity, which throw them into the very midst of those masses who are ignorant of the truth, and which render them open to all who come to them for help. Whose fault is it, then, I repeat, if ignorance stalks like a pestilence through this highly civilized land of ours? Certainly, it is not on account of the want of means, for they stand at the doors of the people and wait, but often wait in vain. The case of the Heathen, the savage in distant countries, is different to this. A 'black robe' makes his appearance, and with the powerful influence which a divine mission lends him, he attracts the simple but benighted soul, who finds in his words an echo to that inward cry which he has been conscious of within him, perhaps for long years, but could not comprehend. There is no indifference *there*, no trifling with grace; he grasps at the hand extended to him, and takes care to hold it fast. It is not so much the want of *means* in this country that is the obstacle, but the want of correspondence. And how is this to be overcome? Certainly, not by the neglect of material means—God grant they may go on increasing yearly!—but also, and I dare to say it, much more by earnest constant prayer, and by generosity in giving to other peoples—poorer in means than ourselves—the bread of life, which is the knowledge of God and of His holy religion."

"We know very well," sententiously answered Miss Margaret, with her *gentle* obstinate adherence to her own views, " that charity begins at home."

"But it does not *end* there, Miss Margaret," said a voice from the window, which proved to be that of Father Neville, who had passed precisely as the good lady was delivering a reply that she believed would disarm the Colonel altogether.

Stanislaus, who until then had remained a silent but far from disinterested listener, looked up with his bright open smile, and said: "Your coming is very *à propos*, Father Neville. Here is my father turned preacher, and Aunt Margaret waxing warm beneath the eloquence of his words."

"I am not warm at all, Stanislaus," replied Miss Margaret, the colour of whose face, and whose restless movements were, however, somewhat contradictory of her words: "I repeat what I said, that charity begins at home."

"And I must be allowed to repeat my response, that it does not *end* there," said Father Neville, smiling kindly at Miss Margaret, the stubborn expression of whose countenance was scarcely consistent with the quiet tone in which she delivered all her sentences.

"If charity *ended* at home," continued the old Priest, gently, "never would our Divine Lord have come down from heaven to save us. It is the very property of charity to expand itself, to give, to sacrifice."

"And cannot all this be done without going to other lands in order to do it?" asked Miss Margaret.

"Assuredly it can," responded Father Neville, "provided that whilst we labour for our own country we forget not the countless souls far away, who have never yet heard the saving Name. We offer Him up daily, or rather He offers Himself by our weak hands, for the salvation of the *whole world*—'*pro totius mundi salute.*'"

Without having heard the previous conversation, Father Neville fell in, as it were naturally, with its strain, for he knew Miss Margaret's views, and the limit of her horizon, and suspected what had given rise to the present discussion. The remark which Stanislaus next made assured him that his suspicion had been well founded, and that the vocation of Francis had been the stone of scandal to his good but somewhat prejudiced aunt.

"Well, I do not profess a knowledge of these things," said the young officer, in his usual bright cheerful manner; "but even, humanly speaking, a man works better, and has better success, in that for which he has an attraction, than in anything else for which he has not the same inclination; and I should fancy it would be the same in those things which directly regard religion."

"Not always," said Miss Margaret, in a tone of decided conviction; "where there is less inclination, less of nature, there is more merit, because we are working more purely for God."

"That holds good in certain things, and, above all, where, remember, divine vocation is not in question," replied Father Neville. "It would be a delusion for anyone to persist in a way which was altogether distasteful, *simply* because he considered it a duty to do what was most repugnant to himself, whilst all the while God was calling him where his faculties would be unshackled, and able to work with their full power in the service of Him who gave them. We must not trifle with the call of God; and believe me, or rather the Holy Spirit, Who says that He conducts all things not only wisely but *sweetly*, to their appointed end. We are not to set up a new school of perfection just because some certain saints have been led in a particular way, and even they, remember, had their *attrait* for the very difficult and repugnant things they did, which *attrait* it was which rendered *sweet to them* what to others, not so attracted, would have been unendurable."

"Well, Father Neville," retorted Miss Margaret, no more convinced than she was in the beginning; "I have heard very solid and pious men, Priests, say that it is all delusion on the part of those who think they cannot do enough in England for God's glory;—it is something like people who pretend to sigh after martyrdom and cannot support the least sharp word."

"No parallel whatever between the cases," answered Father Neville; "moreover, there are many solid and pious persons, and learned too, who do not suffer their interior sight to pass over the boundaries of that horizon they have themselves made, and whose spiritual touch also is not very sensible to the divine Hand; and I must tell you I have had the happiness also of meeting with many learned, and certainly solid and pious men, whose experience, moreover, has been long and wide, and reaching to the point which we are at present discussing, and they have assured me that if a man has really a vocation for the Foreign Missions in vain might they strive to detain him in England; his home work would be a failure, simply because God called him elsewhere, and his *heart* would be *there*, and not where he actually and bodily stood."

"Precisely what I meant just now," said Stanislaus, who was earnestly interested in the conversation. "Reason itself testifies the truth of that."

"And," continued Father Neville, "the good God accommodates Himself to our human nature, and draws our wills, as He Himself expresses it, by the '*bands of love*.' He *forces* none of us, but prefers our free and willing service. No, no; if God calls us to labour here, let us stay and our work will be glorious; but if He draws us to go carry the glad tidings to the poor Heathen, let us beware of neglecting the voice, for if we do we shall have many witnesses against us at the last day, even the poor souls for whose salvation we were designed, and whose cries for bread, the Bread of Life, we have disregarded."

There was an intense earnestness in the old Priest's tone and manner which tacitly imposed silence on Miss Margaret, for she highly respected him, as indeed her good Catholic feeling led her to do all Priests in general, however much she sometimes found their views to differ from her own.

"Well, God grant us all to do His holy will in all things," said the Colonel, cheerfully, " and I pray Him daily that I may never thwart His designs over any of my children."

"That is a prayer most pleasing to God," said Father Neville. " Would that all parents prayed thus, and *acted* on it. There should be great reverence in our dealings with God's designs; whereas too many are inclined to be impertinent, allowing to His authority certain demands, and calling in question, as it would seem, others which surpass their own comprehension. Thus, scarcely a father or mother who would not rejoice if the Lord called their son to the Priesthood; but let Him lay His hand on him as well for the Foreign Missions, and immediately too many forget themselves, and question God's right to put forth such a claim. In the same way with their daughters: few parents refuse their consent to their children becoming nuns in the active Congregations devoted to external works of charity; but if there is question of their vocation to the *cloister* properly so called, that is, to a contemplative Order, there again God's right is disputed, and human views are put forth 'in battle array,' to show why His call must not be responded to."

"True enough," said the Colonel, musingly, and then, after a short pause, he continued : " Francis will be here to-morrow; Agnes also arrives with him. He will call for her at Torrington, and bring her back under his wing. I am pleased it so happens they can pass their last vacation together before the long separation."

The conversation thus gradually passed into other topics, and the question which was so sore a point to Miss Margaret's "principles," or "views," or "prejudices," was not again referred to, at least for the present.

CHAPTER V.

The brother and sister once more at home.—Captain Warnford.—The Departure of Francis.

Perhaps on that bright summer day, so much in harmony with the scene we are about to witness, few happier hearts might have been met with in this world than that which beat in the breast of Francis Willington.

The carriage drove rapidly up to the great entrance of the Manor House, where a group of smiling faces were already assembled to welcome the brother and sister on their first arrival. Foremost was the Colonel, whose paternal heart throbbed with a pardonable pride, as well as with affection, as he saw Francis spring from the carriage, hasten forward with Agnes to greet his father, and then the beloved invalid mother, who, supported on her husband's arm, had come out upon the terrace to receive the children she loved so tenderly. Then there was the new sister, the bride of Stanislaus, to make acquaintance with; and it might be said Stanislaus himself, so very young were Francis and Agnes when their elder brother had left home for India. And good Father Neville, whose blessing both knelt to receive before any other greeting was exchanged with him. And, finally, those of the guests whom they knew, and others to whom as yet they were strangers.

The last year had wrought a marked change in Francis. He had lost the appearance of boyish youth, and although but just past his eighteenth birthday, there was an air of thoughtfulness on the high intellectual brow, and in the quick, dark, deep-set eyes, that bespoke a maturer age. Around the mouth, also, there was an expression of firmness, which told a tale of inward self-restraint, rarely perceptible so early in life; yet, withal, a brightness was reflected over his entire countenance, and an alacrity was visible in his whole person, which seemed peculiarly in keeping with the vocation heaven had given him.

Gifted both by nature and by grace, faithful in corresponding with those gifts, and in devoting them to the exclusive service of the Giver, with his vocation acknowledged, and on the very point of immediate preparation for its fulfilment, what wonder was it that the heart of the young future Missioner, as he stood there, surrounded by loving friends, should beat with a sense of pure happiness, as unalloyed as it is possible happiness can be here below?

Agnes, also, was no less visibly changed than was her brother. She had now attained the age of sixteen, and in one year more was to leave finally the happy Convent School, where she had passed the greater part of the years which had intervened since the day we witnessed her departure from home on that which followed her Confirmation.

There was doubtless manifested in her deportment somewhat of that shyness and modest reserve which naturally result from the associations connected with a Convent School; but not a shadow of that demure affectation which reveals so clearly the concentration of the thoughts on self, and which is no less artificial and displeasing than the frivolous mannerism of a decidedly *worldly* bearing, was to be discovered in her. Her looks, her voice, her manner, though somewhat grave, were eminently simple; and consequently she was speedily at ease, even with those whom she had not previously known, and could therefore derive enjoyment from their society.

But it must be owned that Agnes's crowning happiness was to converse with Francis on all that regarded his vocation—of his studies, of his life at college—and to recall the memories of their past years, in revisiting the spots where Francis had left traces of his early predilections. She took especial pleasure in hearing recitals regarding those Eastern countries whither all her brother's desires tended, and in this both Francis and herself found an adequate and willing informant in one of the guests at their father's house, who, until then, had been unknown to them.

Captain Warnford, such was the name of their new acquaintance, was a friend of Stanislaus, and had returned from India at the same time as himself, but intended, after a sojourn of about three years in Europe, for the sake of his health, to return to his regiment at Bombay. He was a man apparently somewhat above thirty years of age, of prepossessing appearance, and whose manners and entire bearing were calculated to engage the interest of the young, no less than to render him an ageeeable companion to men of mature years and experience. There was, moreover, an expression of suffering in the large brown eyes, and in the lines around the well-formed mouth, that indicated physical pain, or at least a health already injured by the climate of India, which formed an additional attraction for Francis, whose quick eye to discover suffering, and whose tender sympathy for those who suffered, were, as we have remarked, striking characteristics in him, and seemed peculiarly to dispose him for the divine mission of love and mercy to which the Master's voice had called him.

Thus it was that Captain Warnford was the frequent companion of Francis and Agnes in their walks and visits to the old spots so dear to both; and even when several others were of the party, it for the most part happened that, in whatever order they had set out from the house, the Captain with his young companions might be seen returning to it, as it were naturally and unconsciously a little withdrawn from the rest, conversing gaily, and answering the questions of each with evident satisfaction.

The ardent earnest character of Francis was singularly attractive to him, and he saw in him one altogether fitted for the work which was to be his amongst the people of the East, where all the sympathies of the young student tended.

His eye had been also attracted by the youthful Agnes when, standing on the terrace, he had seen her arrive with her brother, and had witnessed the artless yet withal dignified simplicity with which she had greeted her relatives, and received the welcome of the assembled guests. There was something in the fresh innocence of the brother and sister, in their devoted affection for each other, and in the interest which each took in subjects which at their early age ordinarily do not occupy the mind and heart, that rivetted the attention, and was peculiarly refreshing to a man who was obliged to mingle in societies where youth is too frequently represented by a mass of frivolity, egotism, and even artifice.

The vocation of Francis explained in great measure his lively interest in seeking information on various subjects regarding which youths of his age commonly give no very special attention; but that which particularly struck Captain Warnford was the earnest interest which Agnes evinced in such subjects as women, even of mature age, care little or nothing about. Much was to be allowed to her affection for her brother, and the deep interest with which she regarded all that referred to his future career; but the intelligent eye so often fixed upon that young countenance was not slow to perceive that the heart and mind of Agnes derived from some deeper source than sisterly affection the thoughts and interests which so continually engaged them.

That memorable vacation, so happy for both the brother and the sister, was hastening to its close, and as the day fixed for the departure of Francis for Paris approached, many and frequent were the allusions to his journey, and to his future life at the College of Foreign Missions.

One day that he had stolen away for a quiet conversation with Agnes, he said to her:

"Let us once more sing together '*Le desir du Martyre;*' you have not forgotten it?"

"Oh, no," replied Agnes, "I used often to sing it at school when I had the harp all to myself. It reminded me of the days when we used to sing it together, when Madame de Masillon so sweetly struck the chords for us."

"Ah, yes!" said Francis, brightly; "let us go upstairs to the sea room, as we used to call it, with the magnificent view from the great old window—the harp is there, and we will have old times over again."

They found the room vacant. Agnes approached the harp, and struck the first chords of the symphony of the exquisite air of the *cantique* which their dear Madame de Masillon had taught them, and whose sentiments found so faithful a response in the heart of Francis.

" Quand combatterai-je dans l'arène
 Contre la fureur du tyran ?
 Quand verrai-je à mes pieds la chaine,
 Autour de mon cou le carcan ?
 Mes amis sont couverts de gloire,
 Et moi, je ne fais que gemir,
 Il faut pour gagner la victoire } *bis.*
 Mourir, mourir, mourir !

" Il faut rendre ce sol fertile
 Arracher ses épais buissons,
 Il faut que ce terrain d'argile
 Se couvre de riches moissons,
 Mais pour activer sa nature,
 Le *travail* n'est pas suffisant
 Il faut pour l'orner de verdure, } *bis.*
 Mon sang, mon sang, mon sang.

" Du mondain l'immense délire
 Au monde borne ses souhaits,
 De Jésus vivant sous l'empire
 Dans la croix sont tous mes attraits.
 Que de Jésus l'amer Calice
 Abreuve mon dernier soupir,
 Que je succombe dans sa lice,
 Martyr, martyr, martyr !

" Adieu, mes amis de ce monde,
 Il se fait tard, séparons nous,
 Et ne pleurez pas sur ma tombe
 Mais pour moi priez à genoux.

> Je ne veux plus de cette vie,
> D'un dur exil—trop sombre lieu,—
> Nous nous verrons dans la Patrie,
> Adieu—adieu—adieu !" * } *bis.*

Exquisitely the voices of the brother and sister harmonized; and one who heard them would not readily forget the delicate pathos with which those rich clear tones rendered the strains of the melody, which borrowed an additional charm from the soft accompaniment of the harp, which was played by the young artiste in a manner that pronounced her a proficient. In effect they were not alone, as they had believed; for Stanislaus, and his friend Captain Warnford, having passed the door of the apartment just as the singing had commenced, had entered, and had thus been the unobserved audience of the youthful musicians. When the song was concluded they advanced.

"You are singing with voice and *heart*, Francis;—is it not so?" said Stanislaus, approaching his brother, and smiling one of his kind bright smiles; "but I hope you are not going to quit this 'hard exile' just yet. It tells, I presume, of your future career;—that song."

"Yes, Agnes and I have sung it together since we were children ever so young," replied Francis; "but the second verse ending '*La mort, la mort, la mort,*' we

---

* The above *cantique* is one of a collection upon the Mission of Tong King, chiefly composed by Monsgr. Retord, then Vicar Apostolic of Western Tong King.

never used to sing, Agnes, do you remember? It is for us so untrue, and it seems to express the desire of death simply with a view of escaping the miseries of life. The other verses are charming."

"And the music also," said Captain Warnford, who had been a delighted listener, and had moreover watched the countenance of Agnes, as she sung unconscious of the presence of any audience, with the deepest interest.

"Are those sentiments the expression of *your* desires also?" he added, turning to the young girl with a smile which veiled an anxious feeling he did not care to manifest.

"What," answered Agnes, laughing, "have I the desire of martyrdom? No, I have not attained to Francis's fervour; I suppose if I had his vocation I should do so. I like the song and the music, and the associations connected with it," she added, smiling fondly at her brother, "because of Francis, and because it has reference to his dear Foreign Missions."

"And nothing else?" Captain Warnford ventured once more to inquire.

"And because I, too, love all that regards the Foreign Missions. Francis taught me to do so when we were little children," she answered ingenuously. "And some one else has taught me since," she added, with a gay innocent laugh; "but still," she continued playfully, "that *some one* has not yet obtained for me her own desire of martyrdom."

"Oh," laughed Stanislaus, "she means that great aspiring S. Teresa, whose name she had the audacity to take at her confirmation. Am I not right, little one?"

"Oh! how wise he thinks himself, does he not?" said Agnes, laughing, but with some slight confusion in her manner, as she turned to Francis, by which means she hid her face a little from the others. And then she approached the harp once more, and struck the first chord of a melody which she knew was a favourite with both her brothers, and which would tempt them to sing, and thus break off a conversation which the young girl felt was becoming for her somewhat embarrassing, especially as she had not acquired the art of parrying inconvenient questions with the adroitness common to young ladies even of her early age.

Several of the guests had left, and only such remained at the Manor as were numbered amongst the more intimate friends of the family. Amongst the latter was Captain Warnford, whose long and close friendship with Stanislaus entitled him to be regarded by the Colonel as a personal friend, more especially as he found in him a man worthy of his esteem, and capable, on account of a like profession, and residence in the same distant country, of being an agreeable companion, although so much his junior. Thus it was that the Colonel had, in concert with Stanislaus, begged Captain Warnford to pay frequent visits to the Manor during his sojourn in England for the next two or three years, more particularly as the genial climate of the western county in which Willington was situated benefitted his health, and would facilitate its re-establishment.

It was a bright morning, and the household at the Manor had just emerged from the Chapel, where they had heard holy Mass, and where many had that morning communicated, for it was the day of Francis's departure for Paris, and all wished to call down upon the young student and his enterprize the benedictions of Heaven.

Father Neville still knelt at the *prie-dieu* in the sanctuary, and another figure also lingered at the communion rail, his head bent down upon his clasped hands, his heart in closest commune with his God whom he had received into his breast, and regardless of the moments as they sped all too quickly. He was on the eve of the realization of his young life's hope, for he felt that his entrance at the College of Foreign Missions was, as it were, the first immediate step in his actual career. What wonder was it that he lingered longer than usual that morning at his thanksgiving? What wonder that he should taste a drop of the sweetness of leaving all for that Divine Master who had called him to co-operate with Him in the salvation of his brethren;

a sweetness which more than compensated for the sacrifice involved in separating himself *for ever*—as his life of Foreign Missioner would compel him to do—from those he loved with all the capacity of his nature, at once so ardent and so tender? And thus the moments flew, and still the young man knelt absorbed in prayer, and in the emotions, so sweet and yet so strange, that were causing his heart to throb so quickly. At length a hand was laid gently on his shoulder, and looking up he met the kind eyes of his brother Stanislaus, who, leaning down, whispered to him:

"It is growing late: they say you must come to breakfast, or the carriage will be here before you are ready." Then, kneeling down a moment beside his young brother, praying for him to the God of the Eucharist, who had called him to follow Him, Stanislaus again gently touched his arm, and they left the chapel together.

The breakfast was soon over, for hearts were full, and sufficient time for *last words* are more desired by such than corporal refreshment. There was one to whom Francis wished to devote as much time as possible, in order that the balm of his tenderness might alleviate a little the sharp pain of her sacrifice. It was his mother. He went to her private room, where she awaited him, and there in the same deep window looking out to the great rolling sea, where he had first spoken to her of his vocation, he stood beside her now to say his last farewell, at least for several years. She extended her arms to him when she saw him enter, and he, hastening to her embrace, clasped her closely to his heart, and laid her head, as he had done before, upon his manly breast, wherein resided a capacity at once for loving and for sacrificing, worthy of a martyr, such as he desired to be.

"My mother! my darling!" he whispered, after the first few moments of silence, "this is the hour of sacrifice for you and for me;—this is the supreme hour for us to glorify the Heart of Jesus, and to do something for the souls who are perishing. My mother, you know well how I have loved you from my infancy; it is something different from my love of my father, or brother, or sister, precious as they are all to me, precious in a special manner as is my dearest little Agnes; but, but the love of Jesus is stronger than all, and in comparison with which the purest and holiest human love is but weakness itself. Do these words seem harsh to you, my mother? No, no; you know too well the right which the good God has to call for what He has given you, and your generous heart would never dispute with Him that right. I know well, dearest, the thoughts that come to pain you. You think of the hope you had so cherished of having me beside you when God calls you to Himself; of having me, not as I am now, but as a Priest of Jesus, who could dare to speak to you as a father although your son, and who would bring you the Divine Viaticum for your last great journey. Jesus *gave* you this hope, darling mother, in order that you might have more to sacrifice for His love. You think too ———."

"I think, my child," broke in the low sweet voice, half broken with emotion, "my mother's heart cannot help it, of the life of peril, of hardship, of exile, you have chosen—and—and of the horrible tortures and cruel death to which you may be exposed." It was well the mother's face was hidden as she spoke, or she would have seen the countenance of him who looked down on her so tenderly, so compassionately, suddenly lit up with a radiance which to her, at that moment, would have been almost pain. The very mention of a possible martyrdom had sent a thrill of joy through the heart of Francis, which, for a minute, absorbed the sorrow of separation,—and even the purer sorrow of knowing it was himself who was causing such a sharp struggle in his mother's heart. He turned away his head and looked out across the wide sea, and then involuntarily his glance mounted heavenwards. Was it a prayer his heart was offering in that moment of silence? We cannot tell; but a new strength seemed to have been given him to breathe the long farewell, for the love of Jesus and of souls, and to leave the mother for whose sake he sorrowed far more than for his own.

"Is it not true, dear mother, those words of Jesus: '*I came not to bring peace but the sword.*' When He came and visited me with the precious grace of vocation, He brought the sword which should separate me from you, dearest; and it was inevitable but that the sword should 'pierce your own soul' also; but it is a grace, my mother, thus to be visited,—a grace for you as well as for me. When you look out across the great, deep sea, think of the poor negroes far away, who know not as yet the love of Jesus; and let the thought that you have given for their salvation, what is dearest to you on earth, be a consolation. And as your eye rests on the rolling waves, as it loves to do so often, think of that *other* sea, the sea of life, which will so soon be passed by all, even the youngest of us; and then we shall reach the heavenly shore, and home, and Jesus, and Mary, and Joseph: and what a welcome they will give us; and then no more separation, no more tears. Oh! what a joy, darling, *then* to us it will be to have sacrificed each other for Him, and for the souls whom that sacrifice will help to save."

Mrs. Willington raised her head, and upon the beautiful features there rested a smile which had in its expression more of Heaven than of earth. There was in it that peace "*which the world cannot give*," and which, perhaps, only the holy joy of sacrificing something very precious for the love of God, can bestow.

Francis was recompensed. For a little while he had feared that physical suffering might have wrought upon his mother's power of endurance, that she would fall beneath her cross; but now he saw that the Spirit of Jesus was in her soul, strengthening her and rendering her an apostle of suffering and of sacrifice.

Once more he strained her to his heart in a long

embrace, and then, replacing her in her chair, knelt for a moment beside her to receive her blessing. Then he rose quickly and left the room, without turning to cast that *last look* which is so heart-rending, and which the heart, nevertheless, finds it almost impossible to resist.

In descending the stairs he met the Colonel coming to seek him, for the carriage was seen in the distance approaching. They embraced tenderly; and then the noble-hearted father passed on quickly to the room of his afflicted wife, in order to console her in that hour of supreme trial.

A little farther on stood Agnes, her large blue eyes looking expectantly towards him; and Stanislaus and Captain Warnford, and others awaited him in the breakfast-room. There was not much time for the last adieux. Stanislaus was going with him to the junction, so that he would have opportunity of conversing on the way. The brave old Colonel, on leaving his dear invalid wife, had still a few moments alone with Francis, and had for him but blessings, and words of hope and encouragement. Lastly, Agnes waited her turn.

"It is so short at last," she said, trying to force back her tears, that the sight of them might not increase for Francis the pain of the last farewell."

"The pang of parting will pass, dearest," whispered Francis, "and then will come the recompense. You have to help me by your prayers. *You* must be a Missioner too in *that* way."

A bright smile returned to the young girl's lips as she heard her brother's words, and she recovered the courage which, for a little while, had seemed declining. Good Father Neville's blessing was heard, and was felt resting upon them all. In another moment the carriage was driving rapidly away, whilst those who remained on the terrace stood waving their hands to the young traveller, who was seen kissing his hand to them in return, until the carriage was out of sight. All now returned to the house except Agnes, who still lingered, watching the glimpses of the carriage in the distance through some occasional opening in the trees, and listening to catch the last sound of the wheels. She had borne up bravely all the morning, but now that Francis was actually gone, and could not be distressed by the sight of her tears, she no longer restrained them. In turning to retrace her steps towards the house, in order to hasten to her mother, she encountered the gaze of Captain Warnford, who had come back to the terrace. She started a little, for she had thought herself to be alone; then, smiling through her tears, she said with an air of child-like confidence:

"Oh! Captain Warnford, now he is really gone, I feel what a break up it is to the past; it is the first great step leading him away from us entirely."

Nature, for a moment, would put forth its claims, and the young girl turned away her face and shed the tears she could no longer control.

"Dear child, these are the painful moments of life,"

whispered Captain Warnford, gently. "Do not force yourself to check your tears; they will relieve your heart." Then, after a few moments pause, during which he had regarded her with intense interest, he added, in a tone of gentle apology:

"Pardon me for addressing you as I did just now. It was the sight of your grief." Agnes turned towards him, and looking up inquiringly into his face, asked simply:

"How did you address me? I did not notice."

"I called you dear *child*," was the response.

"Oh!" replied Agnes, smiling, "that is nothing; I am accustomed to it; and indeed," she added, "I am truly a child, and very selfish also, to be giving way like this; now I am going to be brave: besides," she continued, quickening her pace, "I must go to poor dear mamma; she feels so very much the departure of Francis. Will you come with me and help me to cheer her?"

"Rather, *may* I come?" answered Captain Warnford, whilst his sunburnt cheek flushed with strange happiness at the confidence that innocent girl felt in him. He had watched her in her relations with Francis, in her unselfishness in awaiting his departure before suffering her keen feelings to manifest themselves, and her generosity in overcoming again those feelings for the sake of the mother who needed consolation. He was to be the witness now of another scene, which would stamp itself upon his memory, and be hereafter one of those reminiscences which, as so many links, would enchain his heart to Willington Manor.

They gently entered the room where Mrs. Willington had remained since Francis had left her. She was not alone. The Colonel sat at her side, having returned to her immediately after Francis had started. He held her thin white hand in both his own, and, in a low endearing voice, was gently recalling the many motives of consolation the vocation of Francis afforded. The eyes of the invalid were closed. The large crucifix she wore beneath her dress was in the hand that was free; and an expression of mental struggle, yet a peaceful struggle, rested on her features. On hearing the door open the Colonel looked up, and perceiving Agnes and her companion he beckoned to them to advance. The young girl flew to her mother's side, and kneeling down, kissed her, saying:

"The sharpest pain is over now, mamma, dear, is it not? We are all going to help Francis by trying to be very good, and cheerful, and generous in giving him to God."

A smile of pleasure parted the pale lips of the invalid, as she looked on the sweet face of her youngest child and returned her caress. Agnes then resumed:

"See, here is Captain Warnford come to visit you; he is such a great friend of Francis, that I am sure he is welcome."

Mrs. Willington extended her hand to him cordially, and very soon, by means of the soothing, filial manner of Agnes, the Colonel's cheerful tone, and the genial conversation and kindly bearing of Captain Warnford, to the astonishment of all, Mrs. Willington appeared to recover rapidly from the trying scene of the morning. Such is the powerful influence of the angel of love—of *unselfish* love—which delights in alleviating the pains of others rather than in cherishing its own.

Such guests as still remained at the Manor, one after another gradually departed, till at length the only visitor remaining was Captain Warnford, who, as if some secret link bound him there, still lingered on, to the satisfaction of all the inmates, for he had become a general favourite.

Francis had announced his arrival at the College *des Missions Etrangères*, and his letters, from the very first, had filled all hearts with joy. In his first letter to his sister he described to her the hall, wherein are displayed the relics of those who, burning with the love of Jesus, have gone out to bear the knowledge of His Name to the poor Heathen; and who, for His sake, have gloried in laying down their lives. He told her, too, of the languages to be studied, which seemed, he said, already to bear him away in thought to his dear East; and of the habits of life to become acquainted with, in order that they might not in the future be altogether strange.

Agnes was reading one of these letters, her cheeks flushed, and her heart beating with an emotion she scarcely herself understood, when Captain Warnford, who was sitting at a little distance conversing with the Colonel and Stanislaus, observed her. As soon as an opportunity permitted he approached her, and said, smiling:

"You have news from Francis, is it not so?"

"Yes," was the reply, "read it; is it not charming? The pain of that morning of separation was small in comparison with the happiness of knowing he is so happy."

She gave the letter to Captain Warnford, who read it quickly, and with deep interest, for he had learnt to love Francis sincerely.

"How happy he is!" said Agnes, half musingly, looking out to the sea as she spoke; "how happy to know what God wills for him."

Captain Warnford did not reply. He listened to the words, and heard the sigh that accompanied them, but he fathomed not their meaning, or the depths from whence they sprung.

At length Agnes's vacation was drawing to a close, and she was about to return for her last year to the Convent at Torrington. There was a gravity in her sweet young face which none could fail to remark; a look, at moments, which partook almost of the character of anxiety. This expression, moreover, increased whenever she met the eye of Father Neville, with whom she appeared to avoid all private conversation. He, however, who had known her from her birth, and watched her in her early childhood, and had cared for her as one of whose soul he would one day have to render an account, was not at ease; and on the evening which preceded her departure, the old Priest called her aside as she was retiring from the drawing-room, and said to her:

"Come into the library, my child; I have a few words to say to you." She was thus obliged to enter, and having done so, she said, half laughing:

"Are you going to give me a parting correction, Father, for all my misdemeanours since I have been at home?"

"No, my child; there is no cause for correction, but I would know if you are leaving home with any trouble at your heart. The gravity of your face is beyond your years." There was a painful pause. Agnes, in her happy ignorance of the art of cleverly parrying questions difficult to answer, said simply, without hesitation:

"There *is* some trouble at my heart, and I cannot tell it to you, because I have been told to speak of the subject that troubles me *to no one*."

"By whom?" asked Father Neville, quickly.

"By one, Father, who has a right to my obedience; if it were not so, certainly I should have no difficulty in revealing it to you, who have known me all my life."

The old Priest appeared satisfied, and desisted from making further inquiries; but Agnes herself spoke again. Turning to Father Neville, she said, looking up ingenuously into his face:

"Father, I can tell you *this*, without any failing in

obedience. I am troubled because I do not know the Will of God for me."

"Oh, my child!" replied the Father, with a sigh of relief, for a ray of light began to dawn upon his mind, "time and prayer, and fidelity to grace and to the inspirations of the Holy Ghost, will clear away all that difficulty. Go in peace, and without trouble, dear child. I will give your intention a daily memento at Holy Mass. Be faithful to the voice of the good Master, and He will not fail to enlighten you."

She knelt to receive the old Priest's blessing; and then, with a much lighter heart than when she had entered, she left the room.

In leaving the chapel after Mass on the following morning, Agnes encountered Captain Warnford. He was paler than usual, and the lines around his mouth more deeply marked.

"You are suffering more than ordinary, Captain Warnford," said the young girl, gently, somewhat with the manner of Francis, and with the same instinct of tender sympathy for those who suffer.

"Oh! it is nothing," he answered. "How soon do you leave?"

"In an hour, I think," replied Agnes.

"So soon! I had counted on a little time to converse with you," said her companion, in a tone of disappointment.

"Oh!" said Agnes, laughing, "I am only a schoolgirl again now, going back to school. Thank you very much for the pleasure you have afforded Francis and myself, and for your great kindness to both of us. I hope you will pay us a visit when I return home next year."

"Do you?" was the quick reply; "if you tell me so, *then* I will come."

"Yes, do come. I am sure I shall say the same then as now," said Agnes; "and, in the meantime, I hope you will take care of your health."

"I start for the Continent next week," resumed Captain Warnford, after a momentary pause; "shall see Francis, and be able to write to your mother and tell her all about him."

"Oh! thank you, thank you; that is so kind," said Agnes, warmly, "but why do you leave here so soon? why not stay, and"—

"I thought of leaving to-day," he said, interrupting her, "but on second thoughts," he added, half to himself, and with a strange smile, as the words passed his lips, "I believe it better to remain at least one day later."

"Stanislaus accompanied his sister to Torrington, and returned the next day in time to bid adieu to his friend, Captain Warnford, whom no solicitations could induce to extend his visit.

CHAPTER VI.

Three years later.—A death.—The first dark cloud.

How swiftly they have fled, those three years since the day on which we saw Francis Willington leave his home for the College of Foreign Missions in Paris.

Even in the tranquil atmosphere of the family circle at the Manor the months glided rapidly by; but how much more so for Francis, who found himself in the very centre of all that most attracted his mind and heart, of all that was capable of developing his energies, and of expanding and strengthening his natural gifts.

He gave himself to each branch of study with the alacrity and devotedness of a true scholastic, whom nature had more than ordinarily favoured with her gifts, and whose aptitude for attaining knowledge was marvellously increased by the fire which the Holy Spirit had enkindled in his heart.

It was this fire which caused him to *desire with desire* the longed-for day when he might follow in the footsteps of his beloved S. Francis Xavier, Blessed John de Britto, and others, across the ocean to those distant shores from whence resounded in his ears the voices of the poor Heathen, asking for messengers to bring them the glad tidings of peace and truth, for which their souls were unconsciously craving.

Oh! happy days of study for the attainment of the one loved object in life. You know it; you, whose vocation has lit up in your hearts a fire which can never be extinguished; which has rendered long courses of study, not only a source of delight for your intellects, but, as it were, a relief for your hearts, already throbbing with that strong, generous love of souls which urges you to abandon kith and kin, and native land, and to pass over the seas to the nations sitting in darkness, that they too may be brought to a knowledge of Him whose glory is the passion of your souls.

Francis Willington had, as it may be easily believed, given satisfaction in every respect. The professors augured for him a brilliant future, and were secretly gratified in being able to number him among their students. The Superiors, and such as were charged with examining and ascertaining the reality and depth of his vocation, were unanimously agreed in their conviction that he was indeed divinely called to the work of the Foreign Missions; and that his remarkable stability of character, knowledge of human nature, and facility in acquiring all that was requisite for Missionary life, even guaranteed a compliance with his ardent desire of a dispensation being sought for, in order that the usual age of Ordination might, in his case, be anticipated.

His twenty-first birthday had passed, and he was free to return for a short vacation to the home he had not visited since the day we have seen him leave it. Nevertheless, Francis did not seek to avail himself of the liberty that would have been granted him. How tenderly he loved his relatives we have already seen; and how real was the enjoyment he experienced when he found himself in their midst; but the love of Jesus and of souls, when once it has taken possession of the heart, goes on augmenting, and predominates there, where otherwise natural ties would dispute with God His claims. If it could have been possible, he would have wished to have deferred his visit until he should have received Holy Orders; but this would be to deprive those who had, after God, the strongest claims upon him, of a legitimate consolation which his filial heart would not deny them, all absorbed as he was even in the great work of preparation for his future life of sacrifice and labour.

Have any of our readers ever experienced that calm, yet thrilling sense of happiness, which, in its intensity, has—to an observer—something of awe in it? This happiness of which we speak, is something far different from that which results from purely religious sentiments—from union of the will with that of God in the midst of sorrows and adversities. It is rather produced by that natural pleasure which the human heart experiences when its good and pure desires, and holiest aspirations, seem drawing near their fulfilment; and when success attends the soul's yearnings, which, from their intensity, seem to form part of our very being.

We have said there is something of awfulness in it, because, unlike that joy which is founded on purely spiritual motives, it reposes rather on those circumstances of life which are liable to change, and which may, therefore, at any moment dash aside the cup of happiness, which had been to us as a foretaste of that tranquil joy which only can be permanent in heaven.

During the three years which had elapsed, one only circumstance had occurred to cast a cloud of sorrow over the heart of Francis Willington; and even in this circumstance—poignant as had been his grief at the time—there was so much that to his Christian heart was consoling, that it was unable to crush, even for a day, the habitual happiness that resided in his soul, resulting from the daily strengthening hope of seeing his life's-dream realized.

This sorrowful event was the death of that mother whom he had loved so tenderly. When first the news reached him, the one sad thought, so stern in its reality, so desolating in its anguish, that he should never again behold her in this life, absorbed every other remembrance, and deprived him of finding consolation even in the memory of his own happy future, which no present sorrow could touch.

The calm, beautiful countenance of his mother, with

that expression which it wore when she had made the sacrifice which had cost her such a struggle, and had given him up unreservedly to the Heart of Jesus, *for the salvation of the Heathen*, was continually before him, opening the bleeding wound in his heart, and causing the intensity of his filial love to become as a fountain of bitterness in his soul.

The letters, however, which reached him from his father, from Agnes—who had not left her mother's side for weeks preceding the death—and from others, were all so replete with consoling details concerning the happiness of his mother, of her entire contentment as to his vocation, and of tender benedictions which she had requested might be sent to him on her part, that Francis soon took comfort from facts so consoling to Catholic filial piety ; and, in effect, it was not long before it seemed to him he experienced the efficacy of his mother's prayers in that happy country to which her patient suffering and generous sacrifice had doubtless hastened her admission.

The memory of this sorrow did not retrench from the deep full joy that now possessed his soul as he steadily pursued his preparation, not only for his Missionary life, but also for the reception of the Minor Orders, in view of which he gave himself up—during the times that study left him free—to exercises of piety and devotion, above all, to the profound meditation, at the foot of the Tabernacle, of the Life of Jesus, Priest and Victim, the Model of those whom He calls to the sacerdotal and apostolic life, the fruit of whose labours will depend on their likeness to the Divine Master, whose mission upon earth it is their vocation to perpetuate.

So much had nature favoured Francis, and so greatly had his apostolic attraction facilitated the culture and development of his gifts, that study, far from having told upon his physical strength, or overstrained his intellectual powers, had but added new vigour both to soul and body. Thus was he well fitted for a career which, beyond all others, necessitates a *physique* unimpaired by premature work, an energy proof against all wear and tear of climate and hardship, and a moral force to persevere in the midst of adverse circumstances and apparent failures.

It was, then, with a strange misgiving at his heart, that, one night, after the day of mingled study and prayer, he felt overcome with so extraordinary a fatigue, and with so violent a pain in the chest, as obliged him —in obedience to rule—to inform the Superior of his indisposition. The Rector was much alarmed, for he discerned in the changed and pallid face before him the indication of serious physical suffering.

The Infirmarian was called, whose practised eye saw that there was question of no light illness in the sudden indisposition of the young, and, until then, perfectly healthy student. The College physician was summoned, who, although he refused to declare in that early stage the precise nature of the malady, owned that it was grave, and would, *at least*, be long and tedious.

For three entire months Francis lay on a sick bed, enduring great suffering, which, by degrees, told fearfully upon the vigour of his constitution; but his physical sufferings were as nothing in comparison with that which tormented him by reason of the check which his illness had occasioned to his preparations, and the secret apprehension that fears would arise in the minds of those whose charge it was to decide as to his fitness for a work which demanded unimpaired health and vigour. His mental sufferings were so much the greater, as his malady in no way affected his power of thought, which was thus left free to contemplate the possible overthrow of his life's one hope, the fading away of the only dream of earthly happiness that ever had attracted him.

Through the long weary nights of pain *that thought* pressed more cruelly than all; and in proportion as the possible defeat of his soul's most ardent desire presented itself incessantly before him did that desire increase in its intensity. The cries of the poor benighted souls far away seemed ever ringing in his ears, and mingled with the night wind as it moaned around the house. What burning prayers ascended from that bed of pain to the Father's Bosom! What touching appeals to the Heart of Jesus! What aspirations to S. Francis and Blessed John de Britto, that they would obtain from on high that cure which the young apostle felt he did not merit. Oh! surely he had already commenced his apostolate: and if—as doubtless there was—much that was human and imperfect in the impatient desire that consumed him, of seeing the hope of accomplishing his project revive, that impatience would find a speedy pardon in the Heart of Him who knew the depths from whence it sprung, and the struggles that were endured in that young apostolic heart in the endeavour to subdue the human will, and render it submissive to that of God.

At the first intimation of the illness of Francis, Colonel Willington and Stanislaus had started for Paris, in order to ascertain the worst that was to be apprehended, and had remained there until the physician could pronounce that the patient was out of present danger. Great, however, was their grief, and that of the inmates of the College, on hearing that *lasting* results *might* be apprehended from so severe and dangerous an illness. All felt that there was absolutely nothing to be done, but to await the manifestation of that Will which "no man can resist." Francis had been ever pious, ardent in desiring the glory of God and all that could tend thereto, attentive to the movements of grace, and consequently diligent in striving to surmount his defects; but until now he had never practically realized the utter nothingness of the creature when the Omnipotent displays His sovereign dominion, and makes His voice resound "*in power.*"

To *know God* had been his aspiration from childhood, and meditation had been for him as the food and nourishment of his pure soul; but in the three months that he lay helpless, and, as it appeared, *defeated*, on his bed of sickness at the Foreign Missionary College, he learnt more of God's greatness, of His claims, and withal of His love, than in his whole previous life. Sometimes, indeed, the ardour of his temperament, and the intensity of his desire, led him to burst forth in accents which bordered on complaint, but very soon grace acted upon his soul, and the ordinary termination to such manifestations was, "But God wills it; God wills it, and He must have His way."

"It seemed *so* near, my Father," he said, one evening, to the Superior, who sat beside his bed watching him with affectionate interest, and anxiously striving to read in that wan countenance some ray of hope for future restoration of health; "it seemed *so* near. All went so well—too well, I suppose—there was not a cloud, not a doubt; and now, O my God! is it then that Thou hast rejected me for the work for which Thou didst inspire me?" He clasped his thin white hands over his eyes, as if to shut out the rich golden rays of the setting sun, as they streamed in from the window athwart his bed.

"No, no; you must not decide that," said the Superior, gently. "Courage and confidence! to-morrow we all begin a novena to Blessed John de Britto, in preparation for his feast. I shall say Mass, and have several Masses said in his honour, appoint a general Communion, and you will yourself communicate, if possible, each day during the Novena. I will myself bring you the Divine Physician, whose glory alone you desire in the recovery of your health. Now for to-night you must try and compose yourself to rest; reject all anxious thoughts as temptations, and repose your future and all your hope in the Divine Heart which in this suspense and trial designs only your greater sanctification."

There was so much unction in the words of him who spoke, such a tone of encouragement and hope, that the invalid received them as a message from on high, and shortly after fell into a more tranquil sleep than he had known for many weeks.

During the course of the Novena a decided improvement took place in the state of the invalid, and, to the astonishment of all, on the feast itself Francis was, by the permission of the physician, enabled, not only to leave his bed, but even to reach the Chapel, and there to receive the Divine nourishment, in the efficacy of which was all his hope for restoration.

Revived hope lent its aid to the work of convalescence, and, slowly though it was, some symptoms of returning health appeared after several months to manifest themselves. Francis was enabled to resume his studies, with management, however, and watchfulness on the part of his Superiors, for his ardour disposed him to pursue them with redoubled application, in order that the time he had lost during his sickness might not retard the longed-for day of his admission to the Sub-diaconate. But although all acute symptoms had disappeared, and a certain amount of health had been restored to him, the vigour and physical energy for which he had been scarcely less remarkable than for the elasticity and force of his mind, no longer distinguished him. There was an habitual languor on the countenance, whose olive tint had been exchanged for a paleness which was relieved but by the hectic flush, which followed after study or conversation in which the ever-present dream of his life had been referred to.

Thus the months passed on, and still no evidence of a real re-establishment, no advance beyond the stage of convalescence to which he had attained. The physician regarded him with much anxiety, and at length gave it as his opinion that the only probable means of total recovery would be his return for the space of a year to his native air, where, freed from the exigencies of college life, and the attendance upon lectures and a course of study, he might regard as the one present and all-important object the restoration of that health without which his desire of labouring in the Foreign Missions was hopeless.

This proposition was a terrible blow to the ardent heart of Francis. Poor, burning, apostolic heart! it must sustain many such an one before its entire purgation will be accomplished; but as yet the anguish of disappointment and suspense was new to it, and the "hot and restless human will" had not yet learnt the difficult lesson which experience alone teaches, that

> "All is right that *seems* most wrong,
> If it be *His* sweet Will."*

There was nothing for it but to submit. And now commenced for that ardent nature that inward schooling, that sharp and ceaseless practice of interior self-restraint, which was to burn away all the dross of human feeling, until the pure gold of divine charity should alone remain, and be the *sole* spring of every sentiment animating that generous and devoted heart. There was, however, one grace he believed he might justifiably demand, before returning to England, and to the scenes which would be as so many links connecting his present life with the memories of his early youth. He desired at least, before returning to his kindred, to have bound himself with a chain stronger than any nature could form; that so, dwelling amongst kith and kin for a while, since God had so ordained it, he might be there as one *set apart*, irrevocably consecrated and destined for the awful functions of the Priesthood. It was in this view that he had humbly demanded that the order of Sub-deacon might be conferred upon him before he left the College, a petition which had been at once accorded, and for the fulfilment of which he now, with all possible earnestness, prepared himself.

* Father Faber. Poem on "The Will of God."

At length the day arrived on which Francis was to breathe the vow which should sever him for ever from the ordinary class of men, and number him amongst the candidates for that sublimest dignity, that office of such exceeding honour that the Angels well may look down with envy upon those upon whom it is conferred, and gaze on them as they officiate at the Altar with profoundest reverence.

"Oh, this is happiness!" he exclaimed, on the evening of that eventful day, as, exhausted with fatigue, and with the intensity of the emotions he had during several hours experienced, he sat surrounded by several of his companions, some of whom had already been admitted to the Priesthood, others like himself who were as yet but Sub-deacons, but all of whom were burning with the same apostolic desire of going forth to carry the good tidings of salvation far away to the nations who were sitting in darkness. "This is happiness," he said, not with the vehement enthusiasm of a transient consolation, but rather in the tone of one whose soul had tasted for long the sweetness of the love of Jesus, and the surpassing happiness of leaving all things to belong to Him alone. Many were the words of heartfelt encouragement that were addressed to him by his companions, who beheld in him a choice fellow labourer in the great work they all had so much at heart; and when Francis went to rest that night succeeding the day on which the Lord had irrevocably "*become his portion*," confidence revived in his heart once more, that surely He who had chosen and called him, and who had now bound him to Himself, would hear the voice of united prayer, and finally enable him to give himself to the work for which alone he desired life, and health, and strength.

It was but a few days before he left for England that he witnessed one of those thrilling scenes which, from time to time, take place within the walls of the College of Foreign Missions.

The ceremony which precedes the departure of young Missioners for the distant countries for which they have been destined, is one of exceeding beauty and deep signification, the witnessing of which has called forth many a latent vocation, and strengthened and established many a wavering one. But if its influence is thus over souls in whom the Divine Whisper is but beginning to make itself heard, what is it not for those whose vocation is perfected, whose hearts are "straitened" until the day of their own departure should arrive? what, above all, for one, who, ripe for the work, is nevertheless deterred from it by a Will which knows no resistance, and which cannot be averted from its secret designs.

As Francis Willington was that day witness of the ceremony referred to, as he beheld seven of his companions standing there before him in all the vigour of health and hope, and heard them pronounce their vow;[*] as he listened to the touching chant of those soul-stirring words: "*How beautiful on the mountains are the feet of those who preach glad tidings of good things,*" whilst the feet of the departing Missioners are kissed; as he heard the earnest and impassioned words of the preacher, who, in that parting exhortation, set before them in glowing colours, in all its aspects, the life that was before them, the grandeur of their vocation, and the vast arena that was open to them, wherein to display their love for Jesus Christ, their devotedness to His Church, and their zeal in labouring to bring all nations to His knowledge and love; as Francis saw and heard all this, it seemed as if his heart dwelt no longer in his own breast, but that the intensity of his prayer—the power of that strong, agonized, secret cry of his soul, that one day he too might be numbered amongst the band of departing Missioners—had drawn his whole being into the Heart of Jesus, where he prayed, and suffered, and lived, rather than in himself. He saw them depart, and then with the scene he had but lately witnessed engraven on his memory—with the words of the parting exhortation still ringing in his ears, and mingling with the solemn chant, whose words had, even in childhood, so fascinated him—he went to

[*] At the ceremony of a "Missionary Departure," the Missioners bind themselves by vow—made to the Superior at the foot of the altar—to be "the Fathers and Servants of the Blacks," and never to return to their native land unless recalled, or to undertake any other work that might withdraw them from their special Mission, *the Evangelisation of the Heathen.*

his room, not indeed to rest, but to pass some hours of intense inward suffering, in which the strong human will, wrestling with grace, delivered him up to a kind of agony.

How various and terrible to flesh and blood are the means by which the Eternal Wisdom purifies and crucifies those souls whom It destines for high purposes, and for eminent sanctity. How many deaths they have to die before the last, which for them is the sweetest of all, and the gate of everlasting life and freedom and victory. How many secret struggles and combats of which the world around them takes no heed; inward sufferings so refined in their nature that common souls would scarcely comprehend them, even if they suspected them.

Francis Willington had entered into the arena, and must sustain combat after combat of the character referred to, and drink in silent anguish many a bitter drop from the chalice of the once agonizing Heart of his Divine Master.

The day at last arrived when, in company with Stanislaus, who, with his usual affectionate solicitude, had started for Paris in order to travel back with his young brother, in case of an attack of illness surprising him on the journey, Francis must quit the scene of his studies, so dear to his heart; quit all the associations connecting him with the future life he so ardently desired to engage in, and return to that which to him was inaction, and, as it were, captivity. As the door of the College closed, and he found himself alone in the carriage with Stanislaus, he threw himself back and covered his face with his hands to shut out every object which they passed, as they rapidly drove towards the railway station. He wished to keep his soul's eye fixed unswervingly upon the Divine Will; but one who well knew human nature spoke truly, when he said:

"But the thoughts we cannot bridle
Force their way *without the will.*"

So it was with Francis. Memories of all he had heard, and seen, and learnt, during his College career; all that had fostered his vocation, and strengthened and intensified his *attrait* for the Missions, rushed back upon him now with resistless power. It was a new thing for Stanislaus to behold that intensity of mental suffering, and nevertheless that quick mastery over self, so as to concentrate within the great sorrow which for a few minutes had shown itself so evidently upon the countenance of Francis. The elder brother felt that expressions of sympathy or encouragement would at that moment be out of place; but before they reached the railway station he had spoken the words his affectionate heart longed to proffer, and he had the satisfaction of seeing that Francis appreciated them, and was even consoled by the knowledge that his brother understood the anguish it was to him to leave a spot from whence it seemed he had to take but one step more in order to reach the cherished object of his desires.

CHAPTER VII.

Old Scenes.—"Now," and "Then."—Agnes grown up.

It needed all the self-control which Francis's strong nature could muster, all the influence which grace had attained over his pure and generous soul, in order to hold back the torrent of feeling which rushed over him as the carriage drove through the well remembered scenes of his childhood and early youth, and as he recalled how, when four years previously he had left his home, no cloud was on his horizon, but only the bright full hope which had seemed so akin to certainty, and which had shone above and all around him, and penetrated his whole being.

How intensely painful is the impression when, returning to familiar spots, we behold everything in nature unchanged, whilst our own fondest hopes are faded, if not utterly blighted.

To the outer world it was an ordinary occurrence. A young man returning from College in ill health, to be at rest and well attended in his father's house. The outer world, we say, beheld no more than this; but perhaps an Eye was looking down from heaven with extreme complacency upon the young Sub-deacon, as with folded arms and closely compressed lips, but with an expression of chastened sorrow in the quick dark eye, he regarded the various well known spots as one succeeded another, until the carriage stopped before the old familiar front of his childhood's home.

There upon the terrace stood the Colonel, who had been pacing up and down in expectation of the arrival of the sick son, whose disappointment his own heart had felt so keenly, and sympathized with so tenderly. The sound of the carriage attracted, in another moment, Agnes to the spot; and then appeared Father Neville, and Mrs. Stanislaus Willington. The meeting was naturally one more of pain than of joy; nevertheless, affection and sympathy have their peculiar balm for sorrow, *soothing* the wound oven though they cannot always heal it.

The thought which sent the sharpest pang through the heart of Francis as he entered the house, was the absence of her whom he had loved more tenderly than any other upon earth. Yes; his mother was gone. He had known how painful would be this impression on his return home, and had prepared himself for it; but when, on entering the dining room, his eye fell upon the loved portrait, bringing before him those beautiful features, those soft earnest eyes which seemed to rest upon him now with so much tenderness, he was for a moment unmanned, and tears started to his eyes. All present understood his emotion, and Agnes stole quietly up to him, and slipping her hand into his, whispered :

"She is happy now, dearest; she has gained the beautiful crown, and all the sooner for her sufferings. She will help you, and obtain for you the desire of your heart."

Francis made no reply: his heart was too full. He only pressed his sister's hand in acknowledgment of her affectionate sympathy. Very soon the habit of self-restraint resumed its power, and Francis was able to force back the tide of natural feeling into the recesses of his own heart, and to manifest the manly, cheerful, and self-possessed deportment that was ordinary to him.

His strength of character, as well as the power which divine grace had obtained in his soul, manifested themselves in a striking manner during the first days of that painful return to his father's house. Not a spot, not a room in the house, or a view from a window, or a part of the grounds, which did not recall the dream of his childhood, which was to ripen into the one absorbing thought and desire of his life.

There was the restless sea, with its ships just discernible far away in the horizon, on which in boyhood he had so often gazed and thought of the distant lands to which those ships were going, where were existing *millions of souls who knew not Jesus;* and as he had gazed, the desire of their salvation had taken a tangible form in his young heart. There was his own handiwork

—his "hut of S. Francis" on the little island in the midst of the river, where he had so often sat and read of the Missions, and dreamt of his own future work. There was his roughly cut altar in the wood, which he had fashioned whilst his youthful imagination had conjured up the extemporised altars erected by the Missioners, as they journey through the forests or pause in their course on the mountain side.

There was the very room he had from childhood occupied, and where he found himself now once more, with its far sea-view seen through the opening in the trees.

There still hung upon the wall the well-known *Horloge Eucharistique*, by means of which he had, whilst still but a boy, familiarized himself with the very spots where, all through the day and night, the Adorable Sacrifice was being offered.. This had ever been to him his devotion of attraction, by which was continually augmented the fire that lived within him. There also were still suspended the picture of his beloved S. Francis, and that of his chosen model and patron, Blessed John de Britto. All and everything brought back to him the long long hope, so trusted, so *all but* realized; and as he looked around him, and memory recalled in vivid colours the bright unclouded past, the sense of present disappointment became the more intensified.

Francis Willington had no ordinary work to accomplish in the Church of God; he was called to glorify

God in an eminent degree, and *therefore* it was necessary that he should be proved in the fire of adversity, in the battle-field of inward struggle, and in the furnace of divine love with which his pure soul burnt.

In these days of trial—early days as yet—in which nature sometimes wrestled fiercely for the victory, the venerable Priest who had known and guided him from infancy was his greatest consolation.

Father Neville knew that ardent, passionate, but yet pure soul, even to its very depths. He knew all its capacity for attaining a very high sanctity; and the more thorough was his knowledge thereof, the more earnestly he desired an entire co-operation on the part of Francis, that so the designs of God over him might not be frustrated.

Moreover, Father Neville could understand, in all their refined anguish, the pangs of disappointment, and the throes of temptation to which Francis was now given up. He could understand them as those only can who have passed through the fire themselves; and thus, knowing, as he did so well, the soul on whom the divine action was operating, and the nature of those operations, so crucifying to the human heart, he was enabled both to administer consolation and to assist grace in the great work it was bringing about for the divine glory in that sensitive and generous soul.

The first day after his arrival, Father Neville, at the request of Francis, accompanied him to visit his mother's grave. A white stone cross marked the spot.

On this was suspended a wreath of *immortelles*. Francis knelt upon the grave, and bowing down his head until it touched the grass that waved in the fresh autumn air, he poured out his soul in prayer, and suffered his tears to flow unrestrained. As he knelt there, the memory rushed over him of the sharp pang *he* had once sent into that heart now cold and lifeless, when he told her of his irrevocable resolution to give himself to the Foreign Missions. Looking up at Father Neville, who stood with folded arms, affectionately regarding him, he said, as if he knew the old Priest would comprehend his thought:

"I might have spared her *that* sorrow, those bitter tears, that sacrifice. See, she has gone home; and I am still here."

Father Neville looked at Francis a moment steadfastly, and then said, gently:

"Do you regret having been instrumental in adding *one* more jewel to her crown? Would you have deprived her of the eternal and special beatitude she now enjoys for having sacrificed to the Heart of Jesus what was dearest to her on earth? And you, would you have wished to have left undone that good work, to have not endured *that* suffering which *your* heart felt no less than hers, for the sake of the poor Heathen, for whose salvation you offered it?"

Francis raised his head; he had kissed the grave reverently and tenderly, and now stood erect once more, regarding the cross, with its wreath of *immortelles* speaking to the heart in their mute eloquence. .

"No, my Father," he replied, in his usual calm, earnest voice, "I would not have deprived her, *indeed,* of *that* additional jewel, or the Heart of Jesus of that glory which her sacrifice, and my anguish in obliging her to make it, have procured. God bless you for recalling me to my better self. Oh! how prone nature is to put forth her claims. These are miseries that make a man long to lie down *there*"—and he pointed to the quiet grave before them as he spoke—"above all, when in the very beginning of the battle one is rendered useless, as I am."

"Nay, nay; there is nature again," said Father Neville, gently. "You have many a battle to fight for the great King yet before you lie down to rest. You say truly, it is but the beginning. He has given you a great and difficult enterprise. You must not lose one of those souls whom He has given you to save; and for this you must be very generous, very faithful; above all, very patient and enduring."

There was a deep earnestness in the old man's words and tone, which sank deep into the soul of his listener, where they found a faithful echo in that *interior* voice which told him that he had indeed a work to do for God, which fidelity on his part only could accomplish.

No less remarkable was the change which had been wrought in Agnes, than was that which, during the four years which had intervened since Francis had left his home for Paris, had taken place in him. If in him appeared now a man of matured judgment, a moral force, and self-restraint more in accordance with middle age than with early manhood: in his sister was discernible a calm earnestness, which seemed to emanate from some permanent train of thought; a stability and strength of character which, although it may exist within, does not ordinarily reveal itself in girls of her age, unless indeed called forth by unusual circumstances.

She had remained at the Convent for the purpose of completing her education longer than had been intended, so that when she finally returned home, she was approaching her eighteenth birthday. From that time she had been the devoted companion of her invalid mother, her solace in hours of extreme suffering, consecrating for this end her many abilities to the service of the loved invalid.

That which especially rendered her companionship precious to her mother, was the deeply religious tone which pervaded all her sentiments, the tender yet solid piety towards all that regarded the glory of God and the extension of His kingdom.

This it was which lent to her conversation a depth and yet an ardour, a breadth of thought, moreover, far beyond that usually met with in persons of her age and sex; and many who would have avoided the frivolous prattle of ordinary young ladies, found in her child-like conversation a charm which they could scarcely explain to themselves.

Since the death of her mother a tinge of sorrow had lurked in her large thoughtful blue eyes, and a deeper gravity had become visible in her whole bearing; but it was when she had received the first intelligence of Francis's illness; when, later, she had learned the dread apprehension of his eventual incapacity for the Foreign Missions, that all her strength of character, and all her religious tendencies and depth of piety manifested themselves.

But although endowed with *depth* of character, Agnes was by no means *reserved;* on the contrary, it was for her a peculiar trial, (one which God permits some souls to suffer,) when she was obliged to use constraint in her intercourse with those who might reasonably expect her confidence. Her frank and simple nature was ill at ease when, from motives of prudence, or for the avoidance of discussions, she was compelled to weigh carefully the expressions that might escape her.

She was to experience this trial, even within the limits of her own family circle.

Our readers will not have forgotten the prejudice which Miss Margaret Willington entertained to the idea of English Priests in general, and her own nephew in particular, leaving England for the Foreign Missions.

Now, when the news of his illness had reached the Manor, Miss Margaret, having expressed her regret for it, as became an affectionate aunt, did not fail to declare it to be her conviction that this illness was sent by a merciful Providence, in order to manifest that the Divine Will desired him to remain in England, and to concentrate there, for the good of his own country, the zeal that he wished to carry away and to exercise far off.

The expression of this conviction had drawn from Agnes, in whose presence it was made, a warm refutation, and she had spoken so earnestly and eloquently to her aunt on the point of *vocation* in general, that the suspicions of the latter were aroused, so that poor Agnes found herself subjected to endless inquiries and pointed questions as to the cause of her evident earnestness regarding the subject under discussion, independently of the interest she naturally had in her brother's success. Agnes, as we have before stated, was no adept in the art of parrying inconvenient questions, and the course, therefore, which she was obliged to adopt was one wholly at variance with and uncongenial to the simplicity and ingenuousness of her character, namely, one of absolute reserve. Whenever her aunt mentioned the subject of Francis's "failure," as she persisted in calling it, the young girl was silent, but her heart burned hotly within her; a fact which did not pass unnoticed by more than one of those who surrounded her.

When, however, that Francis had returned, and that his aunt continued, in her quiet, self-convinced, self-reliant way, to proclaim her conviction, even to himself, the young sister's indignation could no longer be constrained; and one day that the conversation had turned on the unhappy subject, and that Miss Margaret had, with special emphasis, expressed the hope that she should in a few years see her nephew working for his own country, "as English priests *ought* to do," etc., Agnes, with heightened colour and a strange light in her eye, replied:

"Aunt, to say the least of it, it is unfeeling to speak like that. You know the one hope of his life. All his happiness is centred in it: and, believe me, you have not yet comprehended what *vocation* means, if you think it possible to settle down as you say, in a way that is opposed to it."

"Hush, dearest; it is not worth exciting yourself about," said Francis, stopping the young girl, for he saw she was prepared to say more. Then, turning to his aunt with a quiet smile, he added: "Agnes has said truly, aunt; it is not possible to settle down in a way opposed to that of divine vocation. If our Lord does not will to give me health for the Missions, He will teach me how to work for them in another way. The conversion of the Heathen will ever be the one object of my life. It was the Holy Spirit who implanted that attraction in my soul in my childhood;

it is He who has fostered it: and the Spirit of God cannot contradict Himself."

Miss Margaret was silenced, if not convinced, which assuredly she was not, and as soon as possible hastened away, as was her wont when the conversation had not pleased her, and that her favourite views were not altogether accepted as infallible.

Agnes became once more the companion of her brother, as in the days of their childhood, yet in a manner far different. She reserved to herself the care of attending to his health, and was wont to say, in her cheerful accents, that it belonged to her to prepare him for the Missions by doing all in her power to promote the recovery of his strength. To this end, she established herself, on his first arrival, as his infirmarian, and obliged him to obedience in point of repose, diet and the rest, taking care that his hours of study, and the length of his walks, should be regulated by prudence. She was watchful, also, that painful thoughts should be, as far as might be, dissipated by recreation; for this purpose exercising her musical talent in order to divert his attention, and frequently engaging him to accompany her, or, in his turn, to gratify *her* by singing, or by playing on the flute, in which he excelled, and which accomplishment he had been encouraged at the College to exercise during hours of recreation, as being a useful auxiliary in distant and barbarous countries, amidst the fatigues of long and painful journeys through the wild solitudes which

Missioners must traverse in passing from one Mission to another.

But another element mingled now with the deep and ardent affection which Agnes bore her brother: that of reverence. He was no longer her equal; he was consecrated and bound for ever to God by an irrevocable vow: and when she beheld the visible marks of that state which separated him from ordinary men—the tonsure, the soutane, the biretta—she felt that, strong as was natural affection in her heart for the brother of her childhood, it was yet his consecrated *soul* which was, above all, so precious to her now.

Francis, on his side, watched his sister with no less interest than affection, for he could not fail to recognize in her a soul endowed with more than ordinary capacity for glorifying God, and over whom Divine Providence had special designs. Nevertheless, the subject of her vocation had never been approached between them. It was not until about six months after the return of Francis that a circumstance occurred which tended to break the silence which had, upon this point, been hitherto maintained.

There were at the Manor two visitors, one being our old friend Captain Warnford, whose society afforded the invalid inexpressible pleasure; the other, a former school companion of Agnes, who had been invited to pass a few weeks at the Manor, previous to starting for a continental tour, which, as the young lady herself alleged, would terminate for her by her entrance into the novitiate of the *Sœurs de Charité* at Paris.

Helen Sternbrooke had become a convert to Holy Church whilst she was at the Convent at Torrington. Thus Agnes had known her both before and since her conversion. There was much that was congenial between the two young girls; but the principal link which united them was their mutual attraction for all that regarded the advancement of God's kingdom in Heathen lands, an attraction which Helen had been conscious of whilst still outside the pale of the Church, and which probably had been a leading star, designed by Providence for drawing her within the true Fold.

It occurred one day that Captain Warnford and Francis, with Agnes and her friend, were engaged in general conversation, in which Mrs. Stanislaus Willington, who sat at a work table near them, also took part. Miss Sternbrooke had casually alluded to some incidents in the past, which had revealed Agnes's predilections whilst she had been at school.

"Agnes will one day certainly be a Sister of Charity, and go out to China, and be a martyr," said Helen, laughing. "We used to laugh even at school, and say she would never have space enough to work in, so large are her views."

Agnes continued her work without looking up, but she was smiling in silence. Francis seized the opportunity that was thus afforded him of sounding his sister's intentions, and said:

"Is that true, Agnes?"

"What; that I am going to be a Sister of Charity? Oh! certainly not; and precisely for the reason Helen has alleged in my regard: I should not have 'space enough to work in.' I should feel constrained;" and she made a gesture as of one in bonds, laughing as she did so, and feeling the more provoked to laugh, as she knew how droll her words must appear to her hearers, not one of whom suspected her meaning.

"But you were always so zealous for helping on the work of Priests, and above all, Foreign Missioners," persisted Helen, "that I thought nothing else would satisfy you but actively sharing in their labours."

"If it is true that I possess the zeal you impute to me," said Agnes, in the same gay tone, "I must have a territory wherein to exercise it vaster than could be given me as a Sister of Charity. I must be free as a bird in the exercise of my Apostolate. It must not be confined to any particular town or country. I have not what Aunt Margaret would call sufficient 'solid virtue' for *material* hard work, or our Lord does not give me the attraction for it, and I cannot accept the doctrine of going against attraction in everything."

There was an earnestness in her tone which betrayed a deeper meaning in her words than she had intended they should convey. She looked up, and accidentally met the gaze of Captain Warnford. She smiled, for the evident doubts her words had roused up in her hearers, amused her. In that smile that passed between them there was no signification, no sign of a private understanding; there was nothing on the part of Agnes but an accidental glance, and a pleased acknowledgment on the part of him whose eye she met; but Francis, who had seen that smile interchanged, was, for the first time, startled into a vague suspicion, and Mrs. Stanislaus Willington, who, with a woman's quickness had also perceived it, had not been slow in interpreting it according to her own mind.

Agnes quickly changed the subject of conversation, for she was free from that egotism which delights in making self the topic of discussion; but Francis was resolved to fathom deeper when the opportunity occurred, for his sister's words and manner had now increased the anxiety he had—he scarcely knew why—entertained in her regard since his arrival at home.

The weeks passed on. Miss Sternbrooke was still a guest at the Manor, as was also Captain Warnford. The expiration of the time permitted to the latter for residence in England, was approaching, and his return to India was frequently mentioned in the circle to which he had endeared himself.

"Warnford looks anxious: I cannot fathom the reason of it," said the Colonel, one day when it happened that the family group, including Father Neville, were alone together.

"Well," replied Stanislaus, smiling, and with his characteristic ingenuousness, "one thing I know;

when he returned home his intention was to take a wife back to India with him, but he appears as far off from attaining his project as when he arrived in England."

"Oh!" said Mrs. Stanislaus, laughing, "I am of a different opinion."

"Indeed," replied her husband, quickly, for he was much attached to his friend, and deeply interested in all that concerned him. "Do you think," he added, "that Miss Sternbrooke has attracted him?"

"No; I do not," said Mary, laughing at her husband's *naïveté*.

"What do *you* say, Agnes?"

"I never thought about it," was the simple reply; "but I should be sorry if Captain Warnford had become attached to Helen, because I believe she has the intention of becoming a Sister of Charity, and I should regret any pain for Captain Warnford."

Francis watched her closely, and could discern in that calm sweet face but entire truth, without a shadow of duplicity. Somehow, he felt relieved, though he could not explain to himself the cause; but Stanislaus meantime had at last penetrated Mary's thought, and delicacy forbid him to say or inquire more upon the subject in the presence of his sister.

It was a few days subsequent to the above conversation that Francis became the unintentional auditor of a few words which decided him to speak freely to his sister on the subject regarding which they had been mutually so reserved, and which caused him so much solicitude.

He was entering the library, believing it to be vacant, when suddenly a well-known voice said, gravely, but kindly:

"My child, you are trifling with grace. Beware of exposing yourself to the danger of losing the most signal mark of His love that our Lord could show you."

Francis started; it was too late to withdraw, for Father Neville—it was he who had spoken—had turned from the deep bay window which had concealed him, and where he had been conversing with Agnes, and perceiving Francis, came towards him, addressed to him a few friendly words, and then, with a grave and somewhat pained expression upon his countenance, left the apartment. Francis advanced towards the window, where he beheld Agnes standing against the wall, her face paler even than was its wont, and tears coursing each other down her cheeks. She seemed as if she wished to escape his notice, but Francis was determined to satisfy himself regarding his doubts, which had been considerably augmented by the few grave words he had just accidentally overheard.

"What has happened, dearest?" he said, tenderly. "Why that sorrowful little face, and those tears? Come, my little sister, tell me the cause of your pain, whatever it may be."

"I cannot! I cannot!" she answered, with great

agitation. "Come, you are fatigued, Francis. You had better withdraw to your room."

Francis sat down, saying, "I do not go from here until you have told me what great trouble this is that you say you cannot tell me. Of course," he added, "if it is anything of *conscience* I have no right to press you; but if it is, as I suspect, some pain or struggle of the heart alone, tell me, dearest. Am I less to you now than before I belonged to our Lord exclusively? And do you think my heart is become less feeling because I belong to Jesus?"

"Oh, no, no!" she exclaimed, tenderly, trustingly, and with that reverence which had marked her intercourse with her brother since his return from Paris *consecrated*. She knelt down beside him, like a gentle child, and prepared to give him the confidence he desired; but there was evidently some great struggle going on within her breast, which it seemed impossible for her to master.

"I have never spoken to you of a subject which has been always lying near my heart since I was but fifteen years of age," she began; "I mean"—and her voice trembled as she pronounced the words—"my probable vocation to religion."

"No; you have been very reserved with me upon that point, Agnes," replied Francis, gently; "but for all that, I have been very anxious about you; and now the ice is broken there must be no more reserves. What is the cause of your distress at present?"

"I have had trouble from the commencement," said Agnes, feeling now more at ease, "and have been *obliged*, partly in obedience, and partly from other motives, to maintain a reserve, which you know is not natural to me, on the subject of my vocation. The great cause of my past embarrassment has been that they would persist in wishing to persuade me that my vocation was for the active life. They grounded their judgment on my attraction for the work of the Foreign Missions, and said that it was just persons having that marked *attrait* whom they had need of for sending out to distant countries. All destined me for a Sister of Charity, whilst I meanwhile felt that our Lord had called me to work indeed for the Missions, for souls throughout the world, but by means of a different Apostolate. I was told I was headstrong, and self-willed; but I felt that our Lord does not *force* us to serve Him in a way which would be uncongenial to us. The routine of teaching, of active works of charity,— very different in the reality of practice to what persons *imagine* them to be—and the necessary intercourse with seculars; all this had for me, I do not simply say, no attraction, but even was repugnant. I admire those who devote themselves to the active life: for those whose vocation it is, they have not those repugnances, nor could *they* support another kind of life; but for me, the more they spoke to me and endeavoured to persuade me, the more clearly I saw I should never succeed, even if I yielded so far as to attempt a life to which I did not feel myself called. *You* know by experience this inward conviction, do you not, dear Francis?"

"I know it *well*," he replied; "but go on, dearest, and let me hear how affairs stand at present."

"When they found I would not yield, they told me I was not to speak of my own attraction, at least for two years; if at the end of that time I still persevered, it was to be taken into consideration: consequently, the question of my vocation to religion at all has been kept a profound secret. No one has ever known it here, except dearest mamma, shortly before she died, and Father Neville only in part. Not even *he* knows to what Order I wish to belong. Now that two years are more than past, and that I have communicated my unchanged purpose of becoming a Carmelite—to which Order only I desire to belong—my vocation has been considered a true one, and—and," she added, tremblingly, "there is but the time of my leaving which remains to be decided. Father Neville, not knowing *all*, believed I delayed in order to stay with darling mamma until the end, and since then he *seems* displeased that I do not speak openly to him about it, and take steps for putting my intention in execution. He told me to-day, just now, indeed, that I am trifling with grace, and insinuated that I am in danger of losing my vocation."

"Well, Agnes, I am inclined to be of Father Neville's opinion, if you delay any longer. Provided you still have the same ardent desire, *why* would you defer?"

Once more the old troubled expression appeared upon the young girl's countenance, and she was silent; whilst to Francis returned the suspicion which his sister-in-law's words a short time previously had awakened in him. He was resolved to know the truth; and, with the candour for which he was remarkable, he said quickly and bluntly: "Agnes, answer me: has Warnford anything to do with your delay?"

"Captain Warnford!" she exclaimed, looking up into her brother's face with that clear, simple, astonished glance, which, when we meet it, more thoroughly dissipates all doubts than would any number of verbal refutations. "Oh, no; what should *he* have to do with it? he knows nothing of my intention." She paused, for the piercing look of Francis struck her, and then, as by a sudden flash, she became aware of her brother's thought; then also recurred to her Father Neville's warning.

"Ah!" she exclaimed, "*now* I know Father Neville's meaning. He thinks I am in danger of becoming really unfaithful to our Lord, and of taking back the heart I have so long given exclusively to Him. And you, dear Francis, did *you* think that might be?"

"It would not be impossible, dearest; we must be delicate in our way of acting with the love of Jesus," replied Francis, seriously, and reverently raising his biretta as he pronounced the sacred Name. "If you delayed much longer the Heart of our Lord might be wounded, and no one can answer for the ultimate consequences of the least estrangement between His Heart and yours. And you have not told me yet the cause of your continued delay."

"Can you not guess it?" answered Agnes, her tears falling fast as she spoke.

"No, indeed, I cannot; come, tell me, dear, quickly."

"It is my reluctance to leave you in your present state of health and anxiety," she said, with painful emotion.

"Agnes," replied Francis, gravely, yet tenderly, "that is really not a motive for delaying to put your project in execution; and if you make it so, dear child, I repeat Father Neville's words, and tell you that you risk losing your vocation. The love of your brother opposing itself to the love of Jesus in your heart, and preventing you from corresponding with His divine call, might lead the way to a greater infidelity, and finally to the loss of the precious grace which heaven has bestowed on you."

"If all had gone well with you," she replied, her tears still flowing as she spoke, "if this terrible disappointment had not happened to you, if I had known you to be assured of succeeding in your desire, I should not have cared, even if I had never seen you again; I should have known you were happy, and that would have sufficed me: but now such sad associations are connected with the thought of you, it seems so cruel to leave you just now, I, your little nurse, who am always at hand to serve you, and ——." Tears stopped her voice, and Francis interrupted her, saying, gently:

"All those thoughts and feelings are snares of the enemy. It is ever thus when a soul intends to give herself to God; and when the enemy sees he cannot allure her by any gross and manifest infidelity, he assaults her on a side whereon plausible reasons might be advanced. Such things *have* been, as young persons remaining too long in indecision, or deferring at least to quit their home on account of a sick mother or brother, and having ended in their own marriage; yet they would have been as much shocked in the beginning had any one told them it would end thus, as you would be if I said the same thing to *you* now. Shall I tell you what you must do at once, and without any further delay? You must let your intention become known, in the first place. Tell papa this very day. Let Stanislaus and Mary know it, and through them the others. This is essential. Come, courage, little one, '*He who loves father, or mother, or brother, or sister more than*' the good Jesus, is not—you know it—worthy of Him. Having '*put your hand to the plough,*' there must be no 'looking back.' And God forbid that *I* should be any stumbling block to you. If those tears that fall so fast are on my account, dry them up. You are suffering, dearest, for *me*, what once *I* myself suffered when I had to break to our dear mother the fact of my vocation; but you have not *one* pain, at least, that *I* had. We know how much it cost her to give me away for ever for the Foreign Missions; whereas, believe me, you could not afford me a greater consolation in this time of anxiety than the knowledge of your vocation, so much so that I would do all in my power to help you in the speedy accomplishment of it."

Agnes looked up into her brother's face, and the bright glance in his dark expressive eyes, and the cheerful smile which beamed upon his countenance, assured her that his encouraging words proceeded from his heart.

"But let me stay with you until you are better, until your hope has become re-established of accomplishing your desire," the young girl pleaded.

"Until," replied her brother, smiling, and yet with a deeply earnest tone, "until you had no sacrifice— worth the name—to make. No, no, Agnes, the Heart of Jesus demands more generosity from you. *If*, as you say, you feel yourself called, go where our Lord calls you, and let no human motive retard your departure. Think not at all about me. I am in God's holy keeping. I belong to Him irrevocably and exclusively, and He will make use of me in His own time. Your sacrifice and prayers in the holy state you have chosen, will perhaps hasten my recovery, and move our Lord to grant me what I long for. Certainly, *infidelity* on your part would not render me happier. Now, what are you going to do?"

"What you have told me," was the simple reply. "I will speak to all to-day. Poor Father Neville will be so glad to have this long mystery cleared up at last. Oh! Francis, it is such a relief to my heart that I have told you, and that you will not be so very lonely, after all, when I am gone."

Francis smiled fondly at his sister, and did not answer her last words; then he said, cheerfully: "To-morrow we must begin the lessons in the Breviary. I must have the satisfaction of initiating you into one of your most solemn future duties. And now tell me what thought first attracted you towards the Order you desire to enter."

"I read the life of S. Teresa, and then one of her works, '*The Way of Perfection*,' in which she so clearly shows the spirit and the end of the Order of Carmel which she reformed. I did not speak of it for a long time, but during the hours of free time, when I could do so without remark, I read those works again and again; and I used to think so much of that great Saint, and pray so much to her, that I seemed to grow quite familiar with her; and it seemed to me she received me for her own, and instructed me in many ways, and strengthened me in my attraction for a life at once eremitical and apostolic. Her extraordinary devotion to the Holy Ghost; her marked devotedness to the Church, and to all that regards its interests, and her burning zeal for souls, all this established between my heart and that dear Saint a kind of link; and sometimes when I have felt very much alone, S. Teresa has seemed like a friend to me, beckoning me to a land where I should not be alone, but where I might help the Church, as S. Teresa teaches us we can."

Francis looked down at the beaming face which no longer wore any trace of sadness. She, who, but a little while ago was hesitating to obey the call of heaven, through a motive of tender solicitude for her suffering brother, was now animated anew with the courage with which the thought of her high and beautiful vocation inspired her.

The young man read his sister's soul, and all that was passing within her's found an echo in his own. It recalled to him his own early days of promise, of unclouded hope, and, for a moment, a sense of sadness stole over him, as the thought of his doubtful future flitted across him; but instantly he rose above the feeling which nature had evoked, and, forgetting self, applied himself to the sweet task of encouraging his young sister in her design.

"I believe I shall meet with some opposition," continued Agnes, "for the contemplative life, and its mission in the Church, is, generally speaking, so little understood. Persons imagine it to be a kind of selfish existence, into which people withdraw in order to avoid the duties of social life."

"Indeed," replied Francis, "is it so? It is far otherwise appreciated in France, and generally on the Continent. Whenever any disastrous news reached us from our Missions abroad—and always when Missioners were starting—we were in the habit of sending to several of the Carmelite Convents in order to demand special prayers. And it is the same with the clergy generally in France; they regard the Carmelites as their fellow-labourers, and justly so, since S. Teresa, if I mistake not, reminds her daughters, in the very work you have referred to as having been instrumental in attracting you to her Order, that prayer for Priests and their Apostolate is one of their most imperative duties, an integral part indeed of their vocation."

"Yes," replied Agnes, "and that was another motive which inspired me with the desire of being a Carmelite. Oh! Francis, how good our Lord is to me, and how happy I am to day, only ——."

"Only what?" asked Francis.

"It seems so selfish and so cruel to rejoice in my own happiness, when I have, in order to attain it, to leave you suffering, and in the midst of disappointment and sorrow."

"Have I not told you, dear Agnes, that the knowledge of your vocation, and the hope of seeing you set your hand to the work without further delay, is a source of real consolation to me? Why then make yourself unhappy on my account? I acknowledge that the circumstance of my present failure renders our separation more painful than it would otherwise have been, but once over, the thought of your beautiful mission will help me to bear my cross, and the assurance that I am satisfied ought to comfort you."

She took her brother's hand and reverently kissed it. She had secretly hoped to have beheld those hands holding on high the Eucharistic Victim, and extended to give the sacerdotal blessing, but this, too, must be sacrificed for Jesus.

"And now," continued Francis, "have you as yet taken any steps, or have you entertained any idea as to the Convent in which you will enter?"

"Yes," replied Agnes, "I have, since a long time communicated to Madame de Masillon, in my correspondence with her, the desire of my heart. You know her experience and judgment; and she has always said she believed me to be a subject for the Order of Carmel. Now from the beginning I was attracted specially to desire to leave my native country, and I have constantly wished to enter a Carmel in France. On informing Madame de Masillon of this, she referred me to a Convent and interested herself in my behalf with the Superiors. I have had correspondence, more or less constant, with the Prioress, ever since I left school, and her counsels have been to me my greatest comfort; for there have been times when I have felt very lonely, and sometimes even impatient, obliged as I was to keep the thing a secret. So you see, dearest, the ground is tolerably smooth before me; there is but to inform papa and obtain his consent, and then there remains but the question of the time of my leaving."

"And that must be as soon as possible," said Francis, cheerfully, but firmly. "Now you have *sown to-day in tears*, but you have *reaped in joy*, is it not true, dearest? Yes, I read it in your face: it is always thus when we make some sacrifice for God. It cost your heart very much to tell me you must leave me, but it is over now and peace remains to your soul, because you have done what the Heart of Jesus demanded of you. And is He not worth a thousand sacrifices?"

"Oh, yes, and life itself!" cried Agnes, in that deep but tremulous tone which speaks so eloquently of the heart's fulness.

"Yes, but *life* would be easier and sweeter far to sacrifice than other things that God asks us to give up to Him sometimes, for His love, and still to live on," said Francis, quietly. His face was turned away that Agnes should not see it, for he could not chase away the thought of that martyr's life and *martyr's death*, which he had so ardently desired, and which desire—all divinely inspired as it had been—he had been required to sacrifice, *perhaps* for ever. He quickly rallied, for he was making rapid strides in the science of that holy inward restraint which souls united intimately to God learn with such facility, and turning towards Agnes again with his own bright smile, he said:

"Now, before the night has closed upon us, you will have spoken to papa; and before another day is passed all will know—including Aunt Margaret—that you are going to leave home, and father, and brother, and native land, and to become a Carmelite."

"Yes," said Agnes, laughing through her tears at the somewhat comical tone in which Francis had made special mention of Miss Margaret, "it shall be as you desire, dearest, and may God bless you for the comfort and assistance you have given me to-day."

CHAPTER VIII.

The Announcement.—Results.

In preparing to inform her father of her desire to enter into Religion, Agnes felt none of that pain which she had done in breaking the subject to Francis; nor were there any circumstances which would render her departure more than ordinarily painful. On the contrary, there was everything which would tend to palliate the pain of leaving a beloved parent for ever.

The Colonel's own generous character, together with his solid piety, would have aided Agnes in the task which lay before her; but in addition to this, she had the consolation of knowing that she did not leave him in solitude, which is perhaps the most painful trial of any to those whom God calls to devote themselves exclusively to His service. She would leave her father in the society of an affectionate son, whose amiable wife was as a true daughter in filial devotedness to her father-in-law.

Little ones, also, were springing up to gladden the old manor house with their childish glee, and to be the sunshine of the domestic circle.

Already there was a little John de Britto, the eldest of Stanislaus's children, to whom Francis had consented, when at Paris, to become god-father, on condition that the boy should receive the name of his own beloved patron. Then, too, there was the good old Father Neville, the friend of so many years, whose society had been for so long the Colonel's never-failing stay.

Thus, when Agnes drew her father aside and made known to him the wishes of her heart, she did so calmly and peacefully, and without the anticipation of painful results.

The interview, however, was not to conclude without the sanctifying mark of the cross being set upon it. Colonel Willington had been put in possession of his child's whole heart, and although the natural feeling of regret at the prospect of losing for ever the society of one so dear to him, saddened him for a few moments, his faith, his piety, his *unselfish* love for his child, and his solicitude for her *true* interests, caused him at the same time to rejoice for her sake.

"There is one question, however, my dear child," said the Colonel, with a sudden gravity, "that I feel myself bound to ask you, in order to satisfy my own conscience in giving my consent to your desire. Satisfy me fully upon that point, and my consent shall not be withheld from you a single moment. It is this. Are you *quite* sure that your heart is entirely free, and that, notwithstanding your pious desire of becoming a Religious, you have not some little attachment to

Warnford, into whose society you have been so much thrown, and whose admirable qualities you have not failed to appreciate?" Agnes looked up at her father with an expression of profound amazement, as if she were surprised that he could for a moment entertain a doubt upon the point in question.

"Oh! papa," she exclaimed, "if you knew what Jesus makes Himself to a soul whom He attracts to give herself exclusively to Him, you would not think it possible to put any creature, whatever might be his qualities, in comparison with *Him*. Who is like to *Him?*" she said, in a lower voice, covering her eyes as she spoke, and involuntarily giving utterance to the impassioned words of the Psalmist, expressing his appreciation of the Divine Beauty, and His supreme claim upon His creature's love.

"Oh! my child, I am satisfied," said the Colonel; "go, and belong to the good God who has called you thus away from us all, that you may live for Him alone. You have your old father's full consent, together with his blessing." The old man took his child in his arms and embraced her tenderly, whilst tears of mingled gratitude for the favour God had conferred on her, and of natural regret, which, in those first moments of sacrifice would rise, involuntarily flowed.

His emotion quickly passed, and he had resumed his former cheerful bearing, when a shadow passed the window.

"Ah!" exclaimed the Colonel, quickly, as if suddenly recalling something painful, "I fear for *him*."

"For *who*, papa?" inquired Agnes, who had caught the words.

"For Warnford, poor fellow; but it is too late now."

Too many allusions had of late been made to Captain Warnford for Agnes to remain any longer ignorant of their import; whilst on the other side, the Colonel, less prudent than Francis had been—who, although he had had his suspicions aroused regarding the sentiments of Warnford towards Agnes, had, nevertheless, forborne from communicating them to her—did not conceal from his young daughter his impressions, namely, that their visitor, in his frequent sojourns at the Manor, had become attached to her in a way which would now be for him a source of pain.

"I cannot believe that what you say is true, papa," said Agnes; "for, certainly, my intercourse with Captain Warnford has been rather that of a child with an elder relative; but, if it is so, I can only say I deeply regret it, for on no consideration would I have willingly been a cause of pain to any one, much less to one so good and kind, and who already suffers."

She had scarcely spoken the words when Stanislaus and his wife entered the apartment, having just returned from a walk in which they had been accompanied by Captain Warnford, who had left them but a minute before. The new comers were not slow to perceive that a *tête à tête* of no ordinary interest had been interrupted, and an awkward hesitation as to whether to withdraw or to remain, did not fail to manifest itself.

The Colonel soon decided it. "Your coming is *à propos*," he said, closing the door. "We have an announcement to make, and the sooner it is done the better."

Stanislaus looked up brightly, for he anticipated something of an opposite nature; and Mary smiled significantly, as if she guessed her husband's thoughts.

"Our little Agnes is going to be a Carmelite, with the free and full consent of her old father; and I am sure she will have the congratulations of all the rest. Eh! Stanislaus, why do you look so grave? Are you not pleased at the news?"

Stanislaus's countenance had in truth undergone a sudden alteration. The colour mounted even to his brow, and an expression very like indignation flashed in his eyes.

"If I am glad for my *sister's* sake," he said, "I cannot forget that I have a *friend*, whom I consider to have been wronged. You must have known this, surely, long ago," he added, regarding his father almost with sternness; "and you could not have been blind to Warnford's preference for Agnes."

"Hush, dear Stanislaus," said Mary, gently, for she saw that sudden indignation had caused him to forget that he himself had been blind upon the point until very recently; "you were not so clear-sighted yourself, if you remember; and I am quite sure our father would never lend himself to anything that would tend to produce pain or misunderstanding."

"You are right, Mary," said the Colonel. "And as for you, my dear Stanislaus," he added, smiling at, rather than being provoked by his son's impetuosity, "I assure you I knew nothing more of Agnes's intention than yourself until an hour ago. It is true, on her leaving Torrington, the Superior there spoke to me of her *possible* vocation, but added, that it was one which needed well proving, and that the less that was said about it—at least for some time—the better. I acted on her advice. I have, as Agnes knows, never alluded to the subject; and even when questioned by your aunts upon the point, about which they seemed to have some suspicion, I have always evaded it. Seeing Agnes apparently so contented at home, I even thought that she was *not* called to the religious state. On the other hand, she showed herself more disposed for a quiet domestic life than for one of gaiety, and therefore I did not deem it necessary to conduct her to fashionable places at particular seasons, for her 'trial,' as they call it. I took care to provide sufficient society here to meet that end; and I believed if there was a more particular trial needed, it was to be found in the pretty frequent intercourse which she had with one whose qualifications far exceed those of the empty-headed, frivolous fellows ordinarily met with in ball-rooms."

"Good!" cried Stanislaus, breaking out again into indignation in his friend's behalf; "and so Warnford was to be made a tool of, by which Agnes's vocation was to be tested. Hardly honourable, this, I must say!"

Again the hand of his gentle wife was laid upon his arm.

"No, dear Stanislaus," she said, quietly, "it was not so. Captain Warnford was never designedly invited here for that purpose, depend upon it. He came here as any other guest might come; he felt at home with us all, and was always welcome; and you, dear, were yourself his special friend, and pressed him to come, though, to say the truth, not much pressing was required. Our father knew nothing certain regarding Agnes's vocation; and very naturally he thought that if there were nothing solid in her resolution, Warnford would be one likely to attract her regard, and therefore he let things take their course. Come, dear, be reasonable; and, after all, we do not know for certain that your friend's happiness is in any serious degree compromised."

"But *I do* know it: he has spoken to me upon the subject this very day," cried Stanislaus, with more impetuosity than prudence; "and I know how far it has gone. I wish I had never brought him here."

He rose from his chair and walked up and down the room, his arms folded and his colour heightened by excitement. Indignation was, however, giving place to gentler feelings, which, although impetuous, sprung from the strong deep sentiment of friendship which he entertained for his old friend and brother in arms, and from the regret he could not help feeling for the pain he would suffer. Mary quietly slid to her husband's side and whispered to him, gently:

"If Captain Warnford has said anything to you mention nothing of it now: see, Agnes is already afflicted, poor child, at being the cause—although so innocent—of giving pain to any one." Stanislaus turned round and looked towards Agnes, who was resting her face in her hands, weeping silently. Her brother was softened. If his generous heart was aching for his friend, it was no less touched with compassion for his sorrowing young sister, and, approaching her, and taking her hands in his, he said, tenderly:

"Look up at me, dearest Agnes, and tell me you forgive my thoughtless and unreasonable anger. Neither you nor my dear father have been to blame in this painful affair, but I cannot help feeling for ——." A look from Mary caused the words to die away upon his lips, and instead of them Stanislaus added: "May God give you success in your desire. For those whose vocation it is, I can well believe it is a blessed life." Then, turning towards the Colonel, he said: "And you, dear father, pardon my rude and hasty words, just now. You can understand ——."

"Yes, yes, Stanislaus, I understand," said his father, kindly; "it was, after all, a manly sentiment which prompted that little ebullition."

He smiled as he spoke, one of those smiles which reveal entire peace and good understanding between hearts; and then there was a little pause which seemed to indicate a tacit desire to break up the conversation.

Mary Willington drew her young sister-in-law by the hand and led her to her own room, for, with the delicacy of a woman, she knew what she must be suffering, nay, she perceived it upon her pale and sorrowful young face. When they were alone Agnes threw her arms around the neck of Mary, and, hiding her face upon her bosom, sobbed like a child. For some moments her sister-in-law let her weep in silence, pressing her tenderly to her heart the while, and gently smoothing the golden hair as it hung in rich masses over her arm as she supported her.

"Oh! Mary," at length she exclaimed, "it is so sad, so very sad—if it is true, as Stanislaus intimated—that I must really be a source of pain to that good kind friend of his, and of us all. What am I worth that he should have cared for me? But it could not be helped. I could not speak of my intention to become a nun, because they had forbidden me; besides, I never dreamt that Captain Warnford cared for me, except as the young sister of his friend Stanislaus. How should I?"

"It was because of your vocation to a higher state, dear child, that you did not discover it," said her sister-in-law, gently; "your thoughts all turned in a different direction, and, absorbed as you were in the one desire, the one object, that which another would have discerned passed by you unheeded. But now, dear

Agnes, be comforted, for, after all, there is for Captain Warnford nothing *humiliating* in this disappointment; he has no rival but *One*, whose claims he, as a good man, a true-hearted Catholic, full of faith and piety as he is, would not venture to dispute. If I mistake not, his noble character will show itself in this trial; and for you, dearest, you have chosen a Crucified Spouse, and you must not refuse any particle of the cross He asks you to share with Him. I know well the peculiar pain this is to you; to your woman's heart, to *yours* in particular, which is very sensitive; painful also on account of your position, and the state of life you so soon design to enter: but all this has been planned by that Wisdom which cannot err, and by that Heart which has so jealously guarded yours, and prevented it from running away from your first, your only Love."

Oh! what balm those gentle words poured into the young girl's heart, that generous heart which was grieving for another's pain, of which she was the innocent cause.

What human consolation can equal that which a Christian woman of delicate feelings, and of warm and tender heart, is able to afford one of her own sex afflicted with sorrow or perplexities, which only a woman can understand, or a woman's gentle skill, or *tact* as it is called, alleviate?

Gradually calmness returned to the soul of Agnes, but she felt naturally timid at the thought of meeting Captain Warnford, and she crept closer to her sister-in-law, as the shadows of evening closed round them, and reminded them of the necessity of going down to the drawing-room, where the others would be assembled.

"Your poor head is aching, I know," said Mary; "I think I shall forbid your coming down this evening. Come, I will take you to your room; it will be better for you to remain quiet, and I will excuse you to the others."

Agnes gratefully complied with the proposition, and Mary, having seen her quietly settled in her own little room, went down-stairs to the others, not a little anxious as to what might have been communicated to Captain Warnford, and how he had received it.

A glance was sufficient, on entering the room, to assure her that nothing had as yet transpired; and Stanislaus found an opportunity of telling his wife that he intended to inform Warnford himself of Agnes's design that night.

In the course of the evening Francis stole up to his sister's room, for he suspected that her indisposition, upon which plea Mary had excused her absence from the family group, resulted from her having acted upon his injunction, and made known to all the long entertained desire of her heart.

He easily drew from her the details of what had passed, and the cause of the grief which oppressed her. Francis paused a few minutes after she had concluded, and then he said, thoughtfully, and with a tinge of sorrow in his voice:

"It is the seal of the Cross, which Jesus sets upon every work of His. We can but leave it all to Him and pray. *Some* good will result from it, be assured; some glory for His Heart, and merit for ——, for all who suffer on account of it."

How strong and deep a thing is friendship between men when it is based upon Christian principles. Stanislaus Wilfington had had opportunities of appreciating the nobility of his friend's character, and the worth of his manly affection for himself for many years past, but he was about to behold him under a new aspect, and under circumstances altogether unprecedented in his experience at least, in the midst of which Warnford's generous devotedness and delicacy of feeling were to shine forth with redoubled brilliancy.

It was a difficult task which Stanislaus had taken upon himself that night, the more so as that very day Captain Warnford had for the first time revealed to him his sentiments regarding Agnes, sentiments which, ignorant as was Stanislaus of his sister's attraction to a higher state of life, caused him no little satisfaction.

His manner of commencing his painful duty was characteristic of his frank, ingenuous character.

"You scarcely expected to see me again to-night," he began, as he entered his friend's room, all having retired for the night. "I am come to tell you something in reference to the subject of which you spoke to me to-day."

His companion looked at him quickly, and with a

sudden expression beaming on his sunburnt face, which too plainly revealed the hope which lived within him, he said:

"Ah! you have told her, and"—

"Not precisely," replied Stanislaus; "but she has herself this very day spoken to my father for the first time of a desire which she has entertained since she was but fifteen. My sister intends to be a Religious."

He paused a moment, for the sudden change in the countenance of his friend perplexed him as to how he should proceed. There was pain indeed and disappointment, instead of the hope which shone there as a sunbeam but a minute before; but there was something else which Stanislaus could not understand.

"You were quite unprepared for this, were you not, Warnford?" he resumed, after a moment of silence.

"Certainly," was the calm reply, but spoken in a voice whose tone too clearly revealed from what depths of suffering it proceeded. "Had it been otherwise, I should not have spoken to you as I did to-day. Did none of you know this, then, until to-day?" he added, fixing his searching glance upon his friend.

"None of us, Warnford. The poor child was not permitted to speak of it until lately; and I fancy Francis's illness and disappointment have deterred her still further from doing so. Thus it is the misunderstanding has arisen."

Again there was silence. The strong man sat with his hands clasped before him on the table, and his head bent down towards them. His companion could not fathom what was passing in his heart; he only felt that he was in the presence of poignant suffering: but for a few minutes he would not again speak, although he longed to say what his friendship prompted. It was one of those hours of secret anguish through which some have to pass, as through a fire, which is to test their virtue. If the good gold preponderates, those hours of fiery trial will be for them the starting point from whence they pass onwards to higher and nobler deeds, if not visible to human eyes, at least to the eyes of God; but if the gold is overcharged with dross, they will not stand the test, and their after lives will manifest them as they really are.

Arthur Warnford had known how to live in the midst of an atmosphere hurtful to the greater number, without having become infected by its poison. Well informed, his experience extensive, his natural gifts and amiability had rendered him welcome wherever he went. Nevertheless, in India as at home, in his regiment or in the midst of his family, he had ever felt within himself a yearning for some companionship, some friendship wholly apart from the associations which the great world presented to him. That companionship he had found in the innocent young sister of his friend, Stanislaus Willington. It had become the dream of his life, the ideal of his happiness, to take back to India as his wife that young girl, so childlike, and yet so superior in mental gifts to the women he had, for the most part, met with. He would have spoken of it long before, but he could not discern in Agnes anything which testified that she either understood his preference, or reciprocated it in any other way than as a child for an elder friend and almost brother. Within the last few minutes his life's dream was utterly dissipated. It all passed before him in the twinkling of an eye, as he sat there, resting his poor throbbing temples on his clasped hands: the approaching return to India *alone*; the severance *for ever* from that bright pure being whose frequent companionship had shed such sunshine over his life during the last three years. All was over now, and he must go back to the old life with the hope that had been awakened lying dead in his heart for ever. At length he spoke.

"It is better that I leave early to-morrow morning, without seeing your sister," he said, in a voice which indicated the sharp struggle within.

"Oh, no, no, dear Warnford," cried Stanislaus, "do not do that; it will but make things more painful both for yourself and for all of us. As for me, I shall never forgive myself for having brought you here if you are going to be miserable on account of your acquaintance with my family."

Captain Warnford looked up at his friend, and in doing so perceived the expression of deep pain upon his frank countenance. "What would you have me do, then, Stanislaus? Stay here in a position so constrained as mine would be, especially as—if I understand you aright—Agnes knows that I even spoke to you to-day?"

"Yes, thanks to my stupid impetuosity," replied Stanislaus.

"If she had not known, it would not have been so difficult," said Captain Warnford; "but now it would be so very very painful. Perhaps also she would herself prefer not to see me again."

"Will you promise me to stay over to-morrow, at least?" demanded Stanislaus. "I will take care to ascertain about it, and let you know as early as possible. Oh, but I am sure," he added, "it would be so extremely painful if you left suddenly; it would give all an impression that you were deeply hurt, perhaps even estranged from us—my father, poor Francis in the midst of his bitter trial and suspense, and Agnes herself, who will already have a time hard to nature before her final leave-taking; and as for myself, well, it seems a bitter ending to our long and familiar intercourse, it seems as if our friendship itself is to break up."

Captain Warnford rose, and, approaching his friend, grasped his hand.

"No, no, Stanislaus!" he cried, "it shall not be. You shall not all be made to suffer more on my account. You have hard things to bear just now in your family; and I will share them with you. After all, who am I, that I should dispute with the Divine Lover, whom that dear child has chosen since so long a time? Do as you say. Ascertain the wishes of the others, and I will, yes, I will try to remain, if that will cause less pain than my departure."

He turned away a moment, for his voice was broken, and he wished to hide his emotion in order not to increase the embarrassment of Stanislaus.

His Catholic faith and his piety had taught him, without his knowing it, the secret of self-sacrifice, and the inward conviction that the act he had partially consented to, would be not only a delicacy towards those who so much esteemed him, but, moreover, acceptable to God, gave him a strength to suffer, and opened in his soul a source of consolation hitherto unknown to him.

As early as possible the following morning, Stanislaus, having spoken to his wife of the conversation he had had with his friend, and conferred with her on the advisability of informing Agnes of its results, sought his father, Father Neville, and afterwards Francis, in order to communicate to each what had passed on the previous evening.

Francis was deeply touched at what he heard from Stanislaus, for he loved Captain Warnford as an elder brother: but when he heard that through Stanislaus's impetuosity Agnes had been made aware of all, his sorrow was redoubled. He knew too well his sister's sensitive nature, and the peculiar pain it was to her to be a cause of suffering to another; he knew too, how, apart from all this, she was struggling with herself in order to make the sacrifice generously of leaving *him* also in his present state of trial.

"Poor little Agnes!" he said, in a tone full of tenderness. "Do all in your power, Stanislaus, to make Warnford remain, if he can do so without showing what he feels. His sudden departure would leave such a painful impression, such a gloom, upon us all, just at the time we have need of everything to keep up our hearts, for I conclude Agnes will leave us very soon."

All had left the Chapel after Mass that morning, save Father Neville, who knelt within the sanctuary, making his thanksgiving, and another figure, who remained kneeling at a little distance. When the old Priest rose and withdrew to the sacristy, Captain Warnford, for it was he, followed him, and, closing the door, said:

"I wish to speak to you a few words, Father, before meeting any of the family. You know all that has taken place, and the position in which I am. Which will be the best in these painful circumstances for me to do, to leave at once, or to remain, as if nothing had happened?"

The Father paused a moment, and then said, slowly, regarding his companion earnestly as he did so:

"Are you sure that you can remain and appear 'as if nothing had happened,' as you say?"

"Not *exactly* as if nothing had happened," was the answer; "but without manifesting anything of that keen distress, which at present I must bear. I wish to avoid giving pain; and it seems my sudden departure would be very painful to all."

"Yes;" said Father Neville, almost in a whisper; and then, after a longer silence, he said, very gravely, as if by a sudden inspiration: "would you like to do something *for the good God*, something *more*, perhaps, than you have as yet ever done?"

No one had ever said such words to him before, and they sunk down into the depths of his stricken soul, striking a chord, which hitherto no hand had ever touched.

"Yes," he replied, earnestly, "if that is possible to me."

"It *is* possible to you. Stay here, and, by God's grace, overcome yourself for the sake of others. If you left now, in sorrow, it would leave a most painful impression. Besides this, would it not be something so to gain the mastery over nature as to be able to give up generously the treasure you had hoped to possess for your own? to see her leave us all for ever, and to acquiesce with all your heart in God's most holy claim upon her?"

Captain Warnford spoke not for a moment, but his lips quivered as he listened to those last words. At length the answer came, and it was one that thrilled the soul of the old Priest with a joy that he had not known for long.

"Then it would be for God's greater glory if I stayed?"

"Undoubtedly," replied Father Neville, "if you do it generously for God. It is contrary to what *nature* would prompt; it demands the sacrifice of *self*, for God and for others."

"Then I will remain," answered Captain Warnford, firmly, but with an agitation in his voice which told how strong was the struggle in his manly heart. Tears started to the old Priest's eyes as he heard the words and saw how much the final resolution cost; and his own voice trembled as he said: "May God bless and help you, and give you that peace and consolation which He is ever ready to bestow on those who make any sacrifice for His glory."

As that martial figure passed out from the sacristy, and knelt down to adore the God of the Eucharist, and to offer Him the sacrifice he had just made for His sake, few would have suspected the keen anguish that lay at his heart; few would have dreamt of the simple submission he had just rendered to the counsel of the Priest of God, and of the peace, even amidst his pain, which that submission and the generous sacrifice he had made of his own feelings, were already mariting for him.

The first meeting with the entire family, assembled in the breakfast-room, could not be devoid of a certain restraint, which was, however, considerably lessened by the fact of Stanislaus having awaited his friend outside the chapel, in order to assure him that his remaining at the Manor would be a source of consolation to all.

Captain Warnford was himself the first to dissipate the sense of restraint, which, at the commencement, could not but be felt by all. Without assuming an exaggerated gaiety, his manner was cheerful though subdued, and he failed not to sustain the conversation when at intervals it appeared to flag.

But later in the day a new trial awaited him, one of the many comprehended in the sacrifice he had made of remaining there, where now things seemed for him so changed.

Francis, as we have seen, had decided that Agnes's approaching departure should no longer be a subject to be avoided in the family circle, and he assured himself that it would be even kinder towards Warnford, although, perhaps, painful at first, to speak of the thing as a matter of course. Francis himself set the example when the opportunity offered.

It occurred that Agnes was with her invalid brother, bestowing on him some of her care, and conversing with him of the hope of *her* life, which at length appeared so near realization, when Mary and her husband entered, accompanied by Captain Warnford. They were unconscious of the presence of Agnes, for they expected to find Francis alone, it being one of his ordinary hours of study.

"We expected to have broken in upon your solitude," said Stanislaus, "but it must be confessed, in spite of those two great volumes before you, you do not wear a very studious appearance this morning."

"No;" replied Francis, smiling, "Agnes and I have been at our old childhood's game, talking over future hopes, only, ——" he added, with a generous effort to suppress the rising sigh, "they are no longer, as formerly, *my* hopes, but her's."

"But your own are not buried for ever, Francis," said Agnes, who, although she had been advised by her brother to speak of her approaching departure without restraint, even in the presence of Warnford, felt it a relief just then to divert the conversation from herself. "You are really better," she continued, "and perhaps the spring will restore you altogether."

"Oh! yes;" said Stanislaus, cheeringly, "I do not believe you are going to slip so easily out of your trip to the Cannibal Islands. You will go 'to Heaven gloriously, with the loss of your head' yet, as the old books quaintly express it, be assured of it."

None could refrain from laughing at Stanislaus's comic and novel mode of imparting encouragement to his brother.

"I do not know," said the latter; "my hope of recovering health is founded on something far different to the mere recurrence of a milder season."

"On what, then?" asked Stanislaus.

"Upon the efficacy of saying my first Mass. I only await a little more strength before presenting my petition to the Bishop, asking him to ordain me," replied Francis, a bright smile shining in his eyes as he spoke.

"You rogue;" said Agnes, "and you have kept this a profound secret, even from me!"

"Ah, well; you see, little sister, I can have my secrets as well as somebody else," said Francis, laughing; and then, conducting the conversation back to the subject which had been but touched on in the commencement, and which he by no means wished to drop, he added: "At any rate, there are no more secrets now between any of us. And it is better thus. Are we not all of the same opinion?"

Warnford was the first to reply, and he did so simply, and in a manner tending to set all at ease.

"Yes," he said, quietly, "where there are no circumstances that would render it more painful and embarrassing, it is better that between those united by such strong links of friendship there should be no reserves."

An assent, more or less audible, broke from the lips of all, and Captain Warnford felt that he had succeeded thus far in the object for which he had remained at the Manor, in diminishing the pain of others at the cost of self. In the few words he had spoken he had said much, and it was understood by all; but still Francis wished, during that interview, that Warnford, whom he knew to be making such efforts over himself, should become familiarized with his new position, and accustomed to the new light in which henceforward he must regard Agnes.

"Viewing it in the light of faith," said Francis,

upon whom the *grace* of the Priesthood already seemed to rest, although as yet the *character* thereof was not imprinted on his soul, " we cannot but rejoice at the sacrifice which our Blessed Lord has asked of us in calling Agnes to His special service. It is a grace not given to all, and cannot be too highly prized."

"Undoubtedly," said Mary; "I have always felt the greatest reverence for those who give themselves to God in religion."

"But I cannot understand," said Stanislaus, "why Agnes did not choose the life of a Sister of Charity, or some of those nuns who go out to foreign countries helping the Missionaries, knowing her particular love for blacks, and savages, and Hottentots, and such like people. How is it, Agnes?"

"Because," said Agnes, laughing at her brother's dry pleasantry, "our Lord called me to help the Missionaries as S. Teresa helped them, by prayer and penance. Do you not know," she added, looking archly at Francis, "that it is said S. Teresa gained more souls by her prayer and penance than even S. Francis Xavier did by his preaching and miracles?"

"Go, and do likewise, my dear;" said Francis, smiling, "but please to pray for your brother also, that he may follow in the footsteps of S. Francis."

"There is not much fear of my forgetting to do that, dear Francis," said Agnes, tenderly, "or of my forgetting to pray for any of you."

"How long will it be before the day of departure

arrives?" asked Francis, a sharp pain passing through his heart as he forced himself to ask the question.

"As soon as possible," replied Agnes, quietly, and without looking up. "I shall write to the Convent to-day to inquire of the Mother Prioress how soon I may start. My preparations will take but a very short time, and then there is nothing to detain me." As she said the last words she looked towards Francis, and once more the old pain came back in all its poignancy. To leave *him* in his state of suffering, broken down in health and hopes ; *this* was the thorn for her heart, and as she felt its sting, unbidden tears filled her eyes.

Francis perceived her emotion and understood it. He shook his head at her, smiling, and said gently :

"Do not forget what I told you yesterday. Your vocation and your ultimate success will be the greatest consolation to me, next after the realization of my own hope." Then, turning to the others, he said, as if wishing to explain his sister's slight emotion: "Agnes feared to tell me of her long-cherished desire until yesterday, because she dreaded to give me the pain she believed it would be to me."

"And," added Agnes, through her tears, "because she had not courage to leave you, suffering as you are."

"It was natural enough," said Mary, with her usual kindness, " but," she continued, " if it is any comfort to you, dearest, be assured I shall take Francis under my special care when you are gone, and strive to compensate to him, as far as I can, for the absence of his little nurse."

"I know you will, dear Mary," replied Agnes, gratefully, "and your presence here is my greatest consolation in leaving Francis and dear papa."

Stanislaus had risen meantime, and having caught sight of the letter-carrier coming towards the house, left the room.

Not long after Mary and Agnes rose to depart, and Captain Warnford, having remained behind a few minutes in order to say some words in private to Francis, moved towards the door.

On reaching the long corridor in which Francis's apartment was situated, he found Mrs. Stanislaus Willington and Agnes still near, and looking from the large bow window out upon the landscape, beautiful even in its yet wintry aspect.

A servant at that moment came up and demanded Mary's presence in the nursery, Master John de Britto having shown somewhat of the impetuosity which, in early days, had characterized his uncle Francis, and which had afforded him, in succeeding years, a scope wherein to exercise that truest of all mortifications, the discipline of the will.

Captain Warnford seized the opportunity thus presented to him, of saying to Agnes the few words which his noble heart prompted him, in order that there might be on both sides a perfect understanding, during the time which must intervene before Agnes's departure.

"Agnes," he said, "you are on the eve of leaving, in order to enter on a new and devoted life, and it is in view of this fact that I say a few words to you. As Francis said just now, '*there are no secrets between any of us now.*' You know all. I will not touch upon that which, but yesterday, I was on the point of declaring to you. I did not even suspect that you had resolved on embracing the religious life. But my object now is to endeavour to place you at perfect ease in your relations with me during the short interval that remains. They told me if I left, as certainly my natural feelings prompted me to do when first I heard,"—he paused a moment, as if in difficulty how to express himself—"if I had left," he continued, "they said it would be more painful. You can understand *why.*"

He paused again, and Agnes spoke.

"Your remaining here, Captain Warnford," she said, with a gentle dignity, "*is* a consolation to us all. What pain your sudden departure would have given to poor Francis, and to Stanislaus, and papa, and"—she added, with some little difficulty, "to us all."

He had now assured himself that the sacrifice he had made was one bringing peace to hearts, and he was content. But he spoke once more.

"I respect the holy state you are about to embrace," he said, "and may you find in it that happiness I desire for you. As for me, you must regard me—I hope you will—as *a third brother.* It must be henceforth : Francis, for he is the first and dearest, although the youngest, and Stanislaus, and Arthur, or —" he added, with a genial smile, the reflection of that peace which the spirit of unselfishness had shed into his soul, "or if the *eldest* is to take the precedence, the order must be reversed, and it must be Arthur, and Stanislaus, and Francis."

A weight seemed to fall from the young girl's heart as she listened to the gentle yet manly tones that spoke those words of comfort.

"Shall it not be so?" he continued. "Will you have me for your *brother?*"

"Yes," replied Agnes, striving to suppress her tears, for she could not be ignorant of the struggle that strong man's soul had had to sustain, and was even sustaining now, in order to enable him to speak thus. It was sweet to give consolation to one whose claims upon her esteem were so considerable.

"Yes, I will think of you as an elder brother," she said, in a voice as steady as she could command, "as one of our family."

"Then you must call me *Arthur.* You would not call your *brother* 'Captain Warnford.' Call me *Arthur.*"

In a low gentle voice she complied with his request, and then that short interview was over, and Warnford knew what was before him. He must suppress all that could reveal the struggle that human feeling would not fail to raise within his breast; suppress it for the sake of others, above all, for the sake of her whose remaining days in the bosom of her family he would indeed regret to render more painful than the thought of the approaching separation must necessarily make them.

Thus had comparative ease been attained in the midst of circumstances which had been so embarrassing: and when a short time after the same little company met again in Francis's room, and were joined by the Colonel and Father Neville, they perceived that all was on a right understanding, and that "*that peace which the world cannot give*" reigned amongst them.

"Here come Aunts Cecilia and Margaret!" exclaimed Stanislaus, as, at a later hour that day, the Misses Willington appeared, approaching the house. "Agnes, I must really amuse myself with Aunt Margaret at your expense. Will you forgive me?"

"Oh, yes," said Agnes, laughing, "provided you do not give Aunt Margaret any pain."

"Oh! no, *I* will not give her any, but I cannot promise that she will not give herself some pain. She clings so to certain theories, that she seems as if she considers herself injured if all do not exactly adopt them."

"Poor Margaret," said the Colonel, kindly; "it is her weak point; but she is very good."

At that moment the door opened, and the two ladies entered. After the ordinary salutations had been exchanged Stanislaus commenced his harmless assaults.

"Aunt Margaret, there is news for you, fresh since yesterday, and on the most reliable authority. Agnes is going to become a Foreign Missioner."

Miss Margaret, as also her elder sister, looked up in

astonishment at their nephew, and from him to the others. A smile rested on every face, but there was nothing explanatory of the announcement made by Stanislaus.

"What do you mean?" both ladies exclaimed, simultaneously; "some of your mischief again, doubtless."

"I mean what I say," persisted Stanislaus, "that Agnes is going to become a Foreign Missioner, and in a few weeks she will, in all probability, *leave England*."

At the last words Miss Margaret started, for she began to suspect there was something real—some truth conveyed in Stanislaus's speech.

"What does he mean?" she said, turning towards the Colonel.

"Well," said the latter, smiling, "Stanislaus has dressed up truth in a somewhat novel garb, but in order to put an end to mystery, I will tell you at once, that Agnes has resolved—indeed, since a long time—to become a Religious."

Both ladies were amazed at the suddenness of the tidings, neither having even much thought of the vocation of their young niece, but they were no less pleased than astonished, for, with true Catholic instincts, and Catholic piety, which both possessed in an eminent degree, they appreciated at its full value the blessed lot of those whom Heaven calls from a world of frivolity and temptation to a life of devotedness, wherein their energies, their mental capacities, and their hearts, can be exercised to their utmost extent, and in channels the most legitimate.

After warm expressions of congratulation came the natural demand as to what Order their niece intended entering.

"I conclude," said Miss Margaret, "it is that of S. Vincent de Paul, since Stanislaus infers that you will be obliged to leave England for your noviciate; and indeed, in all probability, for the exercise of your vocation, unless they sent you to England, which perhaps they would, in consideration of your being English."

"No, dear aunt," said Agnes, scarcely able to suppress her laughter at the quiet way in which Miss Margaret was settling the matter; "that was but Stanislaus's manner of expressing it. I am going to enter a Carmelite Convent in France. That was what was meant by my becoming a 'Foreign Missioner:' The Carmelites, you know, are specially devoted to every work which tends to the extension of the Church; and of course the Propagation of the Faith, and the Foreign Missions, are in the foremost of that number."

The elder Miss Willington expressed her entire satisfaction at her niece's choice, without any remark upon her preference for leaving her native land. Not so, however, the younger sister.

"It is a beautiful vocation, my dear, and one that cannot be too highly appreciated;" said Miss Margaret, "but what *has* induced you to leave England?"

"Our Lord calls some to leave, not only their father's

house; but also *fatherland;*" said Agnes, gravely, "in addition to which, from the beginning, I felt myself attracted to a foreign country, and especially to the most apostolic of all nations, France."

"Well, I think it is quite *wrong* for young persons to be leaving their own country in these days, when we want all the strength Catholic numbers can afford, and which religious communities so greatly tend to increase."

"My dear friend," broke in Father Neville, somewhat bluntly, "' *the Spirit bloweth where He willeth;*' and who shall dare to control His action? There is a special Providence in all these attractions; and I contend for it, it is wrong to oppose them. It is *not* wrong to leave one's native land, or to stay in it; it is a matter of indifference *in itself*: but it *is* wrong to resist or contradict the guidance of the Holy Ghost. We do not know what we are about when we act thus."

Miss Margaret, whose respect for Father Neville never changed, was somewhat checked by these words, which had entirely banished the playful tone which the conversation—through the medium of Stanislaus—had taken in the commencement. Nevertheless, she had another objection to oppose, which she did in her usual gentle, but self-convinced manner.

"But what is to prevent you, dear Agnes, from praying for the Missions, and the Church, and France, and the rest, as efficaciously in England as in a foreign land? *Your* apostolate does not require your personal presence in the actual places in which you are interested."

"True, dear aunt," replied Agnes, "and for that very reason, you must allow that I do my own country no harm in leaving it, since I can pray for it equally well a thousand leagues away from it as if I were here. When God called me to Religion, and to the Order wherein I hope to live and die, my mind never reverted to any other than the country whither I am going. I made no formal comparisons, nor do I now. I only know there *is* such a thing—for I have been told it by those competent to speak—as vocation to a particular country, and even to a particular monastery."

"Undoubtedly," said Francis, "there is; I have heard of it myself repeatedly."

Poor Miss Margaret felt herself vanquished this time, although, as usual, she remained as inwardly unconvinced as ever; but having ascertained that all was decided as to her niece's choice of *country*, as well as of Order, she said no more; and being silenced upon her weak point, she knew how to render herself truly agreeable, by the good sense and kind-heartedness of which she was possessed.

Miss Sternbrooke, who was present at this conversation, and who was to leave on the following day, started a new subject of discussion by her simple demand for an explanation of the aim and efficacy of a life so "*concentrated*," as she termed it, as is that led by Carmelite nuns.

"You said the other day, Agnes," she remarked, "that in the life of a Sister of Charity you would feel so constrained, and as if you were straitened within too narrow a sphere of action. Now, I pray you tell me what you will do as a Carmelite, where you will be wholly cut off from every work of active charity, and shut up within the limits of a single monastery, and this until death?"

Agnes smiled at her friend's simplicity in having construed her words so literally.

"I did not refer, on the occasion you allude to, to the restraint of *corporal* and *material* confinement. My little solitary cell will be ample space to satisfy me, since within its narrow walls I can share in the greatest apostleship of all, after that of the Priesthood—I mean the Apostleship of Prayer. You are right in saying the Carmelite is cut off from all active participation in any material works of charity; if she engaged in them in any way, she would go out of her element; and if she did not lose the grace of her vocation altogether, she would probably render her life inefficacious for attaining the end of that vocation."

"You are right there, my child," said Father Neville, "each one according to his or her calling; and active works, *material* works of external charity would be as much out of place in a Carmelite, as solitude, long hours of prayer, and rigorous seclusion from the outer world, would be in a Sister of Charity."

The Misses Willington had withdrawn a little apart,

and were engaged in earnest conversation with the
Colonel regarding the news they had so recently learnt,
Stanislaus and Mary joining in occasionally, and now
and then lending an ear to the earnest but amiable discussion going on in the little coterie, of which Agnes
made one, Captain Warnford, also, forming a silent
but deeply interested auditor, and feeling it somewhat a
relief not to be called upon just then to take an active
part in the conversation.

"But you have not yet quite satisfied me," said Miss
Sternbrooke, laughingly, "as to *why* you are so sure
you would not, as a Carmelite, feel that *constraint* of
which you spoke the other day, when I asked you if you
would not be a Sister of Charity."

"Because, dear," said Agnes, "the field of action is
immensely wider for each soul. You look astonished:
but see how easily I can explain my meaning. Whoever is engaged in *active* works of zeal and charity, must
necessarily have his attention concentrated more or less
in those works in which he is actually engaged; he
must labour within circumscribed limits: for instance,
if I were sent to any one town or district, there to
assist in a school or hospital, it would be in that particular spot only that I could exercise myself in the
duties of my vocation. True it is that prayer for other
objects may accompany material labour, but it is difficult where that labour demands the attention of the
mind and heart. What is the tale we hear over and

over again? 'I have so much to do, so many classes to attend to, so many poor to instruct, &c., that I have scarcely time to think of anything, much less of those necessities of the Church throughout the world, which do not come immediately beneath the eye.' Now in that life of solitude which I have chosen, the imperative obligation and end is prayer for the Church, and for all that in any way tends to the extension and triumph of the Church. Now what limit is there to *prayer?* It *cannot* be limited; it is independent of all external accidents or circumstances: in an instant we can, by an interior act, obtain the grace of conversion for a soul, or many souls, whom we have never seen, who are thousands of leagues distant from us. This is the Apostleship of Prayer, the secret power of which S. Teresa knew so well, when she made it an integral part of her great Reform, and shows so clearly in her writings that this is the one essential end of the Order of Mount Carmel.'"

"True," said Francis, "few of the Saints have illustrated so eloquently the immense efficacy of prayer for the Church and for the entire world as has S. Teresa, and thus prepared the way for that great movement which is manifest to-day amongst the faithful; that union of hearts throughout the world in, as it were, one great universal prayer for the triumph of God's cause."

"Well," said Helen, smiling, "I am so glad we have spoken on this point, for I must own I was a little tempted to think the life of cloistered nuns somewhat selfish and ——."

"My dear child," said Father Neville, interrupting her, "your good humoured face encourages me to believe you will forgive an old Priest if he tells you that that thought is a bit of the 'old leaven' of Protestantism not yet got rid of—eh?

"I dare say it is," said Helen, laughing, with perfect good temper. "A Priest told me once it took ten or fifteen years for the *old leaven* you speak of to disappear entirely, and I am only four years old in the faith. But oh! how I love it," she exclaimed, with a sudden ardour which that faith must have grafted into her otherwise quiet and undemonstrative nature.

"And one day, perhaps, will give your life for it in China or elsewhere," said Francis; "blessed for you will be that day if it ever comes."

He ceased speaking with a sigh, for memory had conjured up the ardent wish of his own soul for martyrdom for the faith in a foreign land.

"Well, now," resumed Father Neville, kindly, "you must chase away for ever the thought that a life of prayer—a contemplative life as it is called—is a *selfish* one. It is in fact the reproduction and perpetuation of the Hidden Life of our Divine Lord. What did *He* do for the eighteen years He lived at Nazareth? He neither preached, nor taught, nor healed the sick, but He *prayed*. He was Himself the first great Model of a cloistered life, and His Blessed Mother and S. Joseph were the next. Were *they* 'selfish?' Were *they* 'self-concentrated?' Was *their* life a useless one? Oh, surely not? Neither are the lives of those who, far from the world, hidden from the eyes of men, follow in their footsteps."

"I believe all you say, Father Neville; but do you not think it must be very hard to *persevere* in a life where, for the most part, there is no visible proof of its efficacy?" said Helen, modestly, really desirous now of being instructed in those points wherein she was ready to acknowledge herself deficient.

"*Their fruit shall remain,*" replied Father Neville, gravely, "but it will appear only when the secrets of all things will be made manifest. Then will be seen conversions, or falls prevented, by the daily crucified life and constant prayer of those poor and often despised women who immolate *all* for the glory of God and His Church, and for the salvation of souls. Then will the world recognize how much it owed to those solitudes where the life of Nazareth was perpetuated, and how those who fought in the plain were supported by the prayer of the others who prayed upon the mountain. Theirs is a life of *faith*, essentially so. Their consolation is not for this world. They go on praying for certain objects, but they know not how fruitful has been their prayer: they see perhaps no results; they must await the day of doom. In this they resemble somewhat an author, who sends forth his book to the world. Thousands will read it, thousands perhaps will be consoled or helped by reading it, it will cast its seed into countless hearts. But the author is ignorant of it: he has done his work; it has gone forth like the lightning: but the results, the effects of that work, as it traverses the world, he can never know this side the grave. Then, the life which Agnes has chosen demands a strong faith in order to persevere, as you say."

Helen was silent. There was a somewhat troubled expression on her ordinarily bright young face.

"I fear," said Francis, kindly, for he had remarked her countenance, "that we have a little pained Miss Sternbrooke."

"Oh! no, no," she cried, "not pained, only"—

"Only what, dear Helen?" said Agnes, gently, for she too observed her friend's unusually grave manner.

"She does not like to say her thought," said Francis, "and I will say it for her. She thought we seemed to depreciate the active life. Is it not so, Miss Sternbrooke?"

Before she could reply, Father Neville and Agnes simultaneously declaimed against such a proposition.

"My dear child," said the former, with the utmost kindness in his tone, "when we extol one manner of glorifying God and of serving His Church, we do not in the least intend to depreciate any other. The *end* which each has in view is the same, the glory of God and the salvation of souls; therefore the works in themselves are equally perfect, since intention is the criterion of all things, but for the individual souls who embrace these various ways, or, to speak more correctly, who are *called* to them—and this is what is meant by *vocation*—different graces are given to each, proportioned to the degree of faith and self-immolation which will be required of them. There should be no envying one of another, no spirit of rivalry or jealousy; each should yield to the other that which is their due, remembering only that word of Eternal Truth that '*Mary hath chosen the better part, which shall not be taken from her.*'"

"There, you see it *is* the best, after all," said Helen, smiling, whilst something like a wistful tone manifested itself in her voice.

"It is the best, undoubtedly," replied Father Neville, "in the same way that heaven is better than earth. Faith, hope, charity, are all indispensable, yet, as S. Paul says, of these three charity is the greatest, inasmuch as it will endure for ever, and be the occupation, the very life of the blessed for eternity, when faith and hope shall be no more needed. So, in the same way, when material works of charity, which belong to the active life, that of Martha, shall be no longer required, that is, when this world shall have passed away, the occupation of Mary, adoration, love, contemplation, shall endure; and in *this* sense the contemplative life is undeniably '*the best;*' but all cannot follow it, but only those to whom it is given to do so. Moreover, my child, the fruit of both remains. If our Lord has made magnificent promises to the one, so likewise has

He to the other. There are more ways than one of
converting sinners from their errors, of clothing the
naked, giving food to the hungry, and the rest; all this
may be understood in a literal as well as in a spiritual
sense."

"Yes," replied Helen, thoughtfully, "now I understand better—and am more content," she added simply,
"for I really feel as if I should like to go and labour
for the conversion of those dear little pagan children,
and those good simple people far away, who only want
to be instructed in order to believe, or to comfort and
nurse the sick in hospitals: it must be so consoling to
see one's efforts repaid by souls coming to the knowledge of God and growing in His love. But as to be
praying all day, and contemplating God as the angels
do in heaven, that I really could not attempt."

Francis and Agnes laughed involuntarily at the
young convert's idea of a contemplative religious life.

"Why," said the former, "do you really imagine
that cloistered nuns are on their knees or prostrate
praying all day, as you say? I happen to know some
communities, and when I was abroad I have frequently
had the opportunity of ascertaining some things relative to their life, the Carmelites especially, who are the
most strictly cloistered, and I assure you nothing can
be more erroneous than the idea that the world in
general forms of them."

"But," said Helen, "I have even heard good
Catholics speak very disparagingly of a life which they

consider, if not useless, at least selfish and easy, withdrawn as it is from all the annoyances attendant upon intercourse with the outer world."

"Selfish! easy!" exclaimed Francis, raising himself from the half-reclining posture into which he had involuntarily fallen in the *fauteuil* he occupied, whilst his dark eye kindled with something closely resembling indignation: "let those who say so try it, and then after six months probation let them repeat their assertion if they can—that is with truth. Is daily self-denial of the sharpest kind easy? Is the subjection of will, and judgment, and human pride, easy to flesh and blood? Is the constant immolation of all things, exterior and interior, easy; an immolation so lasting and continuous, and so universal, that that of the Eucharistic Victim alone may be its model? And then, if we come to the charge of selfishness, it is as easily refuted: for all this is undertaken *not* for the selfish thought of personal reward, even in eternity, but for souls, for the Church, for the kingdom of Christ. This is the mission of the daughters of S. Teresa. She tells them so herself. But if all this is too spiritual, too refined, for those good souls who in ignorance rather than in malice charge with selfishness and ease the crucified lives of those true apostles of prayer and sacrifice, let them have a glance at their material life, and then say if it is one according to the inclinations of flesh and blood. Their solitary cell, their three planks for a bed with a straw mattress upon it; their *perpetual* labour, *remember*, out of the hours of choir duties; their short nights and fireless rooms; their perpetual abstinence and long fasts and coarse and insipid food; their monotonous chant, all music being forbidden them, which in my estimation is one of their most trying penances; their menial works, which *nothing* but the love of Him for whose sake they are performed could render interesting, and from which none are exempt, whatever may have been their birth or the cultivation of their tastes: all these things, and innumerable others, which form the daily life of the Carmelite, are certainly not consistent with *ease* and *selfishness;* sacrifice enters into every action of their life, it is their very element, as it was her's whose sacred habit they wear, the Mother of Jesus, our Lady of Mount Carmel."

"I entirely believe all you say," said Helen, "and therefore it is I have been sometimes so surprised to hear Catholics speak disparagingly of the contemplative Orders, and of that of Mount Carmel in particular."

"Ah!" replied Francis, "they speak from motives of prejudice partly, and partly from real ignorance. If they knew the hidden good that is effected by those Orders especially consecrated to prayer they would judge otherwise; it is a want of faith, lively faith. All now tends to exterior and material activity, and good that is operated by invisible means is disregarded, if not disbelieved in altogether."

Agnes had relapsed into silence during the latter part of the conversation, more contented to listen to the eloquent defence offered by Francis in behalf of the life she so ardently desired to embrace than to proffer that defence herself.

The conversation now became more general, and at its termination all felt that a right understanding existed upon all points, not only on those that had been there discussed, but also upon such as were tacitly recognized to be the will of Divine Providence regarding some of those present.

CHAPTER IX.

Departures.

Swiftly sped the weeks of preparation for Agnes's departure. During that short interval the days were "*full*"—in the sense in which the Holy Spirit applies the term—full of triumph for the Sacred Heart, because full of secret self-sacrifice, of generous self-renunciation for God's greater glory, and for the good of souls. One idea seemed to predominate in the minds and hearts of both Francis and Agnes; it was that their lives must be, should be, lives of devotedness, of abnegation, of immolation, and this *until death*. In the mind of Francis, however, was comprehended something more tangible than was the case with his sister, inasmuch as the desire of actual *martyrdom* had formed itself involuntarily within his soul from earliest youth, and had strengthened in proportion as his apostolic vocation had developed itself. The thirst of that baptism of blood still secretly consumed him, and its ardour became so much the more burning, as he saw himself baffled in attaining it. There was a little French song which had been a great favourite with both brother and sister from their childhood, expressing, as it did, the formal desire of the former, and the scarcely less ardent although more vague aspirations of the latter. They often found themselves, almost involuntarily, in these last days of their companionship, singing the self-same strain which, long before, had had for them such attractions; and whilst they sing it together for the last time, on the day preceding that of Agnes's departure, we will transcribe it for the benefit of those in whose hearts it may find some echo.

"Depuis qu'au Golgotha
Le Seigneur de la gloire
Son sang expiatoire
Sur le gibet versa,
Le Chretien sans palir
Affronte les supplices
La Croix fait ses delices
Je veux être martyr.

"Mortels, livrez vos cœurs
Aux vains plaisirs du monde,
Sur la terre et sur l'onde
Cherchez-en les douceurs ;
Mais moi, pour conquérir
La palme que j'envie
Je renonce à la vie
Je veux être martyr.

"Tyran, sombre et cruel
Que tes dures tortures
Me couvrent de blessures
M'immolent sur l'autel,
Cést là tout mon désir ;
Ta fureur, ni ta rage
N'abatteront mon courage
Je veux être martyr.

"Oh ! quand viendra le jour
Où mon âme ravie
Au sein de la Patrie
Verra Dieu son Amour !
De ce bel avenir
Pour assurer l'attente
Dans l'arène sanglante
Je veux être martyr."

They were not alone. Father Neville had been the deeply interested auditor of the brother and sister's last duet. As the last words died away, leaving for a few moments total silence, the old Priest brushed away the tears that had started to his eyes. Many thoughts filled his heart in reference to those two souls, so dear to him, thoughts which were prompted by the words they had just sung, no less than by the separation which was to take place on the following day. But chiefly his thoughts concentrated themselves upon Francis, the realization of whose life's hope seemed now so unattainable, and for whom Father Neville felt that perhaps a longer martyrdom was in store than that which he had so coveted. Possibly something of his secret thoughts revealed itself in the earnest and almost sorrowful expression with which his eye met that of Francis, which was involuntarily raised to his.

"There is a martyrdom for all who love God," said the old Priest, as if in answer to that quick glance, so full of significance; "with the few it is the quick martyrdom of blood, with the rest the long martyrdom of the heart."

"That recals to me some words of S. Teresa," said Agnes, "where she tells her daughters that their '*life is a long martyrdom.*' That thought seemed to console her for the disappointment of her childhood in not meeting the martyrdom amongst the Moors which she and her young brother had actually set out to seek."

"Yes, the thought of martyrdom accompanied her through life," said Francis, musingly, "and was the secret of her quenchless love of suffering in the '*long martyrdom*' our Lord vouchsafed to give her. Is it not a special favour of Providence, Father Neville, that calls Agnes to be the daughter of a saint for whom I have had always a special *attrait*, and whose Order I appreciate more than any in the Church?"

"Yes," replied Father Neville, "it is one of your consolations."

"By the bye, that reminds me," said Francis, "I suppose you know that the *Congregation de Propa-*

ganda File was commenced by three Fathers of the
Carmelite Order?"

"Oh, no," cried Agnes, "I did not indeed. How
glad I am to know it! That increases my devotion to
the Order a hundred-fold. I knew that S. Teresa was
consumed with an apostolic zeal, but I did not know
that it was specially to her sons that we are indebted
for that great work which has been the cause of the
salvation of so many millions of souls. Where did you
learn it?"

"From the best authority," replied Francis, "from
the ancient chronicles of the Order itself, which it was
my privilege to be allowed to read by some of the
Carmelite Fathers whom I knew at Paris, and who lent
it to me.* I knew that many of the Order had been

* We read in the ancient chronicles of the Discalced Carmes, composed in Spanish by the Rev. Father Francis of Holy Mary, Discalced Carme, that the Rev. Father Peter of the Mother of God, one of the firmest pillars of the Reformed Carmel, being in Rome in 1597, where he was honoured with the esteem and friendship of Pope Clement VIII., and with that of the Sacred College of Cardinals, having received orders from his superiors in Spain to leave the foundation of Italy in order to return into his own country, went to take leave of His Holiness, who forbid him, however, to depart from Rome, having designed him to be superintendent of the missions which were just then instituted for the propagation of the faith amongst infidel nations. He remained in this important charge during the nine years that his life continued. During this time Father Thomas of Jesus, of the same illustrious Order, composed an excellent book for the use of the missions. Father Peter being dead, the Pope failed not to preserve the charge that religions had held, to the Carmelite Order, in conferring it upon Father Dominic of Jesus Maria, who acquitted himself of it as an apostle. This new design of the missions, this apostolic

missioners in the East, and it was that which gave me the desire to read the Chronicles, where one sees how the spirit of the mother descended to the sons, and how a life of contemplation and prayer kindles in the soul a burning zeal for the salvation of all men. So you see, Agnes, you are going to be specially allied to the Foreign Missions, as well on account of the heavenly zeal of your future holy mother, as of the actual missionary labours of many of your fathers and brothers. You will also co-operate with me, if God gives me back my health to go where all my hopes tend, more by your prayers and life of hidden sacrifice than you would if you were actually working on the very scene of my labours."

edifice founded upon three stones of Carmel, that is, upon three Discalced Carmes, made such rapid progress that Pope Gregory XV. instituted for this work a Congregation of Cardinals and other prelates, which is called *De Propaganda Fide*, by a Bull given at Rome 22nd June, 1622, which commences by these words, *Inscrutabile Divinæ Providentiæ arcanum, &c.*; and although the Pope wished himself to be henceforth the head and superintendent of the work, he conferred nevertheless upon Father Dominic an honour which he had never granted to any other Religious or private person, which was that of having a seat in that secret congregation amongst the cardinals and prelates of the Church, and of having remitted to his prudence their decrees and their deliberations, because he was considered by each as a sanctuary of the Holy Spirit. Fathers Peter Paul Simon, John Thaddæus of S. Eliseus, and Vincent of S. Francis, were the first apostolic missionaries sent into Persia. The glorious labours of these true sons of Elias and of the seraphic and apostolic Teresa, and of their successors, in the infidel nations of the East, are recorded in the Ancient History of the Discalced Carmes, from which we have extracted the above.

"Oh! yes," replied Agnes, her countenance glowing with hope and happiness, "it is that which makes me love so much the Order of Mount Carmel; the vast extent of the spiritual horizon it has in view. It seems to me the thought of their Apostolic Mission and the claims it has upon them, must assist the Carmelites so much in their laborious and simple life, and help to raise them up above the material miseries that surround us all here below."

"Undoubtedly it does," replied Francis, thoughtfully, and then with a quiet smile, as he regarded his sister's earnest face, he added: "Nevertheless, dear Agnes, S. Teresa's assurance that life is a '*long martyrdom*,' must not be lost sight of, nor the song of our childhood which we have just sung for the last time: '*Je veux être martyr !*'"

"Neither must we forget," suggested Father Neville, "that in all probability our martyrdom will come to us in quite a different way to the one we look for. What matter! the *object* is the same, God's greater glory. This is a never-failing consolation, and one of the mysteries hidden in God; men cannot deprive us of obtaining our end when it is purely the glory of God and the salvation of souls; our *intention* remains the same, although the *means* of carrying it out may be changed. And, after all, it is God Himself who changes the means. He does not will us, however, to change our *intention*."

"Yes, but it is a continual struggle, even where the

intention is very pure," said Francis, in a quiet voice, that told of the knowledge his own soul had of the struggle of which he spoke. Father Neville made no reply, but his lips slightly moved, as if some words, or, most likely, a prayer were silently passing from his soul. It would seem as if he, too, had his life's secret history, the memory of which failed not even now, old as he was, to renew within him some inward strife, which would testify how *living* a victim is the human heart, even to the end of life; and how acceptable, therefore, to the Sacred Heart when it is a victim *willing* as well as *living*.

It was late that night ere the brother and sister separated. Despite the generosity of Francis, and the satisfaction he really experienced in the prospect of Agnes becoming a member of that Religious Order whose apostolate, although exercised in a different manner, has for its special object the interests so dear to his own heart, he felt emotions at the thought of the separation from his sister, which required all his fortitude to keep in restraint.

It was not simply the yielding up one very dear to him; there was another circumstance which rendered the struggle sharper; she was leaving *him* in apparent *inaction*, baffled, disappointed, with his life's sole hope well nigh wrecked.

Separation is easier borne by the one who departs, and who has new and varying scenes to pass through which distract his attention, than by those who remain where every scene reminds them of the absent. Francis felt this painfully, as on that last day he and Agnes had visited together the old familiar spots, recalling to both so vividly their intercourse from childhood.

How mingled are those feelings which agitate the heart during the last hours spent in a loved home. They who have "*left all things*" to follow a divine call can understand it. Deep within the soul there is a joy which only those can taste who have done this, yet it is a joy tempered by memories of childhood passed with the loved ones now about to be left for ever. Then it is that is felt the power of a divine vocation, and that is realized the priceless value of the evangelic pearl, to possess which the soul that is charmed by its loveliness sacrifices '*freely*' everything besides.

But there is one hour in which the Heart of Jesus must indeed be glorified; in which the angels must look down almost envyingly in witnessing the power possessed by beings lower than themselves, of testifying their love to God by so much suffering. It is the hour wherein must be spoken the last farewell. This had at length arrived for the inmates of Willington Manor.

Agnes felt that she must have a little time to spend with Francis in private; for, disguise it as she would, she knew the struggle that was passing in his heart, and her own also in that hour quailed beneath the thought that the adieu about to be spoken *was for life*.

She ran upstairs as soon after breakfast as she could steal away, and having completed her travelling toilet, she hastened to the room of Francis, where he awaited her.

It was Agnes who was the first to speak. "I feel it so cruel, so heartless, to leave you," she whispered. "I am going where I desire to be; for *me* it is the spring time of bright hope and of promise. But oh, my darling, when I think of leaving you like this, as you are now, it seems almost more than I can bear."

"Poor little one," said Francis, stooping down caressingly to his sister, who held his hand in her's. "You feel it to be heartless, and yet your poor heart is like to break with its struggle. You are faithful to the voice of Jesus, and He says Himself He came to bring the sword. Besides, *I* ought to understand better than many others what you are feeling now. If I were well, and had before me the prospect of pursuing my vocation, if my life's hope had not been crushed, your pain in leaving me would be far less: is it not so?"

"Yes, it is that, precisely," said Agnes, in a voice choked with emotion.

"And I too, dearest Agnes, had to leave our darling mother, suffering as you know she was, and to plunge the sword into her heart by following my vocation; that which you have *not* to do in my regard, for, I repeat, your vocation is to me a true consolation in the midst of my own trials."

She looked up at her brother as he spoke, and the calm truthful glance that met her own comforted her. They lingered on that last interview. Agnes was taking her last look at the familiar objects in her brother's room. She was thinking of the hours of secret anguish he would pass there, and her eyes filled with tears at the thought.

Footsteps were now heard approaching, and the Colonel entered in travelling dress, to say that the carriage was heard in the distance.

"Yes, dearest papa, we will come," said Agnes. Then, turning towards Francis, she looked at him a moment, and said, "Is it here we are to say the last word; or will you come down-stairs?"

"I will come down and be with you to the last," he replied.

"Then," said Agnes, "give me here your blessing, for you would not like to give it in Father Neville's presence."

She knelt down as she spoke. He made the sign of the cross reverently upon her forehead, and then, raising her up, said:

"I pray God to give you His blessing now and always, and to perfect the good work He has begun in you."

He stooped and kissed the forehead of his sister, and gently disengaged her hands from his arm, to which she clung as if for support.

"Courage, dearest," he whispered; "this is the

hour to glorify the Sacred Heart: offer up this sharp struggle for Its interests. Come, S. Teresa will help you—will help us all."

He it was—the one whose own hopes were baffled, who was so sharply suffering in soul and body—he it was who led the way, and imparted courage to the sister in the springtide of her hope.

In the dining room were assembled the rest of the family. There were not many to take leave of, for the Colonel and Stanislaus intended accompanying Agnes to her future home in the south of France.

It was soon over—that parting scene—but there was one who met them at the door as they passed out to the hall to whom Agnes had not as yet spoken her adieu. It was Captain Warnford. He stood awaiting her coming, having from delicacy withdrawn for the last hour to his room. She extended her hand to him, saying,

"Thank you again, Arthur, for your great kindness to me all my life. Do stay here with Francis until papa and Stanislaus return. You will be such a comfort to him."

"Yes," he replied, "I will stay and do all I can for him; and one thing I will ask in return, it is that you will pray for me often."

"Always," replied Agnes, "to the end of my life."

So it was they parted. Agnes passed out, following her father and Stanislaus to the carriage. Her hand clasped that of Francis as they crossed the terrace.

In another moment she entered the carriage, and the door was closed. Father Neville had given her his last paternal benediction, and had stepped aside for Francis to approach. One more grasp of the hand, one more adieu, and it was over. Two figures stood on the terrace, watching the carriage until it was out of sight; Francis, and Arthur Warnford who stood beside him scarcely less pale than the invalid himself.

Perhaps at that moment the soul of Arthur Warnford was passing through a greater struggle than was that of Francis. Their trial was so different. To the former, life appeared, humanly speaking, a desert; he had not even the faint hope that Francis still retained of seeing *his* life's dream realized. He must go back to associations altogether alien from that innocent young girl whose interior beauty the man of nearly double her age had so quickly discerned, and learnt to love so deeply. They stood, the brother and his friend, long after the carriage had disappeared from their view, just as Agnes had stood with the same companion at her side, on a former occasion, watching the departure of Francis for the College of Foreign Missions, when the star of hope was shining brightly above *him*, even as now it was shining over his young sister.

"How I envy her!" Such were the first words which broke from the lips of Arthur Warnford, as, giving his arm to Francis, they slowly retraced their steps to the house. "Happy are they to whom it is

given to desire a life such as her's will be. I know
better now the meaning of the word *vocation*."

They walked on in silence for a few moments, for
the hearts of both were too full for many words.
Arthur was thinking of that other occasion when, after
the departure of Francis, he had, with Agnes at his
side, passed over the very ground they now were tread-
ing, and when he had witnessed her devotedness and
self-sacrifice in disguising her own heart's struggle for
the sake of her suffering mother.

They returned to Francis's apartment, and shortly
after they were joined by Mary, who came in her new
character of special attendant upon Francis, bringing
some refreshment, for he had been severely tried by
the events of the morning. Father Neville also soon
appeared, with his genial paternal influence; and thus
it was that, struggling as were at least two hearts there
present, charity and mutual sympathy succeeded in
shedding over all a soothing influence.

Later on that day, when Father Neville entered the
chapel to make one of his frequent visits to the Blessed
Sacrament, he saw Captain Warnford kneeling in the
very spot where some few weeks since he had knelt,
waiting to speak to him in the sacristy. His head was
bent upon his hands, which rested on the sanctuary
rail; he did not look up, but as Father Neville passed
he heard the deep-drawn sigh, and the good old Priest
paused and knelt beside him to put up a prayer for that

soul whom he knew to be so stricken, although so courageous in self-sacrifice.

They had knelt thus some time in silent prayer, when Father Neville perceived that the strong man beside him wept. He rose, and laying his hand upon his shoulder, whispered gently,

"Did I not tell you awhile ago you would glorify God in staying? *This* is the hour wherein to render that glory, the hour of your supreme desolation. Think of it, God's greater glory! Oh, what an honour, what a happiness, to be given in any way the means of promoting it!"

Arthur Warnford raised his head, brushing away some moisture from his eyes as he did so.

"It is *this* thought," he whispered, "that renders the prospect of my life endurable; it is all for His greater glory."

As he calmly spoke these last words his eyes rested on the Tabernacle.

"Forgive me," he said, looking up at Father Neville for an instant; "forgive my apparent want of generosity. I do not regret: but the struggle is great."

As he spoke he involuntarily laid his hand on his breast.

"I understand it," said Father Neville, kindly; "the heart of man is human, and *must* feel and suffer. But close to us is the Heart of One who has felt and suffered more than all of us. Lay your sorrow and all your sharp pain and hard struggle in that Heart, and you will find strength to endure, and at last grace to *rejoice* that at your own cost you have been able to do something for the glory of God."

Father Neville withdrew, but Arthur Warnford still remained alone with the God of the Eucharist, and left not His presence until he felt that virtue had indeed gone out from the Heart of that Hidden God, and passed into his own; then he arose and went forth to continue his work of brotherly love towards Francis.

In about a fortnight the Colonel and Stanislaus returned, having remained a few days in the vicinity of the convent whither they had conducted Agnes, in order to visit her, and to have, as Stanislaus playfully told her, the satisfaction of seeing her safely deposited behind the *grille*, as well as to afford the Colonel a little repose before setting out on the homeward journey.

Captain Warnford, at the request of Stanislaus, remained still a few weeks at the Manor after the return of the travellers, and then arrived the day for his final departure. Here again awaited a severe trial for many. Stanislaus had his share therein, for he knew that, humanly speaking, he should probably never again meet his long-tried and faithful friend. For Francis his departure was also a real sacrifice, and as in most of those trials through which it was the Divine Will he should pass, it was aggravated by the memories associated with his own heavy cross, and which the last adieu between himself and Arthur Warnford so painfully revived. They had conversed together so much, years before, of the life which Francis had chosen, of the countries and the peoples where and amongst whom he would labour; and now Arthur was going back to that East of which Francis had dreamt from childhood; going amongst the poor benighted ones for whose salvation his soul had yearned more passionately in proportion as he saw himself withheld from hastening to toil amongst them. No wonder that when he clasped the hand of his friend for the last time a wistful longing seized on him to go whither he was going, to that shore which had been for him, and still was, as the land of promise which he saw from afar off, and for the attainment of which his soul so thirsted. But it could not be. He must remain and wait on the will of God. And thus once more he saw one dear to his heart go forth to pursue his career in life, and he must be content to stay, like a captive bird beating its wings against its prison bars and longing to be free.

Oh, these struggles of the poor human heart, how God thereby is glorified, when amidst its weakness it *struggles* to the end to unite its will to His!

After the departure of Captain Warnford Francis applied himself with more ardour than ever to study. He suffered himself to be attended, and yielded to all the wishes of those around him, and especially of his sister-in-law, who had now entirely installed herself in Agnes's place of "nurse," as she termed it; but it was almost with indifference that he partook of the medicines and nourishment that were brought him; his hope was built upon other foundations, as he had said himself some time before. One thought, one hope, had taken possession of him; it was that of his ordination to the Priesthood, and the cure he hoped, nay *more* than hoped, from the celebration of the Holy Sacrifice. How his pure soul longed to hold up the Holy of Holies, and to offer himself, in union with the Divine Victim, to the Thrice Holy God! When he contemplated that hour, new life, new vigour, seemed already infused into him; and although these transient improvements were quickly succeeded by a return of the ordinary debility, nevertheless they afforded him matter for steadfast hope, which inundated his soul with unspeakable joy, and communicated already some elasticity to his enfeebled body.

Not very long after the departures related in this chapter, the Bishop—who years before had confirmed Francis and Agnes, and whom we have seen on that occasion conversing with the two children so amiably, in visiting the spots where Francis had erected memorials of his devotion and early *attrait* for missionary life,—was visiting at the Manor. He was deeply interested in the young candidate for the Priesthood, whose vocation he had watched from the beginning. Very earnest were the conversations which the holy prelate held with his young friend, who now solicited him to permit him to enter on immediate preparation for the reception of the supreme grace to which he aspired.

It was at length agreed that he should without further delay be admitted to the order of Deacon, and if the state of his health permitted, that he should, in the September following, complete his sacrifice in being ordained "*priest for ever*," in answer to his ardent but humble demand. This decision arrived at, the tranquil happiness of Francis surpassed all that could ever be understood, save by those who have themselves experienced the same aspirations, and have passed through a similar succession of hope and disappointment, of brightest sunshine and darkest night, and of hope revived again.

In that same month of June the second of the great Orders was conferred upon him, and from that time he gave himself up almost exclusively to study and interior preparation for the immense favour he was soon to receive.

It was a quiet summer at the Manor. The Colonel designedly invited but few visitors, in order that Francis might be free from all constraint. The months were happy ones for Francis, yet it was a happiness which was tempered by anxiety and physical weakness.

Sometimes, in the secret of his heart, he asked himself upon what foundation his strong hope rested of being able eventually to accomplish his desire. None had expressed themselves sanguine of his recovery; his present state did not certainly promise much, neither did he expect to derive any benefit from the care which was so tenderly lavished upon him, but *he hoped in the Lord*, and his trust was in the power of the God of the Eucharist.

Moreover, he knew that his life's desire had been infused into him from on high, it had been the centre round which his whole spiritual life turned. It was a desire manifestly for the interests of God's glory, and for the salvation of souls; and lastly, his vocation had been tried and approved by men of piety and experience. Why, then, should he not hope, even although his present state was, humanly speaking, so unfavourable?

It was in this spirit of simplicity and trustingness that he steadily pursued his studies, and still more his "*preparation of heart*," without being discouraged by the lassitude attendant upon his state of health; nor did his courage fail him, or his faith decrease, as the momentous day drew near, and found him in the same state of debility and suffering.

CHAPTER X.

The Ordination.—The First Mass.

The visit of a Father of the Society of Jesus, who was an intimate friend of the Willington family, enabled Francis to make his retreat preparatory to his Ordination under the immediate direction of a son of S. Ignatius, a favour which he knew well how to appreciate.

During the eight days preceding the one which was to be the greatest, the fullest of his life, all the energies of his soul were called into action, in order to dispose himself for the reception of the grace of graces about to be bestowed upon him. His whole being was penetrated with the awfulness of the functions he was about to take upon himself, yet was his awe tempered by the torrents of consolation that inundated his pure soul as he contemplated the intimacy of his union with the Eucharistic Victim, and the oblation of himself, which he was about to offer, together with that of the Great High Priest, whom he had chosen as his portion for ever. But most of all was he affected by the overwhelming thought of the *eternity* of the Priesthood,

whose character was about to be ineffaceably engraven
upon his soul. "*Tu es sacerdos in æternum,*" were the
words which rung perpetually in his ears. Yes, faithful, or, alas! unfaithful, the impress is sealed *for ever*,
to shine in heaven for everlasting ages as a royal diadem; or—we shudder at the contrast—to burn as a
brand of eternal shame upon the brow, and upon all the
faculties of the lost soul, as a mark of dishonour which
not all the fires which the outraged justice of God has
enkindled will be able to burn out.

Did the soul of Francis Willington quail as he pondered upon this awful truth; or, if he trembled, did he
for that look back, fearing to take upon himself so terrible a responsibility? No, he buried himself in the
abject nothingness wherein he saw himself lie, and
casting himself in lowliness upon the Heart of the
Divine Master, in Whose blessed footsteps he yearned
to walk, he confided in Him alone, distrusting himself,
and hoping all from the might of that love of which he
was the object.

As the supreme day approached, and as those blessed
exercises of his retreat sunk deeper and deeper into his
soul, fortifying him in humility and in love, the sublime
graces attendant on his vocation flowed in upon him
more and more. His inward eye was ever fixed on
Mary, the model of Priests; and as he contemplated the
divine Mother, offering up her beloved Son to the Eternal Father, and herself together with Him, the soul of
Francis was consumed with the ardour of his desires to

consummate *his* sacrifice, and to immolate himself for the souls for whose salvation his own heart yearned with more than even a mother's love.

It was the Saturday preceding the third Sunday in September, the Feast of the Seven Dolours. At an early hour the Chapel at Willington Manor gave evidence of preparations for some unusual event. The Bishop knelt within the sanctuary, saying in private some part of the Divine Office. Father Neville, with two other Priests in the well-known cloak worn by the Fathers of the Society of Jesus, were kneeling similarly occupied at a little distance; whilst a fourth, the Bishop's Secretary, was passing to and fro from the sacristy to the altar, engaged in arranging the various objects which would be requisite in the approaching ceremony.

On one side of the chapel, and immediately in the front of an exquisite statue of the Immaculate Mother of God, knelt a figure, absorbed in prayer and regardless of all that passed around him. It was Francis, the victim preparing for immolation, plunging himself with more and more abandonment into the fires of divine love, as he felt their flames purifying him ever more and more from the alloy of self-reliance, and drawing him more closely into the Heart of Jesus, whose cause he had embraced for ever.

All who beheld him were struck with the expression of profound recollection visible upon his countenance, and the air of self-possessed, yet humble dignity, which characterized his bearing. Nevertheless, as they regarded that pallid face, those sunken yet brilliant eyes, all asked themselves how he would endure the long ceremony, and feared lest his strength might fail under the great mental and bodily fatigue.

Two hours later all was over. The great action had been consummated, and Francis Willington was a "*priest for ever,*" clothed with that sublime character which none could ever take from him, replenished with apostolic graces, victim and sacrificer at the same time, the living representative of Him whose immolation ceases not "*from the rising of the sun until the setting thereof.*"

Beautiful was the expression that rested on his countenance as he passed from the sanctuary to the sacristy when all was ended. But his lips were deadly pale, and no sooner had he gained the sacristy than it was found requisite to seat him in a chair, and to give him some restoratives, so utterly exhausted was the little strength he had.

During the remainder of that day he was obliged to remain extremely quiet in order to avoid a recurrence of the acute pain in the chest which there was reason to apprehend, and to prevent everything which might in the least tax the strength he needed for the solemn act of the following day, the celebration of his first Mass.

The Bishop, with his accustomed suavity, insisted on Francis's apartment being the place of general *ren-*

dezvous, in order that he might be spared the least unnecessary fatigue. Long after was that day recalled to the memories of the holy Prelate and the four Priests who with him were assembled round the newly ordained, the latter radiant in the full deep joy that lived within him, and in the secret hope that never wavered, despite his prostrate strength. He had not spoken of that hope to any; he was *humble* in his expectation, being deeply sensible of his own unworthiness for obtaining the signal favour he confidently awaited, and casting all his trust upon the Heart of Him Who for the first time he was, on the morrow, to hold up in his hands to the Eternal Father, standing himself for the first time thus as mediator between heaven and earth.

The Colonel, as he sat regarding his son with tenderness mingled with a certain pride, could not, however, be without some misgiving as to the ultimate recovery of Francis, and consequently of the realization of his still existing hope of embracing a missionary life. His anxiety was fully shared by Stanislaus; and as to Mary, she sometimes feared that the reception of the supreme grace of the Priesthood was to be the prelude of her brother-in-law's approaching death.

All present—whilst they could not reasonably behold any prospect of Francis being at any time capable of much material labour in the vineyard of the Lord— were charmed by the evident devotedness with which he had given himself to his Divine Master, and by the peaceful yet ardent love which, revealing itself upon his countenance, in his conversation, and in his whole comportment, spoke of the close union which his soul had attained with Him of whom he was now for evermore the representative and the anointed.

At an early hour that evening the little party withdrew, in order to leave him free for that secret outpouring of his soul into the Heart of his Lord and Master, for which they felt he was yearning. As he knelt to receive the benediction of the Bishop, the latter said to him, in a low voice, and with a tone of paternal gentleness:

"To-morrow you must ask our Lord to cure you, in order that you may work for Him."

Francis looked up quickly into the face of him who spoke, a bright light shining in his dark eye, and a flush of colour tingeing his pale cheek as he did so. Had his secret hope—nay, rather, his confident trust—then been divined, or had a similar thought been suggested to the mind of the Bishop? However it might be, Francis felt a singular consolation in the words which had been just addressed to him, and he whispered in reply, as he still knelt, holding the Bishop's hand in his:

"This is my expectation. To-morrow, when I say my first Mass, I confidently hope for my recovery. It is so long that I have offered my life for the poor Heathen."

The Bishop regarded him a moment with great earnestness, then, once more making the sign of the cross above his lowered head, and recommending him to retire early to rest, left the apartment.

At a very early hour the following morning Francis was awake, and panting for the hour when he should for the first time ascend the altar steps as priest and victim, to offer to the Eternal Father the *Lamb slain from the beginning of the world*. He had slept but little that night. He had in spirit taken his place beside the divine Mother standing beneath the cross, and in union with her he had been already offering his own interior sacrifice to the Most High. What more fitting day than the Feast of the Seven Dolours for the celebration of the First Mass, above all, for one who, like Francis, penetrated so profoundly the "height and depth" of what was involved in the sacred character of the Priesthood?

The supreme hour at length arrived. The Bishop knelt at his *prie-dieu* on one side of the sanctuary. Father Neville assisted Francis at the altar. Long after, those who had been present at this memorable First Mass remembered the absorbed expression that rested on his pale countenance, as, issuing from the sacristy, he advanced towards the sanctuary, and ascended the altar steps. They loved to recal, years after, the depth of devotion with which he for the first time performed that highest function which it is given to man to perform, a devotion which was the result of his burning love, and of his appreciation of the intimacy of his union with the Divine Victim immolated beneath his hands.

When, at the *Orate fratres*, he turned round, facing those present, some anxious eyes were directed towards him, for they were aware how his intense emotion must be telling upon his weak and suffering frame; but there was no appearance of faintness on the pale absorbed countenance, no nervous movement in the hands; it was a soul lost in the one great action in which he was engaged, the sublimity of which seemed already to have transformed him, as ages before one had been transformed when entering into the cloud he stood upon the mount, conversing face to face with the Living God.

At the "*Memento Domine*," where the Priest, joining his hands, prays silently for such intentions and persons as he specially intends to pray for, there was something awful in the intense silence which reigned in the chapel. It was as if those present were instinctively aware that the commune being held at that moment between him whom they saw standing before the altar, and the God to whom in secret he spoke, was of a nature even more than ordinarily solemn. When at the Elevation—that supreme moment when the Priest stands between heaven and earth, forming but one victim with the Divine Mediator whom he raises up on high in his uplifted hands, there was more than one bowed head which was slightly raised in order to witness that touching spectacle, the First Elevation;

and there was more than one present who asked himself if aught could be refused to him who at that moment held uplifted in his hands the World's Ransom. The Elevation of the Chalice was so prolonged that Father Neville, who stood beside the young celebrant, made some slight movement as if to recal him to himself. With the least possible trembling of the hands he replaced the sacred vessel upon the altar and continued the Holy Sacrifice.

It was finished: and now must follow the touching ceremony of the kissing of the hands, those pure hands but yesterday anointed, and which but a few minutes before had for the first time upheld the God who formed them.

As he sat there at the entrance of the sanctuary, with his hands spread out in the accustomed manner at the like ceremony, and making the sign of the cross over every one, as each withdrew from rendering the homage so expressive of the faith and reverence with which the Church would inspire her children for the Priests of God, not a shadow rested on his countenance. It was pale indeed, and long suffering had left its traces there, but a strange brightness lit up his features, and his eyes shone as with a light from heaven.

At length all was over, and after having gone to the sacristy to unvest, he came forth, and kneeling in the old familiar place at the communion railing, as from childhood had been his custom, speaking secretly to the Hidden God of his one hope and aim in life, he poured forth now his whole soul in thanksgiving.

How long that thanksgiving would have lasted who shall say, if a gentle pressure on the shoulder had not caused him to look up, and to meet the kind eyes of Father Neville, who whispered to him that he must come to take some breakfast, for that his strength had been already tried too severely?

Francis replied with a smile so bright that the old Priest never after forgot it. Then he immediately rose, and, in genuflecting, remained a moment kneeling before the tabernacle, and finally walked with a firm step down the aisle towards the private door leading into the house.

Some of the poor Catholics in the neighbourhood, and from distant hamlets, were entering at another door, in order to hear Mass, which Father Neville was shortly about to commence.

On seeing Francis, some of them respectfully approached, saying, "Give us your blessing, Father, if you please. We could not get here in time for your Mass."

It was the first time he had been addressed by that name, so sweet to the Priest's heart: "*Father;*" and, as he heard it, the memory of that paternity which he yearned to extend to the millions of souls then sitting in darkness, rushed over him, filling his heart with sentiments which *only* a Priest can know, because they are part of those special graces shed into his soul together with his vocation.

Some there were amongst the poor people who came to speak to him who were natives of "the Emerald Isle," and with their characteristic faith and demonstrative love of all that Holy Church has sanctified, and above all of her Priests, would insist on kissing "the new Priest's blessed feet" as well as his hands. Francis suffered them to satisfy their devotion, and as he paused a minute for that purpose, his heart beat high, for he was carried away in thought by that little scene to the touching ceremony he had so often witnessed at the College of Foreign Missions, on the occasion of the departure of Missioners, when their feet are kissed by those who assist at the public function, and make their adieux to those going forth to bear the *"good tidings"* to the ends of the earth.

Yes, all that his heart had ever desired passed before his mind's eye at that moment, and a thrilling sense of joy took possession of his soul, as he beheld those poor simple people giving him now, as it seemed, an assurance of the ceremony of far deeper import, in which he hoped,—yes, he confidently hoped,—one day, to take part.

Had not the Heart of Jesus arranged the present little scene as a pledge of that other, which, perhaps, at no distant day, should follow? Be it as it may, it was an accidental joy, a brighter brightness shed over that memorable day: and never would be forgotten by those around him the expression that lit up his face as, passing from the corridor leading from the chapel into the house, he was met in the vestibule by the Priests visiting at the Manor, together with the members of the family.

Father Neville watched him from a little distance, anxious to ascertain if the physical change he beheld in him were indeed real, or simply the transient effect of exceeding happiness. So remarkable was it, that he almost persuaded himself it was a reality; but not desiring to be precipitate in his judgment, or to attract the premature attention of others to the evident improvement in Francis's appearance, he resolved to remain, for the present, silent upon the subject. He was not alone however in his observations; and more than one of the little group there assembled whispered to his neighbour: "Surely, he is cured."

The Bishop was awaiting his arrival in the breakfast-room, and Francis hastened forward to meet him before the others were within hearing.

"My Lord, my first Mass has, I believe, had its effect. I think I am cured," he whispered, as he knelt for the Prelate's blessing.

The Bishop raised him up, and, resting his hands on his shoulders, regarded him attentively. After a moment's earnest scrutiny of that noble countenance, he replied: "It does not surprise me if such is the case. We must not, however, in such circumstances, be too precipitate in our judgment; neither must we tempt God by being too secure and free in the commencement. In praising Him for His mercies it is necessary to be humble. Allow yourself, then, to be taken proper care of. The goodness of God will manifest itself sufficiently in you even with that prudence. May He bless and perfect His work in you and give you your heart's desire."

The Bishop had finished speaking before the others drew near, thus they were ignorant of the communication that Francis had made to him, but several immediately commenced referring to the evident change in the appearance and whole bearing of the newly ordained.

"Let us give glory to God for His wonderful works in all creatures, and praise Him for manifesting His power in the weakest and vilest," said Francis, gravely, with a tremulous voice, which caused all present to regard each other in silence, but with faces which seemed to say: "It *is* true, then, he is cured."

Father Neville had heard Francis's words, and then, having his Mass to say immediately, he left the room without making any comment, wending his way back to the chapel, praising God in his heart, for he fully believed in the cure of Francis. The others were silent for a few minutes, and then began conversing upon other topics, for they saw that Francis wished not at present to speak of the change in himself, which none however could fail to remark.

An hour later, Father Neville was standing in the open doorway of his own room watching Francis approaching from a distance, and coming to pay him the visit which he knew he would at the earliest opportunity. There was still the same bright glow upon his countenance, so marvellously indicative of a renewal of health and vigour. The languor which had characterized his bearing for so long had disappeared, and in its place was visible the firm quick step and upright figure of other days, which spoke so well the ardent nature, and the strength and constancy of his character.

He entered the room of Father Neville and closed the door. Then, for the first time, he spoke without constraint.

"Father," he said, "I am cured; the change which was wrought in me whilst I was saying Mass could not be mistaken."

"May God be eternally praised and glorified for that which He has wrought in you," said the old Priest, his eyes filling with tears as he spoke. "Sit down and tell me how it happened."

"You have long known my expectation," replied Francis, "and how it has never been shaken by my continued bad state of health. You know also that I had chosen the day on which I should celebrate my first Mass, for making to God the *vow* of devoting my life to the service of the Foreign Missions, and I have made it *unreservedly;* for even if He had not been pleased to restore my health, the motive and intention with which I should have suffered and laboured even in England would have been the conversion of the Heathen, and the promotion of everything that would in any way further the interests of the missions in distant lands. To-day, when I went up the steps of the altar, I felt so exhausted that it perhaps would have been more *reasonable* in me to have expected that the answer to my offering of myself, and of my vow, would be immediate death ; but God has willed it otherwise. I made the vow at the moment when I was forming my intention for Mass. You know I had long resolved my first Mass should be for the Propagation of the Faith, and I believe no intention could be more agreeable to the transpierced Heart of our Lady, whose feast we celebrate to-day, since no heart, save the Sacred Heart Itself, burns with so ardent a desire of seeing her Divine Son known and loved throughout the world, as does that of our Blessed Lady. When I ascended the altar steps to read the Introit, a sensation which I cannot describe passed through my entire body, and, for a moment, I feared I could not proceed. Turning, however, with my heart towards our Lady standing ' *beneath the cross*,' I gained strength; and immediately I became so absorbed in God that my physical weakness had not the power to distract me again from the great action I was going to perform.

"It was at the Elevation of the Chalice that the decisive change was wrought in me. I cried in my heart to God the Father, and prayed Him for the sake of that Precious Blood which I held in my poor, weak, unworthy hands, to give me health, that I might labour for His glory amongst the poor Heathen, for whose salvation His Son had died, and now immolated Himself anew. Oh, what a prayer that was!"

He paused a moment, and clasped his hands over his eyes as if he were recalling some object he had actually seen.

"That which God wrought in me," continued Francis, "was instantaneous; for no sooner had I replaced the Chalice upon the altar, and risen from adoring, than I experienced the change, and I knew that I was cured. Thus has my prayer been heard,—my sacrifice and my vow accepted. Help me, my Father, to praise the wonderful goodness of God in my regard, Who has not suffered that I should be confounded in my expectation. Let us render thanksgiving also to S. Francis Xavier and Blessed John de Britto, for they have pleaded for me on high whilst I have offered my oblation upon earth."

He ceased speaking, and remained, as it seemed, absorbed in the overwhelming thought of the wonders that had that day been accomplished in him. His venerable companion was also silent, for his heart was lifted up in fervent thanksgiving to heaven for the marvels he witnessed, not only in the cure of which he could no longer doubt, but also for the marvels of grace he discovered in the soul that had been unveiled to him.

They had sat thus some moments lost in emotions which would not permit of words, when at length Father Neville spoke:

"You have then made your vow to-day; and—did you do anything else?"

Francis regarded him with a quick glance of inquiry; and then looking out towards the sea, and with a countenance which bespoke how his conversation was, even at that moment, more in heaven than on earth, he said: "Yes. I offered my life for the Foreign Missions, and for all that can promote their increase." Then, after a moment's pause, he added: "You know, Father, it is but the *formal* expression of what I have done for years past, and it will be renewed with every breath I draw even to the last."

"God bless you, Francis, and perfect in you His work, and the accomplishment of His designs in you. May the great Saints, in whose intercession you so justly confide, continue to help you," replied the old Priest, in a voice full of emotion. They remained conversing for some time and then went to rejoin the others, all of whom were anxious to be in the society of the newly ordained, whose first Mass had, as was evident to all, wrought such a wonderful change.

So assured did Francis feel of the reality of his cure that he would fain have taken steps that very day for returning to his dear *College des Missions Etrangères* in Paris, not wishing, in the ardour of his desire, to lose a moment in the preparation for the career he now believed he might once more confidently look forward to. The Bishop, however, forbade him to do anything that might savour of rashness, all-assured as he might feel of his restoration, and permitted him but to write to the Superiors of the College, informing them of the goodness of God in his regard, and of his hope very shortly to return, in order to make his final preparations for the long-wished-for departure for distant lands.

The marvel wrought in him was fully manifest and acknowledged by all who saw him. He was no longer the invalid of the house, and the object of tender solicitude. He rose at an early hour and repaired to the Chapel, where, for an hour, he made his meditation and recited the Little Hours of his Breviary, before saying his Mass; after which he made, ordinarily, a thanksgiving, whose duration would have been prolonged till a late hour had not a messenger been sent, as usual, to tell him that the family awaited him at breakfast.

There was nothing overstrained—no apparent effort in anything that he did. All was done with the ease of one in perfect health. His appetite was good, that which it had not been since his first attack of illness in Paris; his step elastic, and even the slight tinge of colour which had been wont to appear through his dark complexion, and which spoke of health, had returned to his cheek. It was, in fine, the Francis of other days; the young Foreign Missioner of the future, only with an additional gravity, a dignity which seemed to have fallen upon him, unconsciously to himself, since he had been admitted to Holy Orders; since, moreover, his union with the Heart of Jesus had been rendered more intimate by an habitual spirit of prayer, by sharp suffering, by his more profound comprehension and practical experience of the mystery of the Cross.

Days and weeks passed on, and still not a shadow of alteration which could cause apprehension to the most timid in believing in the marvellous cure; and at length, when two months had elapsed, and the Bishop once more visited the Manor, for the express purpose of seeing with his own eyes if the change he had witnessed at Francis's ordination had indeed continued, he felt bound to give his consent to his returning without further delay to Paris.

Once more, therefore, was the ardent heart of Francis beating high with hope, yet with a *chastened* hope, a more *humble* and a purer joy than he had known before he had drank of the bitter but purifying chalice of disappointment. He had tasted *practically* now of the truth that God is *Supreme Master*, and that the gift He bestows to-day He may at His pleasure recal to-morrow. With this reality engraven by experience upon his soul, he gave himself up to the sentiments of joy and hope which thrilled his breast with a spirit of entire dependence, of humble submission, which mingled as an under-current with all his other emotions. Again, therefore, the inmates of the Manor saw him depart, not as heretofore, as a student, but in all the dignity of his Priesthood, to enter once more the course wherein he thirsted to "*run as a giant.*"

As those who witnessed his departure followed him

with their eyes as far as it was possible, the sentiment of admiration at the wonderful works of God, and the mysteries of His Providence, which are hidden from the prudent according to this world, and revealed to the simple, was universal; and the Itinerarium which they repaired to the chapel immediately to recite together, was joined in with hearts filled with gratitude, and with a spirit of joyous praise.

CHAPTER XI.

Two Scenes from Real Life, which seem to have no connection with our History.

Whilst Francis is in the full enjoyment of that new life, which seemed to penetrate his whole being, preparing himself, with four of his companions, for departure for the distant scene of their future labours amongst the Heathen, which was to take place in the ensuing spring, we must introduce the reader to two dwellings, whose appearance differed no less widely from each other than did the condition of those who dwelt in them, and whose acquaintance we are about to make.

Near the window of a drawing-room at the West End of London, sat two ladies. The younger was occupied in some needlework, in which, judging by the listless manner in which she pursued it, she felt not the most remote interest. The elder, about fifty years of age, but who bore her years "gracefully," was perusing a newspaper, from which she occasionally read to her companion some short portions, varying it with comments upon what she read, which formed a kind of desultory conversation.

"Oh! how weary I am of it all!" at length exclaimed the younger lady, throwing down her work, and resting her head upon her hand.

"Of what are you weary, Clara?" asked her aunt, laughing; "of your heavy labour upon that fragment of work, or of my reading?"

"Of neither, in particular," was the reply, "but of everything in general. I often ask myself, what *is* the use of living?"

"Oh!" replied the elder lady, in an unconcerned tone; "those morbid thoughts *will* occur from time to time: they are the result of some little indisposition, or of over fatigue."

"And for *what* do I fatigue myself?" answered Clara, with a bitter smile of contempt; "for that which affords me no present satisfaction, and which certainly will be no service to either body or soul—for I *have* a soul," she added, with a strange emphasis on the last words. Her aunt laughed.

"Really, Clara, you are inexplicable to-day. I do not doubt the existence of your soul; but you need not, for the sake of your soul, become morose; one would think you were about to adopt the severe maxims preached by Father King, as if that were possible as society exists at present."

Clara's colour heightened as she replied, with some warmth visible in her manner:

"I never heard anything *severe* preached by any of those Fathers; but it is no wonder they inveigh against such a purposeless, frivolous life as the most of us lead."

"You really provoke me to laughter," replied Mrs. Saville; "to hear you talk now you might be a *dévote*, yet a few hours hence you will be one of the most animated, and apparently absorbed in the crowded room where you will be."

Clara did not reply for a moment. She was wincing beneath her aunt's home-thrust.

"It is true," she replied, at length; "for the moment I go with the current, and amuse myself with the objects I pass on the way; but do you think they *really* interest me? Oh! certainly not. I value them for what they are worth—simply that; this heart, the human heart, was made for something greater than all that."

There was something in the tone in which the last words were uttered that told of material in her who spoke them capable of being rendered useful for God's glory, and beautiful in the sight of heaven. They were strangely at variance with the evident worldliness and frivolity of her companion, who was pleased to take occasion from them to return some expressions of sarcasm upon her niece.

"Really, dear Clara, you had better become a *dévote* at once, and join some association of pious ladies, who go about distibuting good books and soup, and patronize all the maid servants out of situation, and orphan children, and—."

Clara stopped her companion with a gesture of impatience.

"Oh!" she exclaimed, "you know I abhor all that savours of the 'Lady Bountiful;' and, as to a *dévote*, I should feel myself a hypocrite if I played that part. I know not what I want—I only know I am weary and disgusted with my present aimless and, to me, uninteresting life. I believe I must go abroad; I *must* find *something* wherein to interest this head and heart."

"Well, if you will wait until the next season draws towards its close I will gladly accompany you on a continental tour," said Mrs. Saville.

"Oh, yes," replied Clara, laughing, "doubtless,—and our tour would be simply London abroad instead of in England. You would direct your steps precisely to every place that you knew there were crowds of people. No, I want to go to places not generally frequented. I want to see nature where I have not seen it before, and to open for myself new fields of thought, wherein I may sometimes refresh myself when I return to the unwholesome atmosphere of fashionable life."

"To what a supreme contempt of us all you have arrived," retorted Mrs. Saville, laughing. "Nevertheless, I shall take my revenge upon you to-night; I predict that the listless *ennuyée* Clara Herbert of the present moment, so sublimely disgusted with 'the world,' will be quite changed—quite another being a few hours hence."

Clara shrugged her shoulders, half smiling at her

aunt's playful challenge, and soon, too soon, perhaps, the sentiment of her *aimless* life was forgotten—at least for a time—in the scenes that succeeded, and in the *divertissements* to which, for want of something better, the vague longing for which was beginning to make itself felt, she gave herself up as they presented themselves.

In a garret, many storeys high, situated in a narrow street, or rather lane, not a hundred miles from the aristocratic quarter we have just visited, were two young girls, busily occupied in elaborately embroidering muslin, whilst rich materials of other descriptions lay around in striking contrast with the poverty of the room and its furniture, as with the humble condition of its poorly-clad inmates. Although extreme poverty prevailed, cleanliness and order were no less conspicuous; and various objects also met the eye, which bespoke the presence of a guardian angel in that poor abode—the spirit of Catholic piety. A large crucifix hung between two narrow beds, whilst beneath it, upon a rough wooden shelf, which served for an altar, stood an image of the immaculate Mother of God. No flowers indeed were there; how could the poor toilers procure them? they could not buy them, for already they had scarce wherewith to obtain the necessities of life, labour though they did all day, and sometimes far into the night; and where were wild flowers to be gathered—even if they had had the time—in that dark murky city? But they had other flowers to lay upon the altar of their heavenly Mother; and they had the sweet practice of depositing each night at her feet a billet, upon which were noted the acts of virtue, the sufferings, and the prayers of the day, and begging her to offer them to the Sacred Heart of her Divine Son for all its interests and intentions.

Such was the abode of Catherine and Maria Dale, the two orphan girls, whose acquaintance we are about to make.

They had seen somewhat better days. Their father, a small tenant farmer in Devonshire, had, in an evil hour, been induced to invest all that he had during many years accumulated, in a large corn factory in one of the suburbs of the great city. Leaving his former country home he removed with his wife and two children to the neighbourhood of his new business, which, for a while, seemed prosperous. Catherine and Maria received such education as is given at the middle-class schools in those convents whose chief object is the instruction of youth. There, also, they were perfected in several branches of ornamental needlework, which, in later times, was to be for them the only source of support.

The fair promises of success which had dazzled the eyes of William Dale soon proved fallacious. The great firm in which he had invested all he had possessed became bankrupt, and he found himself, with his wife and two girls, penniless. Dale was a good honest man, and a fervent Catholic; but his powers of endurance were not great, neither was his character of sufficient firmness to enable him to bear up and struggle through the difficulties that had so unexpectedly fallen upon him. A few weeks only had elapsed since the blow, when William Dale passed to another life, leaving his sickly wife and two young daughters to face their poverty alone. The former was, by her state of health, incapacitated for labour, and hard it was for two girls, of the respective ages of seventeen and eighteen, without friends, without patronage, to earn a sufficient sustenance for their mother and themselves.

As is usual in affliction, their thoughts reverted to those, who, having themselves left all things for God, have consecrated their lives to the relief of others, as far as lies within their reach, and within the limits of their vocation. Catherine and Maria sought the advice of the Religious who had been their kind instructresses. Through their medium they obtained employment for their talents in embroidering and lace work, whilst a Catholic owner of a *magasin des modes* was induced to have them instructed in such branches of needlework as would enable them afterwards to be regularly employed in her own establishment.

Thus did the young sisters commence their battle of life. No toil was too arduous for them, no fatigue too great, for there was a suffering mother to be relieved, who looked to them alone for support. Sweetly, lovingly, with self-sacrifice rendering beautiful the most ordinary of their actions, they continued their work of love, until one day "the *reaper came*" and swept away from them the treasure they had so tenderly striven to preserve from the cold blast of poverty, and then, and only then, the sisters knew in all its bleakness, what, in this bitter world, it is to be *alone*.

Scarcely had the turf begun to grow above the humble grave of Mrs. Dale before fresh difficulties presented themselves. The Catholic owner of the *magasin* in which they had been first instructed, and afterwards employed, died, and the business passed into other hands. The young girls no longer met with the compassion and charity flowing from Catholic faith, which they had found in their previous employer. Hard work, or rather *much* work for *little* pay, was now the order of things; and what was to their feelings far more painful, was the frivolous and even dangerous companionship into which they frequently found themselves thrust, in consequence of the change in the head of the establishment, and in the class of persons employed in her service.

Such was the position of Catherine and Maria Dale at the period of their introduction to the reader.

The March afternoon was closing in, and the waning light was little suitable for the delicate work upon which the sisters were occupied. One of them rose to light with a match the miserable candle which, as they sat close together, was to be placed between them, the rest of the room being almost enveloped in obscurity. No fire burnt in the little grate, and the young girls, shivering with the cold, drew around them each a cloak, whilst every now and again they were compelled to desist from their labour, in order to rub their hands, purple and benumbed with the severity of the weather added to the absence of fire and warm and suitable nourishment. They might—had they wished it—have worked for the usual hours in the house of their employer, in the work-room well provided with fire, and where they would have shared the plentiful meals provided for the other "*young ladies*" of the establishment. But sweeter far to Catherine and Maria Dale was the privacy of their poor garret, where they could as they laboured converse at their ease of Jesus and Mary, and of all that Catholic piety renders consoling to the innocent heart, than the public work-room, warm and well lit as it was, but where they would have found themselves exposed to hear their holy faith and their Priests scoffed at, and to listen to conversation little in harmony with their pious Catholic education.

As they sat at work on the evening in question, conversing in their habitual gentle tone, the younger sister Maria said, as for an instant she laid down her work to rub the poor cold hands, only to take it up again with greater alacrity: "I wonder, Katie dear, if our Lord will ever enable us to employ ourselves in another kind of work. How often we have spoken together about it, have we not? But it is a long time coming," added the young girl, with a sigh.

"We must not lose hope, though, for all that, dear Maria," said her sister. "If only we were in France we could get plenty of employment," she continued, thoughtfully; "in a Catholic country they have so many different works in which we could be employed."

"Oh, Katie," replied the younger sister, her whole face beaming as she spoke, as if her soul had in that moment received a new degree of grace, "if only some of our rich Catholic ladies would begin a work here in London something like *l'Œuvre Apostolique* in Paris, what happiness for us. Only think what it would be to work vestments for distant missions, sacred work, Catholic employers, and such a beautiful object, instead of these pieces of vanity," and she held up the delicate tissue upon which she was labouring, with a gesture of contempt as she spoke; "it would be like heaven on earth for us, in comparison with our present means of living. Is it not true?"

"It is, dear," said Catherine, gently, "and I have often hoped that something of that kind might appear in England. But," she added, more gravely, "there is so much difficulty here for works of an entirely Catholic kind, especially of the kind you mention. In Paris, to begin with, there is the College of Foreign Missions, and missionaries, constantly leaving, to be supplied; then there is the Propagation of the Faith, and the missionary spirit of all the good and pious in

France. If we had in London a College of Foreign Missions, and if there was that desire we see in France of spreading the Faith and of sending out Missionaries to other lands, very soon such a work might be begun as we should wish to be employed in."

There was a few moments' pause, after which Maria said: "Katie, let us begin this very night to pray that all *that* may be brought about. Let us ask it of the Sacred Heart, and communicate for that intention in future every Thursday. Shall we?"

"Willingly, dearest," was the elder sister's earnest reply; and then, looking towards the poor little so-called altar, before described, she added: "I think we must remind Father King of his promise to give us a picture of the Sacred Heart, and beg Sister Aloysia to give us two little blessed tapers to light each night whilst we say our prayers before it."

"Oh, yes," replied Maria, delightedly. "Let us call at the convent on our way to the church this evening, and ask Father King also to-night for his long-promised picture, and so we shall begin our prayers on the last Thursday in March—to-morrow."

Well might many a rich lady of fashion, and amongst them Clara Herbert, have envied the happiness of those two poor girls, whose simple piety opened to them so fertile a source of hope, and who found in the newly awakened thought a brighter sunbeam than projects of any earthly greatness could impart to the votaries of the world.

CHAPTER XII.

The Departure of Francis for the East.

It was the month of June, and nine months had swept away since Francis's ordination. He had completed his course of studies with the brilliant success of which he had from the commencement given promise. He had astonished men whom age and experience rendered venerable, still more by the maturity of his judgment, and by the clearness of his perceptions in every branch of knowledge necessary for his difficult career in Heathen Missions, than by his talent in the acquirement of various languages. To crown all, the state of his health had, since his return to the College, given no cause of solicitude to his superiors. Without being robust he was pronounced sound, neither had any symptom of his former malady manifested itself. Never had a vocation for the Missions been accompanied by more evident marks. Such was the general acknowledgment of all who knew him.

The hour, then, was fast approaching which would witness his departure for those distant shores where he already lived in thought and heart. It was many years since the work for which he had felt himself so powerfully attracted had, as it were, interwoven itself with his every thought, had given an additional energy to every action, to every work of piety, to every prayer. It had been the goal towards which he had never ceased to tend; the golden horizon stretched out before him, which had shed its radiance over his whole life. At length all was to be rendered a reality; the long dream of boyhood and manhood was to become a waking attainable fact, and nothing now remained to be done but to make the immediate preparations for departure.

Four other Missionaries were to embark with him for India, one of whom was destined to be his companion at Madras, from whence, after a time, they were to pass on to a remote Mission, newly established in the interior.

It being the month of the Sacred Heart, special devotions were made each evening in the chapel of the College, and it was after one of these services that the affecting ceremony of the departure took place.

Who that had seen him now in the vigour of health, his cheek slightly flushed with the exceeding happiness which thrilled through his heart, his figure erect, and denoting the buoyant energy of his character, who, we say, would recognize the Francis Willington of a year before, pale, languid, apparently broken down, without hope of recovery?

He alone of the departing Missioners had no relative present at the ceremony. The others were Frenchmen, some members of whose families came to take part in the solemn and touching adieux. Francis preferred it as it was. A word from him would have brought the Colonel to Paris, despite the length of the journey and his advanced age. Stanislaus also had even anticipated that his presence would be requested; but Francis contented himself with letters of adieu, wishing, in that hour of departure, to be unshackled by any natural associations, or by the awaking of sentiments which spring up in the heart on such occasions in the presence of ties of nature. Nevertheless, the ceremony was no less touching in his regard than in that of the others, for Francis was singularly beloved by all, and his warm strong heart had loved those with whom he had been associated at the College as so many fathers and brothers. The vow at length was *publicly* pronounced which made him the *"father and servant of the blacks"* for ever.

The scene which had presented itself before his mind on the day of his first Mass, when they came to kiss his hands as he sat at the sanctuary step in the Chapel of the Manor, was now being realized. The chapel rung with the melodious chant of the antiphon so soul-stirring in the signification of the words which compose it: "*How beautiful upon the mountains are the feet of him that bringeth good tidings, and that preacheth peace.*"*

* Is. lii. 7; Nahum i. 15.

There he stood with his four companions, his feet uncovered, his dark quick eye lowered a little, perhaps to hide the tear that would not be suppressed, as the many persons assembled approached, after the inmates of the College, to kiss the feet of the departing Missioners. It was a moment never to be forgotten—that in which the scene he had from boyhood pictured to himself actually took place. Long after, the sound of those many voices would ring in his ears : the last farewell to the scene of his happy studies, to his fellow-students, to his superiors, would recur to his memory. It seemed to be, as far as is possible in this life after long expectation, the grasping of an object, the *only* object which rendered life to him desirable.

Another circumstance also added a deeper tone to the happiness of Francis : deeper, because more chastened ; chastened, because he had tasted the chalice of disappointment, and had experienced the soul-sickening weariness of hope long deferred. It was the marvellous removal of the obstacle to the accomplishment of his desire, which had followed the celebration of his first Mass. All this crowded in upon his memory and sank down into his heart, mounting upwards from thence to the Heart of God in silent full thanksgiving, which mingled with all his other emotions on that memorable evening.

At length the touching ceremony was concluded. Benediction of the Blessed Sacrament followed, and the moment of actual departure arrived. They went forth, accompanied by the Rector and all the students, as well as others who had been present at the ceremony, singing the *Magnificat*, none of whom left them until they had witnessed the train move off, bearing away the young Missioners *for ever*.

The following evening they arrived at Marseilles, that being the port from whence they were to embark. They found that an entire day must intervene before the ship would sail; and the hours lagged on slowly for those who longed to be hastening towards the souls whose cries for help seemed to come to them across the blue sea which stretched out before them.

Vocation! what marvels are hidden in that word. What divine operations in the soul; what revelations does it not contain of the "*breadth, and length, and height, and depth*" of the love of the Sacred Heart. Yet how lightly is that word "*vocation*" regarded, even by those whose faith should have taught them to esteem more highly a gift of such priceless worth! Has it not been purchased for the soul who is the recipient of it by the Tears, the Blood, the broken Heart of an Incarnate God? Yes, He has bought it "*at a great price.*" He shivered in the crib of Bethlehem, and went away through the desert to live in exile, and toiled through the long years at Nazareth in order to purchase it. He prayed for it on the mountain side, and in the agony, and on the cross. He delivered Himself up to the will of them that hated Him, and stretched out His blessed limbs to receive the nails, and opened His Heart to all the bitter waters of sorrow with which it was His Father's will He should be saturated; and thereby He bought for us, not alone salvation, but the special grace besides, which was to be conferred upon each particular soul that should be in a singular manner associated to His work.

Perhaps if "*vocation*" were thought of from this point of view, Jesus would not so frequently be defrauded of His rights, and not be—at least amongst Christians professing piety—so often as He is "*a sign to be contradicted.*" He is thus opposed by those who are themselves the objects of His special choice and calling, and by those who would pretend to claim a prior right to God Himself over the disposition of His creatures, and who would arrogate to themselves the judgment which belongs alone to the Creator, as to the ways by which His creatures are to attain the end of their existence, that is to say, the greater glory of their Lord and Master, by faithful correspondence with the special vocation He has given them.

Perhaps thoughts somewhat of this nature passed through the minds of all our young Missioners during the hours which seemed to them so long before they could set sail. Certain it is that the heart of Francis, whose vocation had been fostered by habitual meditation on the love of Jesus for souls, beat high with gratitude for that *special* love which the Divine Master had evidenced in his regard by his apostolic vocation. There was, moreover, in his soul that thrilling tranquil depth of joy which frequently accompanies the near attainment of a long-desired hope. Once, and only once before, had he experienced it, and that was when he had been *so near* the goal before his first attack of illness in Paris. But even then it was far inferior to that joy which thrilled within him now. Then his course of studies was not completed, nor had he received as yet the Order of Priesthood. It was rather the success which followed him which rendered to his ardent character the approaching term a *certainty* rather than a *hope*. But now every preparatory step had been taken, every stage had been passed with brilliant success; the sacred character of the Priesthood was stamped upon his soul, which imparted to him the right of proclaiming himself, henceforth and for ever, that which from earliest youth he had so yearned to be, "*the father and servant of the poor Heathen.*" Now he had at last bid farewell to family and native land, and even to the civilized world, and the very hour which had haunted his boyhood's dreams, and sustained him in the trials of a later age, and mingled spontaneously with all his thoughts, giving a character and an energy to his whole inward life, had at last arrived, and he stood actually gazing at the very vessel which, in a few hours, was to bear him with his fellow-Missioners from Europe, and thus launch them upon the course for which their generous souls were thirsting.

The five young men had returned from the vessel,

whither they had gone during that last afternoon, in order to see that their baggage was safely consigned, and to make certain necessary arrangements. They had partaken of their evening repast at an early hour, and had afterwards said together their Matins of the following day. This sacred duty fulfilled, and with the beautiful sentiments which their lips had been uttering shedding their sanctifying influence over their souls, they sat, pursuing a grave yet cheerful conversation, the joy which animated the heart of each being reflected upon their countenances. It was a bright June evening. A fresh breeze had sprung up towards the afternoon, which had cooled the ardour of the mid-day sun, and rippled the blue waters of the Mediterranean, stretching far away in the distance. The sun was fast sinking in the west, and casting over the surface of the sea that golden "*path of rays*" so beautiful to the eye— so fertile in suggesting beautiful thoughts alike to the poet and the saint. For Francis, that golden track across the deep had but one meaning, one suggestion,— the reflection of his whole life's dream, which had coloured every object in nature or in art his eye had ever rested on, and lent a sweeter tone to every sound that fell upon his ear. Not indeed towards the *West*, but still across the great deep sea a golden pathway had opened for him; and lo! he was on the very verge of traversing it; and, beyond—ah! beyond was that vast horizon towards which his soul's eye had ever tended; which his great apostolic heart had embraced with all the charity and zeal with which the Heart of Jesus had inflamed it.

We love to pause upon the scene before us, and to rest upon the holy joy of that sublime and lifelong aspiration, so near, so very near now to its accomplishment.

Somehow, our pen seems reluctant to trace another line, as if some dark foreboding of evil were hovering near, and which must needs ere long be recorded. The five young Missioners prolonged their conversation until the sun had sunk beneath the deep blue waters of the sea, and twilight had deepened into night. Then they spoke of separating for the night—their *last* night on European soil—and of retiring to rest. So gently had the darkness fallen around them that they had not remarked, until the time of separation had arrived, that they were really in such darkness. Having called for lights, they perceived, to their surprise, that Francis was not there; and in passing to their respective rooms, which were all in the same part of the hotel, one of the number knocked at Francis's door, and, without waiting for a reply, opened it and looked in. Scarcely had he done so, than, with a startled exclamation, he turned and beckoned to the others to follow. A sad spectacle met their eyes, and changed the joy which but a few moments before had reigned triumphant in their hearts, into terror and profoundest grief.

In the dim light of a lamp which stood on a table

near the bed, they beheld Francis, half-reclining in a large arm-chair, his face and lips colourless, his breathing laboured, whilst a little scarlet stream was flowing from his mouth. Hastening towards him, they raised his head, and one amongst them rested it against his shoulder. Francis looked at him. The eyes that but so lately shone with the joy of his life's dream, all but realized, now were dim and drooping from the faintness that had seized upon him; yet in that one glance the anxious eye of him who supported him read the cruel anguish that in that short time had made itself the master of his soul. He was not unconscious, and therefore the terrible consequences of that strange sudden stroke from the Master's hand had flashed upon him in all its dread reality. Medical aid was instantly sent for, whilst a telegram was despatched without delay to Paris, to inform the inmates of the College of Foreign Missions, which they had left amidst such unclouded joy one day before, of what had so unexpectedly and sadly taken place. Two physicians arrived within a few minutes, for his companions wished to have a double testimony regarding his state before the despatch of a second telegram giving the medical opinion. At the first glance at their patient both gentlemen regarded each other significantly, and pronounced the case a very serious one—*to say the least of it.*

"He was to embark with us to-morrow morning *en route* for India, on the Missions," said one of the young men, in a low voice, with intense anxiety awaiting the reply. The physicians again exchanged looks, and, with a compassionate smile resulting from professional clear-sightedness of the case, the elder of the two pronounced the words full of such terrible import, and which were echoed by his companion:

"Impossible! Your friend is in a most precarious state." And after regarding Francis fixedly a moment, he added: "I should say this is not the first time he has had an attack of this kind; but if it is so, everything is to be feared now, for his constitution will be radically and permanently impaired. If you leave, gentlemen, to-morrow morning—we cannot deceive you—your friend must remain."

He was about to add more, but was prudently checked.

"This is your firm impression,—our friend cannot accompany us? Your answer, gentlemen, is of the utmost importance," said the elder of Francis's companions, addressing himself to both physicians, whilst he looked steadfastly at them awaiting the reply, the purport of which, however, he already instinctively felt. Both physicians answered, simultaneously, in a tone which expressed their sympathy for the sorrow which had been cast over that little group of departing Missioners: "*His departure is impossible.* It will be a considerable time before his removal even to Paris could be ventured on. The least exertion, in his present critical state, might even be fatal."

The little group collected round the doctors with difficulty suppressed the grief that these words occasioned; but there was no time to be lost in vain regrets. Another telegram must be at once despatched to Paris, informing the Superior of the College of the sad state of the case, and demanding instructions about the care of Francis, who would be left, after their departure, in that hotel, amongst strangers, and in so critical a condition. This done, the little party stayed near the bedside of Francis, whilst one of the doctors remained, at their request, to watch if any change took place, and to lend his aid in case of necessity. The faintness which had resulted from loss of blood, and which had caused him to steal out of the room where he had been conversing with his companions, had in some measure passed away, and in its stead a strange sensibility to all that was going on around him manifested itself, in his gestures, in the quick intelligent glance with which he followed each one of the little group assembled at his side, and in the eagerness with which he sought to catch each word they spoke in subdued accents to each other. From time to time his countenance gave evidence of intense physical pain, but he spoke not excepting when any of his companions suggested change of position, or asked if he wished for anything. Then he answered in a low tone, but with a glance of mingled gratitude, affection, and sadness, which went to the hearts of his brothers in the same sacred calling, whose souls were fired with the same holy desire which animated his own, and who therefore knew how keen was the anguish he was enduring at that hour. Although they had carefully prevented the decision of the physicians from reaching his ear, yet it was impossible for him to be unconscious of the gravity of his illness, especially as he felt only too plainly that it was but a repetition of his former malady, of which he had been miraculously cured.

About eleven o'clock a telegram arrived from Paris, saying that one of the Fathers, together with the physician of the College and an infirmarian, had already set out, and would probably reach Marseilles at noon on the following day, but that the four Missioners must depart, leaving Francis at the hotel. This message brought some consolation to the little party, who yet did not inform Francis of its purport, for they could not determine, by reason of his silence, if he indeed realized the terrible fact that his departure with them was rendered impossible. They watched by his side during the whole night, that night which had been so overshadowed with the sorrow which would be associated for ever in their minds with their last memorable few hours before their departure for their distant Missions.

Very early in the morning a message came to inform them that the vessel, whose hour of sailing had been fixed for 10 a.m., would not set out until the afternoon. They who before had found the hours so slow which must intervene before their actual departure, now experienced a sense of consolation that their waiting must be yet prolonged, which sentiment sprang from the strong fraternal affection they bore towards Francis, which had made them shrink from leaving him thus alone. Now, however, by this providential delay, this would be avoided, as the little party from the College would have arrived, and thus Francis would at least be left in the care of those who knew and loved him well.

As the light of day increased, and they were still in uncertainty as to Francis's consciousness of the necessity of their sailing without him, they felt considerable anxiety as to what they should do when the hour which was at first fixed for their departure should have arrived. It was Francis himself who was to deliver them from their perplexity. The light was streaming in on that bright June morning, and there lay the young Missioner, white and almost helpless on his bed of pain, whilst the fire of burning love and apostolic zeal lived unquenched and undaunted in his soul.

"Charles," at length he said, in a low voice, addressing himself to one of his companions, all of whom he noticed were sitting round him without any appearance of preparation for departure, "what is the hour? It seems growing late; is it not near the hour of sailing?"

"Yes;" was the reply, "but they have sent to inform us that the hour of starting is deferred until the afternoon."

"For what cause?" asked Francis, quickly. On being told that it was on account of some ordinary ship arrangements, he seemed satisfied; and then he asked if they had informed the College of his sudden illness, and if any telegram had arrived with instructions as to what he was to do. The little party of Missioners, like true brothers as they were, felt that the dreaded moment had arrived in which Francis must learn the truth, which would once more dash from his lips the cup of hope and joy which he had so long waited for, and which had seemed at length to be securely his.

His quick eye discerned their hesitation, and, divining the cause, with his inborn delicacy and kindly feeling he hastened to remove their difficulty. Gathering up his strength, he said, looking now at one, now at another, as he spoke: "Do not fear to tell me, my brothers, the worst, the *very worst;* and you know what *that* means for me,—it is not death; oh! no." And as he said these last words his glance shot upwards, as if his soul turned towards heaven with a sense of deep relief in the thought of *that* alternative.

"I did not hear what the doctors said," he continued, "but I feel *here,*" he added, pressing his hand on his chest; "I feel *here* how it is. They have decided that I cannot leave with you to-day; is it not so?"

"It is too true, Francis," was the reply.

"And the telegram from Paris, what instructions does it convey?" asked Francis, quickly.

"*We* must depart, but Père Carrière, with Doctor

Lemesurier and an infirmarian, will arrive here before we leave. It is for this we are glad that the vessel will not sail until evening."

"You will join us later, Francis," one of the party ventured to say, after a few moment's silence, during which Francis appeared plunged in deep thought, or, it might be, absorbed in prayer. He made no direct reply to these words, and seemed rather to evade any allusion to the hope suggested, his only endeavour evidently being to dispel the sorrow which his illness had cast over his companions.

With this view he spoke of the various places they would pass; the incidents they would be likely to meet with; messages which they were to convey to Missioners they would meet, carefully avoiding in all he said, however, aught that would tend to harrow the feelings of those who were leaving him under such painful circumstances. Weakness, and still more, pain, prevented him from conversing long, and then the time dragged slowly and anxiously on for all.

Shortly after midday, to the relief of Francis's companions, the travellers from Paris arrived. They were conducted at once—as they demanded—to the room of the invalid, where they found the whole of the Missioners assembled who had left them but two days previously. What a meeting, and under what altered circumstances!

Père Carrière, like all the inmates of the College, and more especially those who in any office of authority had had special relations with him, loved Francis sincerely, and as he approached the bed, and his glance fell upon the white drawn face before him, tears started to his eyes, and it was necessary that some moments should elapse ere he trusted himself to speak. Dr. Lemesurier, the resident physician of the College, and who had consequently known the malady which had before compelled Francis to suspend his studies, and to return to England, was scarcely less moved. Whilst the Father was exchanging some words with Francis, whose burning hands he held in his own, the doctor was regarding him from a little distance. His practised eye told him all at the first glance, and his kind heart shrunk from the task that lay before him. Francis observed him, and with his old bright smile welcomed him. He approached, and took Francis's hand, and then, laying his own upon the invalid's side, and then upon his chest, he said: "It is here, and here, you suffer; it is the same as formerly. You feel it is so: is it not?"

"The very same, only this time it seized me with such intensity of pain that it caused blood to flow."

"Ha!" said the doctor, in a quick low voice, to Père Carrière, who stood at his side, anxiously awaiting his opinion; "it is as I feared."

"What is the worst?" inquired the Father. "Surely, you do not think it will be fatal."

"Not yet," was the portentous reply, which fell gloomily on the hearts of those who heard him.

Francis, who had also heard them, without however having caught the previous questions to which they referred, believed that they had relation to some possible period when he might rejoin his companions, who were departing that day.

"How long, doctor, do you think it will be before I shall be able to follow them?" he asked, with a manner which bore in it some marks of astonishment, for so intense were his physical sufferings, that more than once in that memorable night the truth had flashed upon him in all its stern reality, that his life's hope was at last crushed for ever. The two words he had heard the doctor speak, inasmuch as he was ignorant of their bearing, had awakened within his buoyant soul a gleam of hope mingled with astonishment.

"Francis," said Père Carrière, "the doctor has just asked me if he shall at once tell you the truth, and I have answered him without hesitation in the affirmative. You were setting forth to break the Bread of Life to others. Accept it now yourself, my son, veiled under the crushing disappointment which the good God has prepared for you. A Missioner—you know it—must be ever prepared to die; so also must he be ready to accept the will of God. Behold it!" The father retired a few steps, as well to hide his emotion as to make room for the doctor to approach closer to Francis, to whom he was about to speak the decisive words which would reveal to him the truth.

"My dear Francis," began the kind Dr. Lemesurier,

"you remember in your former illness I told you that if ever any attack of the same nature manifested itself, it would be beyond remedy, and would prove an insuperable barrier to carrying out your design of going to the Missions. Your present attack is not only of the same nature as before, but in a far more aggravated form. My dear friend, we are in the hands of the good God. His will is now plainly manifested in your regard. *The career you were on the very threshold of entering upon is for you an impossibility.*"

"Even at some future time?" asked Francis, in a voice which revealed the intensity of his mental anguish, added to his physical pain. Then he added in a whisper, "I wish to know the very worst."

"Yes," rejoined the doctor, "it would be to foster a futile hope to think of the Missions—*that career is closed to you for ever!*" There was a dead silence in the room for several minutes after these words had been spoken, which no one seemed willing to break. It was an awful hour for one amongst them,—one of those hours which poor frail nature scarce could endure, if grace for this had not been purchased by the dread agony of One who in the weakness of His own Flesh prayed that *if it were possible His chalice might pass from Him*. There he lay, crushed down in the very hour when hope seemed about to be swallowed up in possession of the object so long sighed for. His white hands,—damp with the perspiration which his mental anguish caused, but burning with the physical pain of which, however, at that moment he was scarcely conscious, so far did the agony of his soul surpass it,— were clasped over his eyes, whilst his tightly compressed lips, and the lines around his mouth, indicated the struggle that was going on within.

He remained thus some minutes, and when he withdrew his hands, his eyes sought those of Père Carrière.

"*C'en est fait, donc, mon Père,*" were the first words that came forth, in a voice scarcely above a whisper, from his livid lips.

"*Oui, mon enfant, c'est la volonté du bon Dieu,*" and bending down, the good Father spoke in a whisper to Francis other words which those around were not to hear. When he had finished, Francis again turned towards the doctor, and said: "Tell me, doctor, will it be long or short?"

Dr. Lemesurier paused a moment, for he did not altogether understand the extent of the question which was addressed to him.

"I mean," added Francis, perceiving his hesitation, "Do you believe my days, weeks, or months numbered?"

"The attack you have now is one from which you will never recover entirely," replied the Doctor; "but, in consequence of the buoyancy of your temperament, it may be even some few years—I could not decide— before death will ensue."

A sigh escaped from Francis, which seemed to say: "Of what avail is my life, *now* that its one aim and object is for ever lost?" He had yet to be perfected; he had yet to learn—practically at least—that life's aim and meaning is never lost, since there is God's will and wisdom to glorify, and the coming of His kingdom to be hastened and extended by the grand APOSTLESHIP OF SUFFERING.

Time was progressing, and all seemed instinctively to dread, for Francis's sake, the hour of his companions' departure. Not a movement, not a sound of a clock or a bell was lost upon him. The window of the apartment where he lay looked out upon the sea, and from it was visible the ship itself, wherein he was to have embarked. He knew that the hour of separation was approaching, and turning towards Dr. Lemesurier, he said: "Doctor, I wish to be placed close to the window, that I may watch them set sail."

"No, no," replied the Doctor, persuasively; "why harrow up your feelings thus?"

"Am I a child," replied Francis, quickly, "or a man?" Then he added, gently, as if conscious that his former words had manifested some irritation, "Do me this favour, Doctor, to assist me to that couch yonder, that I may see the last of them."

The doctor, with some reluctance, consented, and with the aid of some of the others, removed the invalid to the place he desired. His colour changed as his eyes rested on the blue sea, and as the white sails of the vessel met his glance. But despite his inward anguish, and the intensity of his physical suffering, he mastered his emotion, and strove to place at ease those who were departing. At length the moment arrived, and the four young Missioners surrounded him to bid him farewell. Not one amongst them left his side without having shed some tears, which did honour to their manhood and to their apostolic hearts. Père Carrière, with Dr. Lemesurier, and the good infirmarian, were all equally touched in witnessing that parting scene, so unexpected, and under such sorrowful circumstances. The door of the room closed upon them, and they were gone, whilst the Priest, the Doctor, and the infirmarian remained at Francis's side, watching him with much anxiety, more especially as the effort he was making upon himself to suppress any manifestation of the fearful struggle that was going on within, was, without doubt, aggravating the intensity of his physical pain.

Shortly after the Missioners embarked the vessel put out to sea. And Francis watched it all. He saw the white sails unfurled, and the stately ship move on, making a pathway for itself upon the mighty waters. It was evening once more, and the sun, sinking westward in the heavens, shed its golden light across the sea, as yesterday, when Francis had watched that ray, and thought how it prefigured the bright career which awaited him the *other side* of the sea, that lay outstretched before him. With his clear, quick eye he could discern the figures of the four Missioners upon the deck, looking towards the pier; nay, towards the window from whence they knew he watched them. He saw them raise their hats, and he made a sign to those at his side, to wave their handkerchiefs, for he had not strength to do so. Then, with hands clasped, whilst his breath came quick and gasping, he remained with his eyes immoveably fixed upon the vessel as it glided out to sea. In vain did his companions endeavour to distract his attention, in vain did they suggest the necessity of his taking some repose, and of permitting medical treatment to be at once applied. He heeded them not; he seemed not even conscious of their presence; his spirit seemed to have left his mortal body, and by the intensity of his desire to have taken its flight across the deep in that direction whither his gaze was turned. The sun sank down in its sea of gold, as it had done on the preceding evening, and the shadows began to fall, and still his eyes looked ever seaward. Could he still discern that white object in the distance, which began to look so small and indistinct? It would seem so, for it was towards it his gaze remained turned, and not even the paroxysms of pain with which, from time to time, his whole frame writhed, could cause his eyes to flinch.

What passed within his soul during those hours, who shall say? Those around him dared not force him to withdraw from that window, where he seemed as one spell-bound. Dr. Lemesurier feared that such force would be even prejudicial to him; yet a strange anxiety possessed him as to the ultimate effects of that long mental anguish upon a frame attacked by a malady, the gravity of which was alone sufficient to cause the worst fears to be entertained.

Whether it was that his eye could no more discern the object it had been strained to watch so long, or that his physical powers could no longer sustain the effort, they had endured, but his gaze at length withdrew itself, and through the stiff parched lips came forth the whispered words, "*C'en est fait—Oh, mon Dieu! mon Dieu!*" and falling back upon the breast of Père Carrière, he hid his face thereon, whilst one long deep groan broke from his stricken soul, and then all was still.

The one dream of that young ardent life had faded out as the ship had passed for ever from his outward vision. The bright sun that had shed its golden light over his whole existence had set for ever, and the hours of that day, and the scene we have witnessed, and the last groan which fell upon the ears of the bystanders, have told their tale, and are written on high in the history of the Sacred Heart, whose secret designs and loving *cruelties*, (if we may dare so to speak,) and hidden triumphs, will one day be revealed, and form for its special friends and lovers their delight and their beatitude for eternity.

CHAPTER XIII.

A new phase in a life's history.—The Apostleship of suffering.—Father Rebille's secret.

For many weeks Francis lay hovering between life and death. At first, indeed, it seemed as though the latter would triumph, but there were other designs in the book of Eternal Wisdom.

Great beyond description was the grief at Willington Manor, when the news arrived of what had happened, and in a few hours after the reception of the telegram which the Superior of the College had despatched to the Colonel, informing him of the sad tidings, Stanislaus started *en route* for Marseilles, intending to return if death were apprehended for Francis, and to accompany the Colonel to his side. It was a terrible blow for that father's heart, at once so loving and so brave. He had shared in the youthful enthusiasm of Francis, and afterwards had sympathized, with all the ardour of his strong faith and the generosity of his soldier's heart, in the noble desire which he had discerned to be the mainspring and *vitality* of his son's very existence; and in proportion to his joy when he had seen him on the point of entering on his sublime career, so great was his grief now that Francis's hope and aim in life was dashed aside for ever.

It was with difficulty he could be dissuaded from starting at once for Marseilles, but he yielded at length to the entreaties of those around him, on condition alone, however, that Stanislaus would inform him by telegram, immediately he arrived, if there were proximate danger of death. This in effect being the case, the Colonel, being warned of it, set out, and arrived at Marseilles in little more than a week after the occurrences we have been describing had taken place.

After many weeks of almost intolerable pain, during which his mental faculties, however, were keenly sensible of the blow his hopes had sustained, some slight improvement took place in Francis, which rendered it possible and even advisable to remove him, at least as far as Paris. Accordingly, one bright morning, after having looked for the last time from that window from whence he had watched the ship depart, they carried him forth, and with tenderest care and every precaution brought him back, a broken down man, in the hey-day of his youth, with his life's hope crushed and withered as a flower cut off in its bloom, to that College from whence he had gone forth but two short months before, so full of hope and vigour.

Loved as he was by each one who knew him, his disappointment was a common sorrow for all, and nothing that could be done to testify the sympathy and affectionate solicitude of every inmate of the College was omitted.

Several of the first physicians in Paris were consulted as to the possibilities of his ever again recovering. After several weeks of attention, and the most careful observation of the case, the final decision was unanimous that the health of the young Missioner was irrecoverable, and that his future would infallibly be but an expectation—longer or shorter—of death, which alone would put an end to his sufferings.

This decision, far from appearing to be any *additional* confirmation of what before had been doubtful, was for Francis but the seal of authority, as it were, upon his previous *interior conviction*. When the decision therefore was made known to him by the Superior of the College, in the presence of the physicians who had given it, and of some of the other Fathers, no mark of astonishment or of deeper sorrow was visible upon his countenance. With the sad smile that now so often played around his white lips, he said, "Yes, I know it must be so. I felt it would be so *that* day." Then, seizing the hand of the Superior, he added in a whisper: "*That* day, my Father, when I watched the ship put out, and saw them sail without me, I knew—I knew the happiness I had tasted was too great; and when I broke down then, I felt it was all over. They tell me now, then, nothing fresh, nothing that I have not known since *that* day."

The days and weeks wore on, and still Francis was an

inmate of the College. He was waiting there simply
until it should be pronounced practicable for him to
return to England, and consequently he found himself
in the midst of associations at once very dear and very
painful; very dear, because of their relation with all that
had been dearest to his heart on earth, very painful,
because they recalled but too vividly the utter frustration
of his hopes. In one sense he felt as though the links
were broken that had bound him to the College and its
inmates. He was there no longer as one preparing to
carry on the work that there was propagated, no longer
as one preparing to labour in the vineyard; but as a
visitor, a disabled member, cut down before he had even
borne the burden of one day's toil and heat, much less
gathered the palm of martyrdom which he had secretly
coveted. He was there *by favour*, awaiting until he
should have sufficient strength to bear the journey to his
quiet English home, whither he was to return—to die.
Such were the sad thoughts that welled up from the
depths of his heart, as he lay there during those long
summer days.

At length the day arrived when it was pronounced
safe to undertake the journey, and Francis was called
upon to endure another trial, scarcely less painful than
that he had sustained in taking leave of his four
companions at Marseilles, with whom he was to have
sailed for the East.

He was now to bid adieu for ever to all those with
whom he had been linked by the *strongest* of all ties,—

that of one common interest, one common sympathy, in a great and a noble cause; more sacred than the ties of flesh and blood, because its source is altogether supernatural, and its object God Himself; more powerful, because it reaches not only the affections of the heart, but penetrates even to the most intimate recesses of the soul, and is strengthened by the light and perceptions of the intellect. These are friendships whose foundations are cast above, and which will be perpetuated and perfected there, where they will add an additional joy to our beatitude.

In heart and soul, indeed, Francis would never be severed from those whom he was now leaving, but all *active* co-operation with them, he felt, was at an end; and he was leaving, besides, all those associations which bore special relation to his one only aim in life, and this separation was not, as it had been before, with the possible hope of re-union; it was now unconditional, and for ever.

It was over. The last adieux had been spoken, and Francis had torn himself away from the scenes and the country, and the Fathers and brethren, who were so dear to him. Once more he had been on the sea, but only to cross to his English home, instead of to the distant shores towards which his heart still turned. Each stage in his journey, and each object that pre-

sented itself, brought his crushed hope in all its reality
before him. The waves, as they dashed against the
vessel, and the very fact of being on the *sea*, which,
from his childhood, had ever presented itself to him as
the friendly track which was to conduct him to the far-off
haven where he would be; the arrival on his native
land, which he had believed he had left for ever, and
the old accustomed English faces, and costumes, and
manners, all presenting so striking, and in his circumstances so painful, a contrast with the sights and
people that would have met his eye if his landing had
taken place at his wished for destination. But the greatest trial of all was yet to come, and as such it will be
recognized by those who have ever experienced the like.

There are passages in life whose exceeding sadness
seems almost unendurable, and such an one is the return
to a familiar spot after an exceeding sorrow has fallen
upon us; above all, if that sorrow is of a nature to have
deprived us *for ever* of an object dearly beloved, or of a
hope whose realization was the sunshine of our very
existence.

To see each old familiar scene and object the very
same as when we dwelt amongst them formerly, and our
life was full of promise; to recognize that it is ourselves
alone in whom there is so sad a change, and that it is
our *changed selves*, our own crushed hopes and blighted
happiness, that cast the shadow over the beauty of all
that meets our eye, and render it so redolent of sorrow;
Oh! these are things that bring in the waters, even to

the very depths of the stricken soul, and waters whose bitterness the blessed cross alone can sweeten.

Thus it was with Francis Willington on that golden August evening, when, in company with the devoted Stanislaus, who had gone to Paris in order to conduct his brother home, and to watch over him on the journey, he drove through the scenes of his childhood, where in youth had germinated and been fostered the sole aspiration of his life, scenes which were naturally so dear to him, but which, when his hopes were matured, he had rejoiced in quitting for ever, in order to plunge into the glorious arena which had opened itself before him.

For the second time he returned to his old home, broken down in health, thwarted and baffled in his hope, but this time, unlike the preceding, it was with that hope utterly crushed for ever. On either side the avenue beyond the shrubbery, and stretching out before him on all points of the landscape, his eye beheld the yellow corn-fields, ripe for the harvest; and as he watched them waving in the gentle breeze of that bright August evening, he was again reminded of the hope, whose harvest day had been for him so near, but which harvest never had been—never would be gathered. Was it his guardian angel that whispered to his broken spirit that thought so full of balm, that followed his sad reflection, as he watched the corn-fields ripe for the sickle? "*Not in this world;* but that hope which it was not permitted thee to gather *here,* is laid up for thee in the house of thy Father above."

Such was the tone of his thoughts when the grey old mansion appeared in sight. Now, indeed, he had need of all his strength, or rather of all the grace which God ever gives in proportion to the trials which He lays upon us.

There, on the terrace, stood the Colonel, waiting to receive the son whose sorrow his own heart felt so keenly,—waiting to give him that reception, which, by reason of the painful cause of his return, must be twofold in its tenderness. By the side of the Colonel stood the venerable old Priest, Father Neville, a little more bent, his grey hair fast changing into white, but otherwise the same Father Neville as formerly, only that now a shade of sorrow, not remarked before, rested on his countenance.

And now Francis was at home once more, the object of the tenderest solicitude and affection, all vying with each other in testifying their sympathy with him by their services of love.

Even the domestics showed that they comprehended well the sorrow of him who was come back amongst them, him whom many of them had known from childhood; and old Philip wept without restraint, as he grasped the hand which Francis extended to him at their meeting.

As he lay down to rest the first night after his arrival, in the old familiar chamber which he had particularly requested might be his once more, it seemed to him that not even until that moment had he realized to the full how utterly frustrated was his life's desire. And when, on the following morning, his eyes opened on the familiar objects of his boyhood, so different to those he had dwelt amongst of late, and oh! how widely different to those towards which his mind and heart had been for ever turning, he closed them again as if to exclude something too painful to support, and forth from the quivering lips, on the stillness of the early morning, broke once more that low groan, giving some relief to the anguish of his stricken soul: "My God! my God!"

The months wore slowly on, at least, slow they seemed to Francis, the vigour and energy of whose mind and whole character were strangely, painfully, at variance with his now broken health and wasting frame. There were times when fierce struggles went on within his soul, when he needed all the interior strength which his deeply religious mind procured him, and which enabled him to unite his sufferings and his great sacrifice to those of the Divine Heart for Whose interest he offered every pang he was enduring. It was on one of these occasions, when the exhaustion of his bodily strength seemed mocking at the ardour of his soul, and when all things seemed in league to sever, if possible, his will from that Divine Will to which he had entirely given himself up, that Father Neville found him one November evening reclining in his room up stairs, it being one of those frequently recurring days upon which he was unable to come down and join the family party. The kind old Priest at once remarked the struggle that was going on within, and sitting down beside the invalid, and resting his hand caressingly on his shoulder, he said some few words of encouragement, which, however, succeeded only in eliciting from Francis an acknowledgment of his inward strife, and from Father Neville himself a confidence which, whilst it caused Francis to value his venerable friend still more, at the same time diverted his thoughts from his own sad reflections.

"Oh! dear Father, you do not know how terrible it is;" he said, clasping both hands together tightly over his eyes, "this burning heart that never *will* be at rest; this ceaseless thought of all that has been and *would* have been, but for this utter helplessness."

"But for the Master's Will," gently suggested Father Neville.

"Ah! that is the saddest thought of all," replied Francis, mournfully, "that after having given up, as I thought, myself entirely into the hands of God, that He might accept me and my crucified will for the same cause, the salvation of those whom I shall never cease to regard as my own—the poor Heathen, I render myself unfaithful to God and to them, by taking back what I have offered."

Father Neville knew the unswerving fidelity of that

soul, whose persevering devotedness to the cause of the poor Heathen had ever excited his admiration; he knew also how faithfully he was struggling to keep his will in conformity to the Divine Will, and what interior combats he was for this enduring. He saw, moreover, how poor human nature seemed sometimes on the point of carrying off a victory, which, although but transient, caused Francis afterwards profound affliction, from the sense of infidelity which overwhelmed him.

"You do not *really* take back any part of your offering," he said, gently; "you are only *tempted* to do so. God permits this for your greater merit in the exercise of patience, humility, and submission to His adorable appointments."

"It seems as if I alone must be useless, and miss the object of my life," resumed Francis, after a pause of a few moments, which followed Father Neville's words. "See here, a letter from Mapleton," he said, holding up an opened letter; "you remember, he was with me at S. Edgar's, and preceded me to the College at Paris, where afterwards we studied together, and from whence I saw him depart about a year before I was to have followed. He tells me of the glorious harvest of souls that might be garnered in the various parts of India, where he has been, if only there were more labourers. He writes at length of his missionary work, his life, his hardships, which are to his heart such a source of joy; and as I read, my own heart throbs with its burning desire, and then I look at myself and see a wreck: I am as one paralysed, who has his limbs and faculties entire, but which are useless to him. All those I have known are gone, all have attained their aim in life, Mapleton, and so many others whom I have seen depart for distant lands, and Agnes, and Helen Sternbrooke; and I alone remain stranded on the shore, baffled." There was no wilful murmuring in the tone in which he said these words; it was but the quiet outpouring of his own sad thoughts. The kind old Priest was profoundly touched, but there was a strange expression upon his countenance, as Francis's last words rung in his ears: "*And I alone remain, baffled.*"

He remained for some moments with his hand supporting his head, buried, apparently, in profound thought. At length he spoke. "Francis, shall I tell you a life's history? Many years ago, an English Priest, doing missionary work in a populous district, felt himself called to a vocation still higher, that of Religion. He sought, after mature deliberation and long and earnest prayer, admittance into the Society of Jesus. The Bishop in whose diocese he was, so strongly opposed the step that the Jesuits hesitated to give him a trial, perhaps believing that his lordship had some special grounds for his unwillingness to relinquish his hold upon the services of the Priest. However it was, it was agreed to by all that the Priest should go to Rome, and that if four of their Fathers there decided it to be a true vocation, the Priest should carry their agreement and supplication to the Sovereign Pontiff, begging from his Holiness himself the approval of the step he meditated, namely, to relinquish the secular body of the clergy and to enter the Society.

The four Fathers agreed in favour of the Priest, and, with a heart beating as high with hope and promise as ever yours has, Francis, he started for the Vatican, his testimonials in his pocket, and where he found awaiting him the friend who was to present him. But what more awaited him? The Sovereign Pontiff received him with affection as a father, but with a firmness which admitted of no doubt, refused to grant the desired approbation, in consequence, he said, of the communication he had already received of the valuable services that the Priest was rendering as a member of the secular body. So well was the case pleaded that the supreme approbation was withheld, and the Priest was bidden to return to England and continue to labour as he had before. The Vicar of Jesus Christ had spoken, and must be obeyed. At first, before it transpired that this decision was the result of a communication received from the good Bishop, who had formed too high an opinion of my poor services, I was tranquil and contented in my disappointment, for I thought it was in consequence of some interior light that his Holiness had thus settled the matter. When I learnt all, however,—." Father Neville suddenly stopped, for he became aware that he had betrayed his secret by unconsciously adopting the first personal pronoun instead of the third, which he had used until then.

"Ah!" exclaimed Francis, grasping the old Priest's hand, and gazing earnestly into his face, "it is then as I began to suspect. *You* are that Priest, and I am listening to the history of your own disappointment."

"The rest is soon told," resumed Father Neville. "When I learnt the cause of the Pontiff's decision against my entering into the Society, my soul sustained a conflict which I like not, even at this distant day, to recall. I fell ill with fever, and my life was despaired of. Shattered in health and hope, yet with that inward peace which the blessing of Christ's Vicar sheds into the soul, I returned to England. But my life went on as on clogged wheels. It was thus when I met again your father, who was returning from India to settle down at the Manor. We had been old friends, and I told him all my trouble. No one but himself knows my life's history. He has been my true friend until now."

"And you have been his," said Francis, affectionately, "and the comfort of us all."

"I have laboured in the interests of the Society in a literary way," continued Father Neville, scarcely noticing the interruption; "I have thought as a Jesuit, felt as a Jesuit, and, to the best of my limited capacity, worked as a Jesuit, without having the consolation of *being* a Jesuit. Say, Francis, are you the *only* one baffled in your life's hope? Even at this far-off day the wound is fresh, and the mystery of the divine permission is the only balm it knows."

The old man ceased, and laying his white head down upon his clasped hands, he wept.

For a few moments there was silence, for Francis was too much affected to reply; moreover, he felt a profound reverence for the sorrow until then unknown to him, the intensity of which was now so manifest.

"Father Neville," he said at length, as he saw the old man raise his head and dash away his tears, "Father Neville, you have indeed helped me. Thank you for having told me all this. And how patient you have been, and self-forgetting in sympathizing with me, whilst your own heart was aching the while."

"Ah! Francis," said Father Neville, "He knew well the human heart who said: *'What doth he know who hath not been tried?'* Often, when I have seen you struggling, and have heard by passing words how hard the cross was pressing, it was to me as my own young days over again. But come; we must do the will of the good Master *cheerfully*, and be faithful to Him to the end."

"Yes," slowly responded Francis, "*to the very end.*"

Father Neville alluded no more to the subject of that day's conversation: but it frequently afforded Francis matter of thought, and he felt admiration for the grandeur of that long life of secret cross-bearing; and when nature was sometimes making its voice heard within his own soul at the thought of his baffled hope, a glance at the God-serving, cheerful old Priest before him, was as a silent monitor, speaking more eloquently than any words.

CHAPTER XIV.

Clara Herbert.—The Letter from Agnes.

A year has flown since the return of Francis. Very slowly, yet surely, disease is making its insidious inroads upon his constitution, and conducting him gently but surely to the tomb.

The vigour of his mental powers, the ardour of his soul, however, do but augment in proportion, it would seem, as his body wastes.

The dream of his boyhood is still the dream of his fading days, the goal to be attained the very same; the same movement impelling his every action, and lending a colour to his every thought. He has learnt many lessons within the year that has passed; chastening, elevating lessons taught by the Divine Master Himself, in hours of suffering and prayer. He has struggled in many an inward strife, and at last he has learnt to rest contented with the Will that has destined him to labour for the Heathen by means of an apostolate that costs him a *living* martyrdom, instead of that martyrdom of blood for which he had so longed.

Amongst the visitors who at different periods were

found at the Manor, were occasionally some who regarded the work of the Foreign Missions from a somewhat different point of view to that from which it was beheld by most of those with whom the reader has been made acquainted in the course of this narrative. Some there were who, to judge by the sentiments they expressed, considered a lively interest in the conversion of the Heathen, and efforts to promote their evangelization, as a *wrong*, in some sort, offered to their native country.

Belonging to this school was a certain Father Fairclough, whom Stanislaus had often met in visits to the North of England, whom he had invited to the Manor more than once, and who was generally a favourite there.

It was not until after the return of Francis, that Father Fairclough's *views* regarding the Foreign Missions manifested themselves. The fact, however, of the young Missioner actually residing at the Manor, stricken down in the flower of his youth, caused the subject of the Missions to be frequently alluded to by the guests assembled there, and thus it was that "*out of many hearts thoughts were revealed*," and many conversations bearing on the point in question brought about.

At the period in our narrative at which we have arrived, several visitors were staying at the Manor, amongst whom was Father Fairclough.

There was also another and a very different person at present an inmate of the hospitable old mansion, and whose visit there was, in all probability, a turning tide in her life, as she herself failed not to suspect before her sojourn ended.

Our readers will perhaps remember that in a former chapter we introduced them to two ladies residing in a fashionable quarter of the great metropolis, and that in the desultory conversation to which we listened, we discerned in the younger of the ladies a tone of bitter discontent with the aimless life she was leading, which made us suspect, we scarce knew why, that beneath the worldly manner of Clara Herbert, was a heart which longed for better things, and a character capable of accomplishing them.

The same lady we find, strangely enough, domiciled as a guest at Willington Manor. She had, it appears, been educated at the same *pensionnat* as Mary Willington, and although since their school days they had met but seldom, yet there was something elevated in the character of Stanislaus' wife, in her conversation and tastes, which always had a charm for Clara Herbert, and seemed, as she said, to remind her that life was *real and earnest*, and that her own was passing away without an aim or meaning.

Some there were who more than suspected that Clara had had, in her earliest youth, an attraction for the Religious life, but that the pleasures of the world had choked the good seed, and that vocation, if indeed there ever had been any, was stifled in its commencement. There were times, however, when she sighed wearily after having a fixed object in life, to which she might legitimately devote the energies of her soul.

It had been on one occasion, when this desire was pressing upon her more than usual, that she wrote to Mary Willington, as it were to one apart from the atmosphere of frivolity in which she lived, and to whom she felt it would be a relief to unburden her heart, at least so far as to give vent to some of the bitterness that was fretting her within.

The result of this letter was a cordial invitation from Mary, in the name of all at the Manor, to pay a visit there, so that by change of scenes and associations, she might "regain vigour for the battle of life." It was thus that Mary worded her letter, and little she guessed in what way and by what means that vigour was going to be imparted.

It was Clara Herbert's first visit to the Manor, and its cheerful hospitality, and the agreeable and high tone of the conversation, so superior to that which in her own circle she was in the habit of engaging in, charmed her, and at the same time disposed her to open her heart unreservedly to the new and happy influences which now surrounded her.

From her first arrival, she had been much interested in Francis, the sanctity of whose state, together with the circumstances relating to him, and his evidently approaching death, inspired her with a profound respect akin to reverence. With a natural quickness of perception, she had discerned in the young Priest a depth of holiness which opened, as it were, to her wearied heart a place of refreshment from the heat of the world, and she was never more contented than when listening to the conversations which took place between Francis and those around him; but although powerfully attracted by his discourse, she felt some strange inward pain when conversing with him herself.

"I know not how it is," she said one day to Mary, "I feel in the presence of Father Francis a certain *safety;* there is in him something which seems to shed a hallowing influence over my whole being, and yet, strange to say, I feel a kind of shyness when I converse with him. It seems to me as if he reads the very depths of my soul, and this makes me quail before his eye, and experience a certain awe in speaking to him."

"Why, dear Clara," replied Mary, smiling, "you are such a —a "—

"Wretch," said Clara, supplying herself the word, and discovering some emotion as she said it. "I feel," she continued, "just this—that Father Francis, without any effort, stirs up within me whatever there is of good. Sometimes I am on the verge of saying something of this, and I fear to seem, and perhaps to be, hypocritical. I am sure his eye reads my soul, and if I said what I feel under the impulse of better influences, it would seem to him such an inconsistency."

"If," replied Mary earnestly, "you feel that he reads your soul, you need not fear his suspecting you of *hypocrisy*, at least; and as to inconsistency, Francis knows enough of human nature not to be surprised at seeing much of that, especially in one like yourself, whom, I am convinced, feels an immense disproportion between what you *might* do, and what you actually do for God: is it not so?"

"Indeed it is," replied Clara, with something of the old bitterness in her tone; and then the conversation was cut short by the entrance of some of the other guests.

Miss Herbert had not been far wrong in her impressions that Francis read her soul pretty accurately.

From what he had heard of her, and still more, from what he had seen of her since her sojourn at the Manor, he felt convinced that there lay beneath the surface a fund of goodness, and a power to perceive and appreciate good, above what is ordinarily met with. He had seen how, in certain conversations, her eye had lighted up, and although she had been silent, how much interest was evidently awakened within her, when she had heard discussed such matters as referred to the glory of God and the good of souls. She had been present sometimes at the amicable disputes—if we may so call them—which had arisen between those who entertained dissimilar views regarding the urgency of the work of the Foreign Missions, or the active part which it was incumbent upon all true Catholics in England, as elsewhere, to take in it. This subject had been for Clara Herbert a new field of thought; it had unfolded before her mental vision a new and more vast horizon than had ever before presented itself, and it was evident to the quick eye of Francis that this spoilt child of the world, whose better self had been warped by the fevered atmosphere in which she had lived, opened her soul with an instinct of true Catholic charity, to embrace the new object, for the first time presented to her, and to embrace it in all its vastness.

Such observations as these had excited in the *priestly* heart of Francis an interest in that soul so *nearly* spoilt, and he set about thinking what could be done to provide for it a nourishment for want of which it was, though unconsciously, famishing. An opportunity was not long in presenting itself, and Francis seized upon it anxiously.

Miss Herbert was one day with Mary alone in the private room of Francis, where he remained when he was not sufficiently well to join the family group downstairs, but where he was willing to receive any who wished to visit him.

A letter had that morning arrived from Agnes for her brother, and Mary was pressing him to read it aloud for the benefit of herself and her friend.

"What will Miss Herbert care for a letter from a Carmelite nun?" said Francis. "There is not a single mention in it of anything of what is called 'the world.' It is as a missive from *another* world, where God's interests only form the theme of all their thoughts."

"*Do* read it," said Clara; and then she added, a

little bitterly, and as it were in allusion to the first words Francis had said: "Even such a worldling as I may derive some good from it."

"Very well," replied Francis, "then here it is, and if you become *ennuyée* before the end, remember, you have only yourself to thank for it."

The ladies went on with their work, and Francis, unfolding his sister's letter, began as follows:

"Carmel de ——
"Mois d'Aout, 18——

"My dear brother,

"May the Holy Spirit be with you for ever. Amen."

"It was thus," interrupted Francis, "that St. Teresa always commenced her letters, and her daughters continue the custom to this day." Then he resumed:

"It is very long since I have given myself the satisfaction of writing to you, and it was with much pleasure that I received from our dear Mother Prioress to-day, the suggestion that a letter from me might be agreeable to you, and that I might write to you at full length.

"As to your health, dear brother, I will not waste time in expressing vain hopes, which we must at last believe it does not enter into the designs of God to fulfil. I can only comfort myself in the confidence that you are meriting treasures for eternity, and which, I believe, you think more of, procuring by your suffering and self-immolation, glory to God, and actual graces for innumerable souls.

"For myself, it would be impossible to express the happiness I experience in the life I have chosen, at once eremitical and apostolic. As time flows on, the more clearly I see, the more intensely I appreciate the beauty and the efficacy of such a vocation. If only people in the world knew what is the true end, the mission, of the Order of Mount Carmel, how different would be their appreciation of it. They imagine we retire into these cloisters to live selfish lives, to pass our time in idleness and uselessness: but how far is this from the truth? Our *material* works, indeed, are of the commonest order, and designedly so, that our thoughts may not be diverted (by absorption in material actions, as is too frequently the case,) from application to the dearest interests of our heavenly Spouse. Every work, every action of the Carmelite, whether it be of religion or otherwise, has for its end, with the sanctification of our own souls, the exaltation of our holy mother the Church, the assistance of her Priests, and the extension of God's Kingdom throughout the world. Thus no limit is placed to our zeal. The nations are ours, to gain or to regain to the sovereignty of Jesus Christ. Sinners are ours to reclaim, by ceaseless prayer, to the Heart of our King and our Spouse; and there is not a region upon earth, not a remote island far out in the wide ocean, which the charity, and the prayer springing from that charity, of a Carmelite, does not embrace.

Say, my brother, is there anything of constraint, of narrowness, in such a vocation as this?

"True it is, if we wish to attain our end, I mean the end for which our glorious mother St. Teresa assembled us here, that is, to help the Church, save souls, and contribute efficaciously to make God and His truth known and loved throughout the world, we must be truly *hermits;* our *cell* must be our earthly paradise; but at the same time, what can be more *apostolic* than such a vocation, since it is an apostolic spirit which is to animate the whole body of our life, and every detail which makes up that life?

"I have often smiled since I have been here, in remembering how certain persons, knowing my attraction for the Foreign Missions, used to suggest to me the life of a Sister of Charity, or some other of the congregations engaged in active works merely, and to remark upon the unfitness of a life strictly enclosed, as is the Carmelite, to one in whose soul there existed such an *attrait.* I cannot help feeling that such persons think (without intending it) unworthily of the great mission of Prayer, and also of the immense share it has in the work of the world's redemption. Surely it is because the Life in the House of Nazareth is yet unknown, that there are found those speaking this strange language. The great work of this divine and hidden apostleship commenced *there,* and continued there during the greater part of our Lord's life, whilst to active works He consecrated but three years.

"What did He during those long thirty years, which so few think of, and fewer still think of imitating? Was not He praying for the coming of His Father's Kingdom, and the sanctification of His Father's Name by all peoples and nations? And this is precisely what the Carmelite, taking Jesus for her model, does in her little cell, whilst her hands are occupied, as were those of the Mother of Jesus, in needful common work.

"From all that I have told you, dear brother, and I might tell you a great deal more of the life which your little Agnes has chosen, or rather which the divine Master chose for her; you will see how integral a part the work which is so dear to you forms in my thoughts; and it is a source of great joy to me to feel that, whilst I am fulfilling one of my most imperative duties as a Carmelite, that is to say, praying with all the energy of my soul, and consecrating my penances, trials, and whatever, by God's good providence may occur, for the coming of His kingdom to every nation, and to aid those who labour in the vineyard, that I am by that united with you in the one great object for which you have lived and suffered, and—will die.

"Many Missioners departing from this dear apostolic-hearted country send to solicit our prayers, and to ask us to give the Mission to which they are going a special share in our works of piety. You may imagine how the heart of your little Agnes thrills when such demands arrive; and you may believe she does not forget the Missions and the Missioners.

"Pray for me, ever dear brother, that I may be faithful to the great work—the only work for which I desire to live—to contribute to the utmost of my power to the extension of God's reign on earth, and this by the *hidden* means of which the world knows so little, ceaseless prayer and self-immolation.

"Adieu, my ever dear brother. We are united in the Heart of Jesus in one desire, one hope, one love. *Cor unum et anima una.*

"Your Sister,
"TERESA XAVIER."

Francis folded the letter, and remained a moment silent, then, looking towards Clara, he said: "Well, Miss Herbert, what do you think of the glimpse you have had of a Carmelite's vocation? Are you *ennuyée?*"

"Oh! Father Francis, do not say that," was the reply; "all that you have just read to me is life and health. It is like breath from another and a happier world." She said no more; but she rose and walked to the window, and looked out on the great sea, that which had so often been a resource for others when their hearts were too full for words.

Francis watched her, for, with an instinct of zeal, he felt drawn to render help, if it were in his power, to a soul who seemed to be opening itself to the salutary rays of light and warmth which before it had not known. He was hesitating how to break the ice, when Mary said, half playfully: "Clara, suppose one day you should become a Carmelite? It is not altogether impossible."

"Quite impossible," said Clara; "such a high vocation is not for me: besides, it is said vocation always pre-supposes attraction, and I have none whatever myself for the religious life of any kind. Besides," she added, with a little of the old bitterness discernable in her manner, as if she were annoyed with herself for engaging in such conversation, "it is really ridiculous to speak of myself in relation to anything good or useful, or—"

"Hush," interrupted Francis, half smiling, but really earnestly desiring to check the rising bitterness he had not failed to discern. "All such assertions must be looked upon as heretical. There is *no one* who may not do good in some way or other."

"Oh, well," was the still bitter reply, "just as the reptiles from which we naturally shrink, who may be said to glorify God by making us exercise forbearance or mortification."

"But you have a rational soul capable of knowing, loving, and serving God," replied Francis, gravely; "the glory, then, which the irrational creatures render to God in serving man, bears no resemblance with that which the most insignificant amongst us can give Him. I have no right to preach to you, I know, but you must excuse me if I tell you plainly you must beware of leaving undone the good you might do—of frustrating God's designs."

"That is already done," was the still bitter reply.

Francis paused a moment, and just caught sight of the tear that was dashed hastily away, as if she proudly shrunk from discovering how deeply she was moved, and then he said gravely, but with great kindness in his tone: "Supposing such to be the case, is it yet too late? Oh! no. You know little of the divine patience if you think so. He is waiting for you now, and preparing for you another opportunity of, let me say it, of repairing the past."

Clara turned round quickly, for her head had been for some minutes turned away. For one instant she looked full into the young Priest's face, as if to read his thought. What did he mean? What did he know either of her past or of her future? His quick penetrating eye was bent upon her.

"How I wish I had courage to speak out to you, Father Francis," she said at last; and now there was no bitterness in her tone.

"I *intend* you to do so one day," replied Francis, smiling. "I am not going to let you off. But you are not quite ready yet."

Mary, who was quietly pursuing her work, taking a secret interest in the conversation, which she hoped might be the commencement of good for her friend, laughed at Francis's conclusion, and she had the satisfaction of remarking that much of the difficulty which Clara had until now experienced in conversing with Father Francis, from that time began to pass away.

CHAPTER XV.

Divers "Views" on the Work of the Foreign Missions.

A few days after the conversation related in the preceding chapter, another of a somewhat different character took place, but which no less prepared the way for the exercise of Francis's zeal with regard to Clara Herbert.

The Colonel had that morning received a letter informing him that one of the sons of a dear friend had just decided his vocation for the Foreign Missions, and that it appeared probable that a second son would shortly follow him. The Colonel's correspondent was known, not only to the family at the Manor, but also to some of the guests then staying there, and the news that morning received consequently formed subject of conversation in the course of the day, and was the means of eliciting sundry *"views"* regarding the *"legitimacy,"* as some expressed it, of letting Priests go out of England, when there is so much to be done "at home."

"As for that," remarked the Colonel, in reply to some observation of Father Fairclough, "it is, to say the least of it, no good to seek to deter men from following their vocation. If a man *is called* to the Foreign Missions it is useless to think of keeping him at home. It is a *special* call, just as is any other, and we know who is the absolute Dispenser of such things."

"What I feel about it is," said Father Fairclough, "that youths figure to themselves something exciting. The relations they hear of Missionary life please and excite their imagination, and thus they are turned away from a line of real usefulness which is offered to them in the great needs existing in their own country."

"If it is but their imagination that is pleased," replied the Colonel, smiling, "it will soon be proved that they have no vocation for that kind of life. Solid vocation implies something more than the gratification of mere fancy or sentiment: there is a rigorous training to be endured, and sharp realities to be faced before these men are pronounced to be truly called to such a mission, such a life."

"Well, granting that," replied the persevering Father Fairclough, "I believe that very often a certain influence is exercised by which young men are induced to undertake a life for which, if left to themselves, they would have had no particular attraction."

The good Priest's objection provoked a smile from more than one present, and this time it was Father Neville who replied.

"Setting aside," he said, "what the Colonel has

just now so truly asserted, that only a true vocation will be able to stand the test of regular training and the sharp realities which will be proposed to prove its strength and endurance ; I assure you, experience has fully made known to me that if any bias is exercised regarding young men's vocations, it certainly does not lie on the side of the Foreign Missions. On the contrary, care has to be taken that vocations which are not so marked and strong in the commencement—but which, if left free to the action of the Holy Spirit, will become solid—are not dwarfed and stifled by counter-influence, and by the narrow maxims of mere national or insular prejudice. True, this would have no effect upon a very decided vocation ; but such is not given to all, and Almighty God sometimes gives one that is less pronounced, in order that the recipient may glorify Him, and establish himself in the course destined for him by means of struggles and greater difficulties. Sometimes people thwart God's designs by exercising an undue influence, in consequence of private prejudices, or 'views,' as they are called."

"Well, I confess," retorted good, sturdy Father Fairclough, "loyalty as an Englishman forces me to keep in view the interests of my own country before every other ; and I am always jealous when I hear of men, who might do so much good at home, carrying all their zeal and energy abroad."

"My dear friend," rejoined the Colonel, laughing, "are we not *all* English, and I believe true lovers of our country, and desiring her welfare, above all, her religious welfare? But I cannot agree that love of country excludes the possibility of seeing national short-comings. Now I confess, when I recall the former *spiritual* as well as temporal wealth of England, and when I consider how very little she has ever done towards evangelizing the nations, I blush when I look to France, Italy, and Spain, and see how, century after century, they never flag in the first great duty of Catholic charity, which is to make God known to *all* nations. As *this* is the mission of the Church herself, so is each one of her children called to co-operate with her therein. As to France, her Catholic and Apostolic zeal has never been restrained by her misfortunes; on the contrary, in proportion to the greatness of her troubles at home has been her generosity in propagating God's truth in infidel lands."

"But," objected Father Fairclough, "look at the number of Priests in France, and other Catholic countries, as compared with England. *They* can afford to let some of their Priests go abroad."

"But we must remember, also, my dear friend," replied the Colonel, "that the number is in proportion to the size of the countries, and although I am one of the very first to allow that the number of Priests, even in this little island of ours, is far below what is adequate to our wants—and I offer my poor prayers, such as they are, each day to obtain an increase in their ranks—yet I firmly believe that a little more zeal for the conversion of the Heathen, a little more generosity in a wider field of charity, would merit for us blessings at home, which it is very possible a certain selfishness has been the cause of depriving us of. '*Give, and it shall be given unto you,*' was spoken ages ago by One Whose word is infallible, and we have seen it exemplified in the case of France, whose unflagging devotedness to the interests of God has, I doubt not, merited for her the preservation of that lively faith and intensity of piety for which she is remarkable, despite the revolutionary and infidel spirit which has taken possession of so many of her children, and which threatens her with so many evils."

"For my part," rejoined Father Fairclough, as if, defeated on one ground, he was determined to try his strength on another; "I don't think Englishmen are fitted for the Foreign Missions, that is to say, a *Catholic* Missioner's work. As for the emissaries of Protestantism, of course it is easy work enough for them, they sustain but little, if any, hardship or danger, it is with them a sure means of getting a comfortable livelihood; but as for *our* Missioners, who suffer privation, hardship, and danger of every kind, I really do not think our national character is adapted for that. They will make good, zealous Priests at home, but for the *Foreign Missions* —."

At this moment a pair of hands were laid upon the good Priest's shoulders by some one who had just entered the room and approached him from behind, and then a voice said: "What treason are you speaking, my good Father? What insult are you offering to all your compatriots?" And then the voice was lowered, and Francis, for it was he, whispered so that only he whom he addressed should hear: "And what esteem are you making of the grace of God, by the help of which the most unfit can do all things, and without which the most able can do nothing?"

Father Fairclough turned round, and, perceiving Francis, endeavoured with the true kindness of which he was possessed, to give a softer colouring to the sentiments he had just expressed.

"No, no," said Francis, smiling, "I know well how varied are the views held by many in this country on this subject, and I believe it proceeds from want of thorough understanding of the matter. However, I can speak from some experience; and I can affirm that when the vocation is given, Englishmen are as capable of making as devoted Missioners as are men of any other nation. He who calls them dilates their hearts, and infuses into them a thirst which cannot be quenched, a thirst for carrying His Name and the knowledge of His love to the nations where He is as yet unknown. It is a *special* call which only the Master of souls can give; and where the vocation is a true one, no human influence can deter the soul from following it, therefore is it in vain for people to endeavour to make men settle down at home, if the Master's voice has called those men to labour amongst the Heathen. People may rail and murmur, if they will, about men leaving England, but what is spoken above cannot be gainsayed; and the will of God is, that the people of this country should give generously and cheerfully, for '*God loveth a cheerful giver*,'—not only money but also *men*,—imitating thus France, which has given, age after age, her life's blood, so to speak, in her sons and her daughters, for the extension of God's Kingdom throughout the world. Then, I am convinced of it, England will draw down upon herself graces and blessings, which will result in the exaltation of our holy religion here, and there will be opened to her people a glorious field for the exercise of their zeal, and for the application of their temporal wealth."

"True," said the Colonel, after a few moments pause, for Francis's earnest and burning words seemed to have rendered Father Fairclough mute. "I own I have always felt much humiliation as an Englishman and a Catholic, that whilst so many souls, who know not the name of God, toil and enrich us with their wealth, that whilst they send from their shores wherewith to pamper our bodies, and adorn them and our dwellings, we, on our side, have done little or nothing to convey to them the message of mercy, and the means of attaining eternal life. *Our* communication with the heathen lands is exclusively of a mercantile nature."

"And yet," broke in Father Neville, who until then had been engaging disjointedly in a side conversation, and listening, during the pauses, to the discussion we have been relating, "I saw only a week or two ago that upwards of two hundred millions of human beings, who are subject to England's dominion, are as yet in ignorance of God. What an awful responsibility does not this lay at our door!"

"But after all," persisted good Father Fairclough, "charity begins at home."

"But does not *end* there, however. Come, you must acknowledge that," replied the Colonel, smiling at the sententious remark of his friend, and the weak and worn-out objection it implied.

"Did our Lord live, suffer, and die for the salvation of His own people alone?" broke in the low but earnest voice of Francis. "Oh, no," he quickly added, "but for that of the Heathen also, and one of His last injunctions was: '*Go, teach all* nations.' Should we obey that injunction, if we made this little point of the globe the ultimate term of the Gospel dispensation? No, no; the Catholic heart, which draws its life from the Heart of Jesus, must necessarily, like the Divine Master, embrace every tribe, and race, and corner of the globe, where human hearts beat, and human souls, for whom His Blood was shed, cry out to us for help, in order that that Blood may be applied to them. We must not, we cannot, shut up and restrain the charity which has been breathed into us by the Spirit of Christ within the narrow limits of our own little island, dear though it is to us."

"Ah, yes, that is true," gravely replied Father

Neville; "the whole bearing of Catholic dogma, I had almost said, rests upon those words, or are involved in them, 'PRO TOTIUS MUNDI SALUTE!' For *all* He died, and daily immolates Himself anew upon the Altar; and His universal charity must be the rule of our's as well in prayer as in action."

"Ah, yes," said the Colonel, thoughtfully; "as our faith is *Catholic*, and not of *one only nation*, so also must be our charity; then we must necessarily do all in our power to help on the evangelization of the Heathen."

"And in so doing," said Francis, "I am convinced of it, English Catholics will draw down upon their native land an abundant flow of graces."

"If we think of it in quiet meditation," said Father Neville, "it seems to me that the Incarnation itself teaches us our duty towards the Heathen. Our blessed Lord left the bosom of His Father to come and live in exile amongst us, in order to teach us to know that Father. We find the same effects of divine charity in the Immaculate Mother of God. No sooner did she bear within her the Divine Infant, than she was *impelled* to go and convey salvation, 'good tidings,' to the house of Zachary; and we know the result, the sanctification of the great Precursor whilst yet unborn. The *principle* is the same,—the communication of good. It is a divine instinct, and one which, if corresponded with, will not fail to arouse us from our lethargy, and to *move us to compassion* for the poor benighted Heathen."

At this point the little company began to separate,

and the conversation was brought to a close: but there was one who had listened attentively to all that had passed, and who had felt her heart strangely moved.

It was Clara Herbert, who lingered still, as if she wished to say something to Francis, who, on his side, had observed her, and had seen the lively interest she had taken in the conversation, although she had not joined in it. Francis, however, did not remain in the library, and despite the suspicion he had that Clara would have spoken to him then, he quietly passed out, and returned somewhat fatigued to his own room.

CHAPTER XVI.

How Clara Herbert found "something to do."

Several days passed, and still the proposed conversation between Miss Herbert and Francis had not taken place.

There was evidently some secret work going on within her soul, for her former want of interest had entirely disappeared. She seemed occupied with some grave thoughts, and not unfrequently her eyes told of secret tears. Francis was not unobservant of these things, and hoped for good to come.

At length, one evening, when the others had for the most part gone for a quiet stroll through the grounds, Mary asked Clara if she would be content to remain with her, because Francis, being more than usually suffering, could not accompany the walking party, and so she intended passing a quiet evening with him. Clara gladly agreed, and thus the opportunity occurred for the conversation which was to bring forth such happy results.

"I am glad to see you, Miss Herbert," said Francis. "I have had no opportunity of asking you what you thought of the lively discussion the other day, regarding our duty towards the Heathen. You were quite silent, but for all that, I think you were interested in the subject: am I not right?"

"Yes," replied Clara, "I *was* interested, but I am always silent on such occasions, for I feel so ignorant and foolish, such conversation being so new to me."

"And the subject of it also, I suppose?" rejoined Francis.

"Yes; it opens a new train of thought, a new horizon, as it were, before me. I only wish.———"

She paused, but Francis quickly said: "Well, what do you wish?" And then, seeing her still hesitate, he added kindly, for he saw the propitious moment had arrived: "You wish, perhaps, that you had had such an horizon long before,—such a scope for the occupation of your heart and mind: is that it?"

"Yes, it is that," was the reply; "but now it seems too late."

"No, no, not too late," exclaimed Francis and his sister-in-law together, and then the former continued earnestly; "tell me, does the work you have heard of frequently since your stay with us *really* much interest you?"

"It does indeed," was the reply; "and if I had been faithful in the beginning," she added, a little lower, "perhaps I might have had a vocation to devote myself to it as a *Sœur de Charité*, but I have no desire for the *Religious* life now, and in no other way *could* I help such a work as the Foreign Missions."

"I cannot agree with you there," answered Francis; and then, after a short pause, he regarded Miss Herbert, and said: "Come, let us see. About what age are you, if I may ask?"

Mary laughed as she exclaimed: "Well, Francis, what a question to ask a lady!"

"Oh," said Francis, with the quiet smile that had become familiar to him, "surely a dying Priest may venture such a question;" and the expression of his features told how his thoughts were tending towards the country whose eternal shores he was so soon to behold.

Clara looked up, and replied simply, yet with a shade of embarrassment, "I am nearly thirty."

"So much the better," replied Francis. "If it is God's will that you should one day carry out the project that has suggested itself to me, a few years added on to your present ones will be an advantage."

"But," said Clara, somewhat sadly, "I have lived so long without having any object or aim in life, that I cannot believe I am capable or fit for anything. Besides, I have wasted grace already; and oh! what a folly my life has been, and yet I hated it."

Francis looked a little uneasily towards his sister-in-law, for he could not but feel that poor Clara was speaking to him thus confidentially in virtue of his Priestly dignity, and that she had, in her trouble, overlooked the presence of his gentle nurse. Just at that moment the door opened, and a bright little child ran into the room, exclaiming: "Mamma, mamma, come, come play with me. John de Britto happy boy now, he has found mamma ;" and the little fellow began to clap his hands, and to draw his mother towards the door. Francis quietly waved his hand, as a signal to his sister-in-law to withdraw, and then, left alone with the soul he so much desired to help, he said, referring to her last words:

"We have *all*, more or less, wasted grace, but supposing that you feel you have not corresponded with some *special* grace in the past, why should that discourage you for the present or the future?"

"My life has been such a lie," she said, almost passionately; "I was so strongly attracted to good when I first entered into 'the world,' as it is called, and then vanity and love of pleasure lured me away. For *then*," she added, "it was not mere empty, frivolous pleasures which captivated me; it was only afterwards, when the misery of the consciousness of neglected and resisted grace tormented me, that, in the very bitterness of my soul, I gave myself up to the frivolities of a mere fashionable life, and all the while I have despised it. I have been secretly longing for something higher, greater, nobler than anything that I met on my way. I have hated my aimless life. If I had met any one who would have spoken to me as you have, of things that may become objects to live and work for, all might have been so different. But what am I worth now?

I am not fitted for Religion. As to occupying myself in the world, in teaching children, and in visiting a few sick poor, or giving good advice, and the rest, certainly I do not feel that *that* sort of thing is my vocation. I scarcely know what it is. I only know I want to live for some object. That which has interested me more than anything I have ever heard spoken of is the conversion of the Heathen; but what could *I* do towards that, except, indeed, to pray ?"

"If you could do no more than pray for the knowledge of God's Name to be spread in Heathen lands, you would have yet something noble for which to live," said Francis, gravely; "but in addition to prayer, there is another way in which you can help the work."

His companion looked up quickly, and a flush spread over her ordinarily pale countenance, whilst her eye suddenly lighted up with a strange brightness.

"Oh! Father Francis," she exclaimed, "why did I not meet you sooner?"

"Because God's *hour* was '*not yet come*,'" replied Francis; and then he continued in the same low tone: "I know I have no right to speak to you thus, but '*the charity of Christ presses me*,' and my sacred office gives me a confidence in addressing you, which certainly of myself I should not have. Your soul and its wants have become known to me just as I am drawing near to the tomb, and on that very account I speak to you as one who already belongs more to another world than to this. I want, before I go, to animate as many souls as

I can to generous devotedness to the cause of God, in the conversion of the millions of poor Heathens, who are crying out to us: '*Pass over the seas, and come and help us.*' Individual souls, as well as nations, will draw down upon themselves benedictions of grace by their unselfish apostolate, and therefore not only the *saved* would be enriched with eternal goods, but also those who make efforts for their salvation."

"Tell me how such as I am can share in this great work," was the humble but intensely earnest reply; "for truly this is indeed something to live and work for, if only one knew how, but that is what I do not see."

"Listen," said Francis. "It is a grain of mustard seed that I want you to sow, which eventually may become a tree and bring forth much fruit. I have long thought how advantageous it would be if some lady, endowed with an apostolic heart, and with sufficient resources, would endeavour, under guidance, of course, to form a society—no, no," he interrupted himself, smiling, "that word *society* frightens you,—to seek out, then, and collect a certain number of pious Catholic young women who had the ability and will for doing needlework *exclusively* for the benefit of the Foreign Missions."

Clara Herbert's eye again brightened, and Francis, encouraged by the interior welcome his suggestion had evidently met with, continued:

"You do not yet know," he said, "the wide field

my proposition opens to your zeal, and all the nourishment it will provide for heart and mind, or the plentiful occupation it will afford you. The benefit of such a work would be threefold *at least*. First, the material assistance procured to Foreign Missions by the provision of suitable, or at least decent vestments, and requisite ornaments; then, the employment of poor virtuous Catholic girls, which would involve not only their material relief, but also, by engaging them in a class of work conducive to interest their piety, would be a benediction for their souls, and very probably would be for some amongst them a means of attaining a real apostolic spirit, and consequently sanctity; thirdly, it would bring before the notice of others the work of the Foreign Missions, with its needs, and might, and would probably be the means of interesting many in an object as yet scarcely known in England, and certainly whose importance is not adequately appreciated. What do you think of my project, and how do you feel personally regarding it?"

"With my whole soul I would devote myself to it," was the fervent reply, "for I see, as you have said, that it would open a field capable of interesting both heart and mind, in one of the most intimate concerns of God's glory. But how would it be organized?"

"I told you in the commencement it would be, like many other good works, but a grain of mustard seed. You would simply begin by making inquiries of the Fathers of the Society of Jesus, if they knew of any pious girls in want of needlework, especially such as could be capable of Church work. After a time, if you succeeded in this first step, you would have recourse to some Catholic ladies, in order to solicit their contributions, in alms and materials."

"And supposing we succeeded so far," said Clara, anxiously, for her generous heart was fully interested in the project, "where should we send the things that had been prepared?"

There was a moment's pause, during which the eyes of Francis were directed across the sea to the horizon of gold-tinted sky which bound it, whilst an expression passed over his face which seemed to tell of prayer and expectation.

"For the present," he said, "they could be sent to the *College des Missions Étrangères* at Paris; but if God grants my ceaseless prayer, there will be one day a similar College in England. Your labours would then be referred to it; thither you would send the work prepared, and learn from thence, also, what was most required. This would place you in immediate communication with those having experience of the Foreign Missions, and the fact of preparing things for Missioners actually departing, and who would thus, in some sort, be known to you, would be a spur to your zeal, and an interest ever fresh. It is true," he added, with a pensive smile, "as yet there is no prospect of such a blessing for our country as would be a Foreign Missionary College in its midst, but what cannot be hoped from ceaseless prayer? If I knew that such a blessing were in prospect, how gladly I should sing my *Nunc dimittis!*"

"I will join my prayers to yours, Father Francis," said Clara.

"And by prayer," replied Francis, "you will keep alive in your soul the fire which our Lord desires to see enkindled over the whole earth. Then, besides all this, all those who were engaged in the *material* work for the Foreign Missions, in the way I have in view, would have provided for them also some spiritual nourishment, in the way of special prayers to be said, and communions to be offered for the same glorious intention, so dear to the Heart of Jesus. As for yourself, you would see, as the work progressed, new and extensive demands would be made upon your zeal. You would be what may be called a zelatrix, to sustain the zeal and devotedness of others, and to seek always new allies, as well as labourers as contributors."

"Oh! Father Francis," exclaimed Clara, with confusion, "I, who have so much to do to repair my own coldness, to take upon myself to animate others to fervour in anything! Oh, no; besides, I have told you I could never give good advice and talk much, as those good ladies ordinarily do who set about pious works in the world."

Francis smiled. "Certainly," he replied, laughing; "I am one of the last who would counsel you to *that* kind of apostolate. I believe you when you say you are not called to it, nor is it required in the work I have in view. Persevering devotedness, the endeavour to interest others in the conversion of the Heathen:—not by telling them drily what they '*ought to do;*' but by gathering facts continually, and by bringing them into notice, doing so *agreeably*, and in such a way as to awaken the interest of all within your reach; by the example of *self-sacrifice* in the cause; by all these ways you can be a zelatrix, and a very efficacious one, without setting up for a 'preacher.'"

Clara's countenance now brightened, and gave somewhat the impression of a calm, clear sky, when a cloud has passed away. There was now no bitterness, no discouragement; the beacon had appeared for which she had long looked out in vain, and "*forgetting the things which were behind,*" according to the advice of the Apostle of the Gentiles, she "*stretched forward to the things that were before.*"*

"I know not how to thank you, Father Francis," she began; "it is a new life which has been shed into my soul to-day."

"By whom?" quickly rejoined Francis, who, ever jealous for the honour of his Divine Master, was wont instantly to turn the conversation whenever any one seemed to refer to *him* any good that was done. "By the Heart of Jesus, whose hour of triumph in your soul has arrived to-day. Now tell me, do you know any persons likely to enter into this project? One important point must not be forgotten, in order to render the work

* Phil. iii. 13.

enduring, by the real devotedness of all who are allied to it, and that is, its co-operators must be such as have a *true attraction* for the work of the conversion of the heathen lands; just as in the Missionary Colleges it is not sufficient that a man desires to be a *Priest*, he must desire, moreover, and in a special manner, to be a *Foreign* Missioner, otherwise he cannot be admitted; so in this work, comparatively insignificant as it is, yet in order to ensure the *end* for which we desire its establishment, all those engaged in it must have a *primary* desire of devoting their labour to *the* object; they should have *specially* at heart the providing Missioners going forth to infidel lands with what is necessary for the Altar; although for the poorer members of this apostolic work it must be for them *in addition* a means of livelihood, for this forms part of our project. Now, do you know any whom you think would be suitable subjects to whom to propose the work ?"

Clara paused a moment, and was about to reply in the negative, when, suddenly recollecting herself, she said : " I know none personally, but I remember some months ago Father King spoke to me of two sisters who, he said, were desirous of obtaining employment from *Catholics;* he seemed to be much interested in them, and asked me to try if I could do something for them."

" And what did you do ?" inquired Francis.

His companion blushed, and replied with a smile, yet with some little confusion also : " I only gave him some money for them, and told him he could ask me for more if he wanted it for them."

"And did he ask you again?" inquired Francis.

"No; it did not seem to be precisely *money* that he wanted. I think he wanted me to go and see them, and interest myself in them, but——"

"But?" echoed Francis, with a quiet smile.

"But I was too selfish, apathetic," continued Clara. "His wanting to engage me in the work of 'pious ladies' irritated me. I lived but for myself, because I had not found *the* work which was to draw me out of myself."

"But Miss Herbert of the past is not Miss Herbert of to-day," said Francis, kindly. "Now," he continued, "when you return to London, ask Father King concerning the sisters he mentioned to you on a previous occasion, and ascertain if they are fitting subjects to commence with. Meantime, pray earnestly about this affair, that by God's help it may succeed to His greater glory, and for the good of souls."

"And for my own soul, I hope," said Clara, with emotion. "I repeat it,—to-day new life seems to have been given to me."

"For which," replied Francis, gently, "thank gratefully the good Master, and say to Him in return: '*What shall I render to Thee for what Thou hast given to me?*' and if I mistake not, He will answer in the interior of your soul: 'Help Me to make known My Father's Kingdom to those who sit in darkness.' This you can do by fully entering into the work I have proposed to you to-day, and for which our Lord has disposed your heart."

"Henceforth," was the low earnest response, "this shall be my object in life. Thank God! thank God!"

She knelt down, asking, with a humility her soul had never known before, the Priestly benediction of him who had that day opened before her eyes a glad prospect of better things, an horizon which was to dilate her heart more and more, and inflame it with Catholic and Apostolic charity.

Francis blessed her, saying a few words of encouragement, and then she withdrew to seek Mrs. Willington, to whom she imparted the happiness which she had derived from her interview with Francis. From that day Clara Herbert was a new being.

CHAPTER XVII.

A year later.—Apostolic seed.—The approach of the term.

A twelvemonth has passed away, in which time many changes have taken place, even amongst the few personages brought before our readers in the course of this narrative. Some of these changes are of a nature to be observed; others more concealed, but whose result is of a character tending to strengthen the hidden life of the Church, and to extend the Kingdom of God, and whose source, under God, may be traced to the influence of the sanctity of one who is fast approaching the term of his short sorrow-stricken life.

In vain shall we now look for Francis amongst the family group assembled in the drawing-room, or leaning on his brother's arm, walking on the terrace or through the grounds near the house.

It is several months since he has left his own room, and for some weeks he has but moved from his bed to an arm chair near the window, where he can feel the cool breeze coming from across the sea, over whose expanse his eye so often wanders, just as in other days, —days of hope and promise—he had looked out and thirsted for the salvation of the souls on the distant shores beyond.

It was *another* shore now to which his soul's eye was ever turned, wistfully longing for the day when the consummation of his sacrifice should be accomplished, and when he should at last be free to go and see unveiled the triumphs of the Sacred Heart, for the love of which he had offered up his life.

His inner life, since the crushing of his one great hope, had been one of almost ceaseless struggle. He had indeed bowed down with loyal submission to the Master's will, and the spirit of murmuring had found no place in his devoted soul; but the vigour of youth was there, and the energy of a strong character and burning zeal, whose constraint was as a consuming fire within him. The intensity of interior suffering which all this produced was, in some sort, a relief to his apostolic heart, for every pang and struggle was consecrated to the one object for which he had vowed his life.

But there were hours of keener, darker suffering even than this, in which he was permitted, for his purification, to drink of the chalice of desolation; hours in which his life seemed wholly useless for the cause for which alone he cared to live. But God had spoken to his soul in these dark seasons, and gradually, as the life of nature became weakened, that of grace grew stronger, and after storms which had seemed to shake his soul to its centre, *there was made a great calm*, in which he was enabled to see all things from *heaven's* point of view, and to recognize how precious to the Heart of the Crucified is an apostleship of suffering.

"Father Neville," he said one day, to the devoted old Priest who sat beside his couch, and with whom he loved to converse, "when I look across the sea, and remember how, in times gone by, I used to love to think I could hear the voices on the shores where I longed to be, crying to me, and saying: '*Pass over the sea and help us,*' and how I used to figure to myself the dear souls coming to meet me on my arrival there, I think that, after all, things are not so much changed; and when I look over the great wide sea, it is only *another* shore I figure on the other side, and that instead of the same souls asking me to come and *help* them, they are only beckoning to me to come and join them in the praises of the 'Great Spirit' they have learnt to know and love, and in whose presence they now rejoice. Think you," he added, with a bright smile, "they will own me as their father, although it was never given me to toil amongst them as such?"

"Assuredly," was the reply. "God sees not as man sees. In the eyes of *men*, you have never actually laboured amongst the Heathen, but you have loved them with a father's heart, have prayed for them, have suffered—oh! how much—for them, and," he added, almost in a whisper, although they were alone, "have *vowed* to give your life for them, and THAT VOW HAS BEEN ACCEPTED. 'Greater love than this no man hath,' according to the testimony of Truth Himself; and the souls for whom you have given yourself, seeing, as do those who are saved, all things in the light of God, will recognize you as their father, their apostle."

Would that selfish worldlings, who know nothing of the mighty power of the love of God and of souls, could have seen the radiant happiness that beamed on the young Priest's face, as the words he heard thrilled through his soul.

"For this," he said, "how sweet it has been, and is still to suffer; and the sweetest thing of all—to die!"

One day, not long after the little dialogue related above, Mary Willington entered Francis's room with a letter for him in her hand.

"See, dear Francis," she said, "here is a budget from Clara; I hope she gives you abundant good news. Please to tell me about the progress of her work, for you know how lively an interest I take in it." And delivering the letter, she sat down to listen.

Before, however, listening ourselves to the contents of the letter, we will briefly relate the success which Miss Herbert had met with in carrying out Francis's apostolic project, and the hope it afforded of future progress.

On her return to London, after her eventful visit to the Manor, which we have lately recorded, she made inquiries after the two sisters recommended to her some time before by Father King, as objects of interest for her charity.

Father King was surprised at the new spirit with which Miss Herbert made her inquiries; and Clara, authorised by Francis to do so, imparted to him the project she had at heart.

Father King, himself full of apostolic zeal, was charmed at the proposal, and promised to second with all his power a work so conducive to God's greater glory and the good of souls.

His experienced eye was not slow in perceiving the cause of Clara's change, and he prayed that many other souls who were known to him might find, as she had so happily done, an object in life worthy of occupying their hearts and minds, and of contributing to the glory of God.

Now the two sisters to whose humble abode Clara Herbert found herself one day wending, were no other than the Dales, whom our readers will probably not have forgotten.

It will easily be conjectured with what joy they listened to Clara's proposition, and how simply they told her of their long-conceived desire of an engagement in just such work as she spoke of. Now that Miss Herbert's generous heart was roused from the lethargy which had for a time paralysed its energies, she manifested all the strength of character, and ability for affecting good, of which she was possessed. Accordingly, she lost no time in commencing the enterprise. Being possessed of considerable fortune, this was not so difficult as it would otherwise have been, and it was with the devotedness which henceforth was to characterize her, that she rejoiced in consecrating to the apostolic work entrusted to her the necessary funds for establishing it on a permanent footing.

However, having herself ascertained the benefit of doing something for God's interest, she endeavoured by every means to make known the opportunity thus offered, as widely as she could, and it was not long before she found several in her own sphere of life, who, if they did not as yet feel disposed to take an *active* part in the work, were willing at least to contribute to it alms and materials, and in their turn also to speak of it to others.

Many pious young women, moreover, to whom gradually the work became known, solicited employment in it, several of whom declared that they would gladly sacrifice higher payment in order to be associated to a work which satisfied their piety, and which brought them into relation with persons devoted to God, and to the interests of His Church.

Things had been thus steadily progressing, when, on the day in question, Mary Willington put into Francis's hand the letter from Clara.

It was a statement of the position of things, and of their progress since last she rendered to him an account, and ran as follows :

"My dear Father Francis,

"I am convinced it will afford you true happiness to hear that the apostolic work you entrusted to me is rapidly progressing, and has already been productive of the most happy results.

"When I remember that it is but one year since you spoke to me of your project, and when I see the progress it has, in this short space of time made, and the apostolic spirit it has called forth in many souls, I can but praise God that He put it into your heart to conceive such a means of procuring Him honour and glory. As for the good it has done for me, you know it well, and I need not take up the present letter in dilating upon it. I will only add, however, that my aunt is utterly perplexed at the change which has been wrought in me, and sometimes not over well pleased, for my time being much occupied in the work, it is impossible for me to accompany her everywhere, and at all times, as formerly; moreover, *having found something worth living for*, a tangible object to interest me, mere pleasure is to me so insipid, that it is with difficulty I can support the slavery which 'the world' imposes. My aunt, however, being truly Catholic, and really good at heart, has contributed several gifts to our work; and the very fact of my occasional absence from places of amusement which I might be expected to visit, offers an opportunity for making the work known, inasmuch as my aunt invariably tells the plain truth regarding my mysterious absence, and I have found persons whom certainly I should not have suspected of taking any interest in such a matter, to my surprise, asking me minute details regarding it, and telling me that they would be glad to contribute towards it. So you see, the grain of mustard seed is taking root and spreading.

"Our first contribution, or packet of vestments, altar linen, and the rest, is just ready to be sent off as you arranged, *for the present,* to the *College des Missions Etrangères* at Paris. But oh! for the day when we shall, in answer to prayer, have such a College in our own country. What a blessing it will be! Those who are now regularly engaged, and who have joined in the work, have really at heart the object it is designed to help, so that it is not only for those poor girls a means of earning a modest livelihood, but also a source of refreshment to their souls. They recite daily specified prayers for the propagation of the faith in Heathen lands, for the increase of apostolic labourers, and for all the interests of the Foreign Missions. For the same intention also, they communicate twice and sometimes thrice in the week. On the Sundays and Holidays of Obligation, we assemble at the house that you know I have hired for a time, where all the work is carried on, excepting by such members as are infirm,—we have two or three—and these I permit to work at their own homes, where they are visited by the others from time to time, as well as by myself; in this house I have fitted up an humble oratory, and it is there that we assemble on Sundays for special devotions. The chaplet is said for the Foreign Missions, and some other prayers, and then we have appropriate missionary hymns.

"One friend lately contributed a harmonium, and some of my own acquaintances have now and then volunteered to accompany me, and to take part in our really devotional singing. At these re-unions we also have some reading about missionary work in foreign lands, with a provision of interesting details, whereby fervour is kept up, and an apostolic spirit maintained and increased. Works, such as the 'Annals of the Propagation of the Faith,' and of 'The Holy Childhood,' 'The Christian Missions,' and 'The Messenger of the Sacred Heart,' and the like, are circulated amongst the members, who can take them to their own homes for private reading.

"The name by which our fervent little band of labourers love to be called is, the '*Helpers of the Foreign Missions*,' and I assure you that title is no misnomer.

"At the Communions, in which we all unite, they wear a red ribbon round the neck, to which is attached a medal of the Sacred Heart. They wear also this badge at our private re-unions, and whilst at work at the house of the associates, but they never wear it ostensibly at other times.

"I think, dear Father Francis, I have now given you full details of all that regards this dear apostolic work, and I know what a joy and consolation your Missioner's heart will derive from hearing how greatly God has blessed your project and our united efforts. You will pray for it, I know, as well as for me, who can never sufficiently thank you for showing me so effectual a remedy for the *ennui* of an aimless and frivolous life. Earnestly begging your blessing, believe me, with great respect and gratitude,

"Ever your devoted servant in the Sacred Heart,
"CLARA HERBERT.

"I long for your permission to sign myself by the title I value so much,—

"'HELPER OF THE FOREIGN MISSIONS.'"

Francis had just finished reading this letter, and had expressed to his sister-in-law his entire satisfaction at its contents, when little feet were heard pattering outside the door, which opened, and John de Britto, (Francis's little god-child,) and Francis, (Stanislaus' second boy,) entered and ran to their uncle.

"What do you want up here now, my dears?" asked their mother, fearful lest they should fatigue the invalid. Francis however, answered for them, as he extended his arms to give them an affectionate welcome:

"Oh! you forgot," he said; "this is the first Friday of the month, on which they come for the name of their new Mission, for which they will have to pray during the month."

This was a little practice of devotion which Francis had commenced a year before, and in which his two little nephews had already become much interested.

At the commencement of each month, they were told of a certain Heathen Mission for which they were to pray; the spot was shown to them upon an atlas, and all that Francis could relate to them conducive to engage the interest of those innocent hearts, and to awaken in them a spirit of Catholic charity, he failed not to do, and his endeavours had been already fruitful.

The little boys, well instructed in their programme, or rather with the eager simplicity of early childhood, proceeded to a small altar opposite the couch whereon Francis reclined. Upon this altar was a statue of the Sacred Heart, at whose feet on one side stood a smaller one of Our Lady of Dolours, and on the other, of similar proportions, one of S. Joseph. Over the altar was the large "Eucharistic Clock," indicating the hours at which the Holy Sacrifice was being offered at the several places throughout the world, marked on the dial. On one side of this dial hung a picture of S. Francis Xavier, dying on his desert island, *in sight of* the shores of China; on the other, a representation, which Francis had himself designed and painted, of his beloved patron, Blessed John de Britto, standing on the shore, on the memorable occasion when he had witnessed the ship, that was to convey him back to his dear Mission in the East, sailing down the Tagus without him.

Fresh flowers were daily placed by careful hands upon

the altar, and little Francis, and John de Britto, who,
though so young, were already learning to perform the
office of acolytes, proceeded on the present occasion to
light two tall wax candles that stood on it.

Having done this, they knelt down before the altar,
and looking back towards their uncle, as if to testify to
him their readiness to begin, he, from his couch of
suffering, pronounced in a low voice, a touching, simple
prayer for the conversion of the Heathen, and for an
increase of apostolic labourers; then an act of consecra-
tion to the Sacred Heart of Jesus, with a resolution
to try to make It everywhere known and loved.

The children followed aloud, word for word, the act
pronounced by their uncle, Mary also kneeling down,
and heartily joining her voice to theirs. Then Francis,
in a low, sweet voice, intoned a simple air, which the
little ones took up, and sang a canticle to the Sacred
Heart, which, in touching, child-like words, implored
Its help for the Negroes. Lastly, approaching Francis,
they were told the particular countries they were
especially to pray for during the ensuing month, and
this concluded the little re-union, as far, at least, as
regarded the religious or ceremonial part.

Then the little voices began clamouring for information; an atlas was brought forth, that they *might put
their finger* on the spot which was entrusted to their
prayers; then the route conducting to it must be traced,
and endless questions answered as to the savage tribes
or idolators inhabiting those countries. And thus it was

that habits of Catholic piety and apostolic zeal were being sweetly and insensibly engrafted into those innocent souls.

"I should not wonder in the least," said Mary, thoughtfully, as she tenderly regarded her little ones, "if they both become Foreign Missioners. John de Britto especially, seems to give already evidences for such a surmise."

"Well, you know," replied Francis, smiling, "you *would* insist on my being his god-father, so you must take the consequences."

"Oh! if such is his vocation," answered Mary, "or if both of them should be called to such a work, I should not grudge the sacrifice."

Francis regarded the children for a few minutes, and then said, half musingly: "Will their lot be that of their uncle, I wonder?" And then, as if fearing there might be in those words the least tinge of regret, he added: "God knows best how to form His Missioners." Then, speaking to the children again, he said: "Do you know, I am going a great journey soon?"

"Where are you going, uncle Francis?" both exclaimed with one voice. "Are you going to your Negroes?"

Tears started to the eyes of Francis as he heard those simple words, and then, looking down at his Missioner's *soutane*, which he had continued to wear ever since he returned to England, saying he should be a Foreign Missioner until his death, and that therefore he should never cease to wear the badge of one, he said, answering the children: "Yes, you see I am ready; yes, I go to my Negroes; but it is a long, long journey—you must pray for me."

"When are you going, dear uncle?" asked John de Britto, his great earnest eyes fixed gravely on his uncle's face; "I should like to go with you. May I go with uncle Francis, mamma," he added, turning to his mother, who was brushing away her tears; for although all at the Manor witnessed their beloved Francis wasting away daily before their eyes, yet none could bear to think of his death as near.

"You must wait till Jesus says He wants you, dear," said Mary, tenderly, to her little child, fondly kissing him as she spoke.

He was contented with the answer, as simple little children always are. Why can we not always remain contented, simple children! Then he turned again to Francis: "What country are you going to?" he asked.

"The most beautiful that can be imagined. Look, far away beyond, not only that great wide sea, but far beyond the sky, and there my Negroes will know me. And when I am gone, you must pray that more Negroes may come and join me in that bright land; and one day you and Francis, and papa and mamma, and grandpapa, and all of you, will come, and we and the Negroes shall all be one great family."

The children looked fixedly at their uncle, as if they

would question him further regarding his mysterious journey; but Francis, not wishing to make them sad, began to ask them about their play and their gardens, and so turned their attention to other subjects.

Happy children, in whose young hearts and minds was cast the seed of future harvest!

CHAPTER XVIII.

"Preparations for Departure" once more.—Nunc Dimittis.

Ever since Francis's return to England, it may be said that he had been by stages withdrawing further and further into solitude with God. For a short time he had been able to go down-stairs each morning to say Mass in the chapel, but very soon that became impossible, and it was granted as a privilege that he might say it in his private room adjoining his bed-chamber, which was in effect a kind of oratory. But for many months he had not been able to celebrate on account of his increased exhaustion, resulting from the almost continual pain which he suffered, more especially in the early morning.

In consequence of this, a still further privilege was granted, which was, that Mass should be said twice a week in his apartment, and even daily, whenever a second Priest was staying in the house, which frequently occurred.

Things had gone on thus through the winter months which succeeded the incidents related in the preceding chapter. But the spring had brought a change, which, although all were prepared to witness, having long expected it, yet which struck profound sorrow into every heart when it actually arrived.

They loved to rally round his bed, and listen to the words that fell from his lips,—words which would long be cherished up in their memories with reverence and affection. For all he had expressions of earnest gratitude for their devotedness to him; for all, words of encouragement and hope.

The venerable old Colonel would sit, his hand clasped in that of his dying son, and drink in the torrents of heaven-inspired consolation with which he fortified that father whom he loved so tenderly, and who had so shared his apostolic charity, and so freely co-operated in the designs of God in his regard; fortified him, we say, for the severe blow his aged heart must sustain when the hour of separation must arrive.

One day, Father Neville was sitting at the bedside of the invalid, speaking to him from time to time, but much more speaking to God *for* him, for it was a day succeeding one of those nights which were now but too frequent, when racking pain utterly banished sleep, and left him in the greatest exhaustion.

"Pray for me, my Father, that I may persevere to the end—the very end," he had just said, in a low, feeble tone; "*the Mass is not ended yet.*" These words were in allusion to the thought he had always before him of uniting his sufferings, and above all, the immolation of his life's hope, to the immolation of the

Eucharistic Victim, and of reproducing in his own dying life the Sacrifice of the Altar, of which he was the minister.

"It is solemn High Mass, Francis," said Father Neville, gently, thus humouring his train of thought, or rather his spiritual attraction.

"Yes, yes," was the reply, whilst a faint but radiant smile lit up his wan features. "Yes, there must not be a single part or ceremony omitted;" and then, in a whisper, he was heard repeating disjointed parts of the Mass, whilst his upraised eyes, and the movement of his thin white hands, plainly indicated that he was in spirit standing before the Altar of Sacrifice, offering himself in union with the August Victim, as ever had been, and still was his wont. "*Suscipe Sancta Trinitas hanc oblationem . . . pro totius mundi salute.*" And then again, as if appealing for prayers that he might persevere in his oblation, "*Orate fratres ut meum . . . sacrificium acceptabile fiat apud Deum Patrem omnipotentem.*"

His room was as a species of oratory, in which the different members of the family loved to pray, and to unite themselves to that pure sacerdotal soul, who day and night was immolating himself to the glory of that God whom he had chosen for *his portion*, and for the one apostolic object to which he had vowed his life.

None were excluded from entrance there, and as they passed the threshold of the apartment, and heard the quick, short breathing of him who lay there in the shadowy light, awaiting the final summons, or as he, following his supernatural attraction, beautifully expressed it, "the '*Ite missa est,*'" they felt that veneration which insensibly steals over the soul when we enter a hallowed porch, and which makes us inwardly convinced that "*indeed the Lord is in this place.*"

Even the domestics failed not each day, at stated times, to steal in quietly, and kneeling before the altar, to offer their prayers for the happy death of him whom some of them had known and loved from his childhood.

The devoted old Philip, whom perhaps some of our readers may not have forgotten, could with difficulty leave the apartment after his daily visit, to which he looked forward with singular devotion, saying that he " felt so near heaven whenever he went to the room of Father Francis." On Sundays, as a singular privilege, he was permitted to prolong his visit, and after having prayed for some time fervently before the altar, he would withdraw to some retired part of the room, and there remain reading some pious book, which he occasionally interrupted to look up towards the sick bed, and if possible, through the half-opened screen between it and that part of the apartment which formed the oratory, to catch a glimpse of the face that was to the old man's heart so dear and so familiar.

He used to bring the choicest flowers from the hothouse for the adornment of the altar, that Francis might see them, especially of the kind which he had loved so much when a boy, because of the thought of their Eastern origin.

One day that Francis was somewhat easier, he heard the old man coming towards the door, for the sound of his wooden leg, despite all his precautions, could not be avoided. He entered, and was gently approaching the altar, a magnificent bouquet of choice exotics in his hand, when a voice from the sick bed made him quickly turn round, and with a thrill of pleasure advance towards Francis, who was as yet partially screened from him.

"Philip, is that you?" said the low, weak voice.

"Yes, Father Francis, may I come to speak to ye, sir?" and without waiting for a reply, he opened a division in the screen, and approached the bed.

"The Lord bless your dear pale face," were the first words that spontaneously burst forth from the old man's lips, as he looked on the countenance that bespoke so evidently the nearness of death.

"May He bless *you*, Philip," was Francis's gentle reply, as he raised his hand to make the sign of the cross over the white head that was bent down to receive the blessing he prized so much.

"You have brought me beautiful flowers, Philip. Ah! yes, how beautiful!" And for a moment the mind of the sick man seemed to have fled away to another and a nobler Object, whose Beauty he had seen reflected in the flowers that met his outward eye. Philip smiled delightedly at the evident appreciation his flowers had found.

"I mind, Father Francis, how, when first you came back to us, broken down, I daren't bring you they kind of flowers, 'cause they made ye think too much of the Indies, where you'd never more hope to go, but somehow, ye don't seem to mind it now."

Francis smiled at the old man's delicate discernment.

"Nearer home, Philip," was the low answer; "and so the Father's will becomes more clearly seen. Do you understand?"

"Aye, aye, Father Francis, I do indeed," answered Philip, in vain striving against the tears that would not be restrained.

"Well, Philip, a little while, and you will come home to *me*, and then—no more tears, no more pain or sorrow," said Francis, gently laying his hand on that of Philip. The old man seemed soothed, and soon after, with the good instinct which affection and respect engender, moved away to another part of the room to say his prayers.

As time went on, Francis's sufferings augmented, and were so continual, that sometimes those around him believed that his wasted strength must succumb at once beneath them. He was no longer able to recite his Breviary, but amidst his sufferings, disjointed portions of it were ever rising to his lips, and discovering the love he bore, and the consolation he found, in that treasure of the Priestly state,—the Divine Office. Even amidst the delirium which the fever, owing to intense pain, sometimes occasioned, passages of the Psalms would escape from him, and frequently could be discerned such verses as he had been in the habit of applying in particular to the conversion of the Heathen nations, with which the Divine Office abounds. At other times he would seem to be in spirit amongst his dear Negroes. "See, see," he would cry out, "they believe, they ask for Baptism;" and then he would extend his arms as if in the act of pouring water on the head of some neophyte. "They are mine," he would exclaim at other times, "I have given my life for them. They know me, listen to them; but no, no, you do not know their language." And then he would relapse again into silence for a while.

It was on one of these occasions that his aunts had been visiting him, and had been the silent witnesses of his delirium, to which the supernatural attraction in his soul had evidently lent so much colour.

On returning to the drawing-room, where they found the Colonel and Father Neville in much anxiety, and in the anticipation of approaching sorrow of a more than common nature, both ladies sat down, and Miss Margaret, whose tears were falling fast, was the first to speak.

"Well, I am now indeed convinced," she said, in a low voice, "that when God calls a soul to a particular work, it is in vain for man to meddle with it. I own," she continued, in a somewhat apologetic strain, "I maintained for a long time that Francis would have done better to have settled down in England, and laboured for God here; but it is clear *vocation is from God*, and none can overthrow His designs, provided the soul to whom the vocation has been given is faithful. Truly, our dear Francis gave his life for the Heathen, and even in dying, even in his delirium, they form his one thought."

"Would that many others, Miss Margaret, had had the opportunity of learning the same truth that you have learnt," said Father Neville; " our Lord would not find His designs so often opposed."

"Yes," resumed the old lady, "I wish Father Fairclough could have been here now, to see and hear dear Francis; even *he* would, I think, be convinced of the uselessness of trying to oppose a real vocation. I used to join in all his sentiments when he was here last year, but the sight of Francis dying, and as much a Missioner in heart as he was the day he started for the East, which he was never to behold, has entirely changed me."

"God be praised for it," said Father Neville. And then he added: "The Catholic Missioner's life is a holocaust, in which each day nature is offered up on the altar of sacrifice; but at each conversion the Missioner's heart takes new courage, and counts as nothing his pains and privations. So is it now with Francis. He said to me yesterday, in accents I shall never forget: 'Life is beautiful only in proportion as it is one of suffering.' The sentiment of a true

Missioner, for he knows well that sufferings are the price of souls."

"I am sure," said the Colonel, gently, to his sister Margaret, "that you no longer feel any jealousy at men devoting themselves to *Foreign* Missions, despite the many wants at home."

"Oh! no," was the earnest reply; "when God wills it, there is nothing to be said. I see it now plainly."

"Besides," said the elder Miss Willington, "the souls of the poor Heathen, who have never heard the Name of Jesus, are as dear to Him as those of Englishmen; and I know not how we could wish to keep all the fervent and intrepid Missioners at home, when there are millions and millions of souls ripe for conversion, if only there were labourers to gather them in. For my part, I consider the cause for which our dear Francis has lived, as one of the very noblest, and the thought of how he has loved the Negroes and all the poor Heathen, and given himself for them, makes one recognise better than anything else the beauty and the power of divine charity in the soul."

They were here interrupted by a messenger from Mary, requesting the presence of Father Neville upstairs, as Francis had recovered from his temporary delirium, and had asked for him.

The old Priest found Francis in less pain than usual, and after some little conversation, at the request of the latter, he sat down, and began reciting his Office, which was for Francis always a source of great pleasure, even when he could not audibly unite in it.

Meantime the day wore on, and the second delivery of letters arrived. The Colonel, as he sat by his fireside in the drawing-room below, for they would not let him remain too long in the chamber where his heart was, lest it should prove too much for him, read several letters hastily, and apparently without much interest, until at length one seemed to rivet his attention, and even strangely to agitate him. What could have had this power at a moment when his whole being was concentrated in the one thought of the approaching death of his beloved son?

He read the letter, put it down, and mused a few moments, re-read it, and then, folding it, there broke from the old man's lips these low words: "Thank God! thank God! he will know it before he dies." He continued to sit, as it were, absorbed in thought for some minutes, then rising, and taking the letter in his hand, he slowly left the room, and ascended to the chamber of Francis, where he found Father Neville just concluding his office, whilst Francis, soothed by the low murmur in which the kind old Priest had, for Francis's sake, recited it, had fallen into a gentle sleep. Mary sat at work at a little distance, and Stanislaus, who had entered a few minutes before, stood near the bed, tenderly regarding the brother he loved so deeply, and whose approaching death his manly heart felt so keenly.

The Colonel had been seated but a few moments when Francis awoke from the light sleep which for a little while had overtaken him. A deep sigh broke from him, and those who surrounded him heard him breathe forth the words: "*Usquequo, Domine, usquequo?*" as if the weary spirit was panting to be free. The Colonel stood up and bent a little over him.

"Dear Francis," he said, gently, and then, taking the language of the Church, which was so continually on the lips of the dying Priest, he said: "*Ecce evangelizo gaudium magnum, quod erit omni populo.*"

Francis looked up into his father's face, and pressing his hand, replied in words which had ever been ringing in his ears, and which in the present instance he gracefully applied to his father, as being the messenger of some good tidings to him, although he little guessed the extreme appropriateness of the words he was about to say to the tidings that were shortly to be imparted to him.

"*Quam speciosi pedes evangelizantium pacem, evangelizantium bona!*"

No sooner had the Colonel imparted the tidings with which he came laden, than all present felt the peculiar fitness of the passage with which Francis had greeted his father's announcement.

"My dear, dear Francis," resumed the Colonel, much affected, "how glad I am to be able to tell you that the prayer you have put up so long has been granted. I have just received from undoubted authority the information that a Missionary College for the training of Priests for the conversion of the Heathen, is actually set on foot in England. It is not a *project* only, but steps have already been taken for ensuring the establishment of this work, so deeply involving the interests of souls and the extension of the Church."

At the first words his father had spoken, Francis had unconsciously clasped his hands, and raised his eyes up —up above the loved faces that were around him, till they seemed to have found their Object; then there broke over his features a light and a smile, whose radiance seemed to be a reflection from heaven itself. "*Nunc dimittis servum tuum in pace, quia viderunt oculi mei salutare tuum.* My God, I thank Thee, now I die content. What joy! what joy!" The sunken eyes closed, and from beneath the lids tears streamed down the thin, white cheeks. It had been granted him to taste this ineffable consolation in recompense for his devotedness, and as a foretaste of that joy which only the Blessed know, when the results of persevering prayer and self-sacrifice shall be unveiled. Who shall say, the pure, deep joy, even in this life, which flows into the soul when it experiences beyond doubt that its trust has indeed "*not been confounded;*" when it "*tastes and sees*" that its prayer has been answered? But how is this joy increased a hundred-fold, when the object of the prayer is one which involves any of God's dearest interests, as was that for which Francis had prayed with so much ardour?

The gratitude, the happiness, which inundated his soul, were as a pledge of that endless joy of which so soon he was to be in possession. It was as "*the stream of the river which maketh the city of God joyful.*"

He remained for some time silent, his eyes closed, and his whole being apparently absorbed in the sentiments of profound thanksgiving which penetrated him. At length, looking at his father, he said : " Will you read me the letter, dear father, which has brought this blessed news ?"

The Colonel willingly complied, and not Francis only, but all who were present, listened with the deepest interest. It was from one personally known to the Colonel, informing him of the steps that had been already taken, and of the preparations that were actually being made for a College solely devoted to the formation of Priests for the Foreign Missions, and soliciting him, as a Catholic whose interest was well known in all that concerned the extension of the Church, to contribute to a work of so apostolical a character.

" I know," said Francis, when the letter was finished, "that you will help in this."

He held the Colonel's hand, and was looking up into his face. A tear fell upon his forehead from the old man's eyes. There was something so touching to see the dying Priest pleading, even to the last, for his Master's cause.

"My dear Francis," said the Colonel, in a voice broken with emotion, "You know how I value any work that has for its object the conversion of the Heathen, how *doubly* dear that object is to me *now*. Your dear mother's fortune, which, had you lived, at my death would have fallen to you, I shall not touch; neither will Stanislaus his share of it,—he has just asked me to give you this assurance. The whole will be devoted to the interests of the Foreign Missions. There could not be a nobler work of charity, or one certainly dearer to our hearts."

Francis held his father's hand in one of his own, and that of Stanislaus in the other, whilst, with an expression that spoke more eloquently than words, he looked up alternately into their faces.

What a moment that was! What a recompense for sufferings, and pain, and sharp disappointment, endured for the one great cause: and yet this joy was but the faintest foreshadowing of that which was so soon to dawn!

CHAPTER XIX.

Departure of the Missioner.—"Ite Missa est."

"There in the twilight, cold and grey,
Lifeless, but beautiful, he lay."

The night succeeding that day on which the events took place related in the preceding chapter, was a very anxious one for the inmates of the Manor.

A change appeared to have stolen over the invalid. He was no longer restless, neither did delirium occur at intervals, as before, although those who watched him perceived that he was suffering exceeding pain, whilst he was consumed with burning inward heat. But the calmness that was reflected on his features, and the stillness with which he suffered, seemed a figure of that high sanctity wherein the soul suffers martyrdom, and consumes gently and silently with the fire of love, contented in her anguish, because it is God's Will.

It was with difficulty the Colonel could be prevailed upon to take some repose, and it was not until Stanislaus, who, with the faithful Mary, was going to remain all night with Francis, promised to call him at the least sign of an immediate change, that at length he yielded.

As for Father Neville, notwithstanding his age, he would not leave the sick room, and would only submit to take some short repose on a couch from whence he could see any movement the invalid might make.

He resolved to celebrate the Holy Sacrifice at an earlier hour than usual, in order to ensure to the dying the Holy Viaticum, with the additional consolation of hearing Holy Mass.

Accordingly, about six o'clock, Father Neville stood before the altar in Francis's room, with little John de Britto at his side for acolyte, whilst the rest of the family, and several of the servants, knelt at a little distance. It was a touching scene,—that *last Mass* to which Francis was to unite himself on earth. He followed every part of it, repeating the words as if he himself were celebrating, and sometimes the vehemence of his devotion was such that he pronounced them audibly. After having received the Holy Viaticum, he entered into a profound recollection, and his soul continued henceforward to converse but with God.

The physician, who arrived in the early part of the morning, announced that he had evidently already commenced his agony, and that, in all probability, the end might be expected that day. All were wondering if he would speak to them again, and longing for a last look of recognition, as only the last look of the dying *can* be longed for. They had not long to wait. It was towards noon that Francis opened his eyes, and beheld his aged father and Father Neville standing close beside him, whilst Stanislaus and Mary stood on the other side of the bed.

The dying man made a movement with his hand towards the Colonel, took his hand, and kissed it, as he whispered: "Dear father, give me your last blessing, I am soon going."

For each he had some word of tender affection and grateful acknowledgment of their devotedness to him; then he murmured the name of his little god-son, John de Britto. Mary brought him, and lifted him up, that Francis might lay his hand upon his head, which he did with peculiar earnestness. Shortly after, he fell back again into recollection, in which began that utter solitude of the soul with God, which is the immediate precursor of death.

His eyes were not continuously closed: often they rested upon the crucifix, which he held tightly clasped in his hand; sometimes upon the distant sea stretching far away to the horizon; whilst at others he would appear entirely absorbed in the thought of the Mass, to which, throughout the whole of that day, he seemed to be uniting himself.

From time to time, Father Neville suggested to him some act of conformity or love of God and His holy will, especially when it was evident that some fresh access was augmenting his physical sufferings. On one of these occasions the old Priest said, gently: "Patience yet a little while, dear Francis,—the Mass is nearly ended."

A bright smile lit up the features of the dying at these words, which told how well they were comprehended. The words, "*Adveniat regnum tuum,*" "*Vere dignum et justum est,*" and "*Suscipe Sancta Trinitas hanc oblationem,*" were continually bursting from the lips that were quivering with the strength of the agony, whilst the sweat of death stood out in large beads upon his brow.

The day wore on, and the *Mass was not yet ended*. The evening sun was shedding its golden light once more across the sea, and streaming in at the window of the death-chamber. Suddenly, Francis turned towards the light, and his eyes, now fast becoming veiled, were riveted upon the golden pathway they had before so often followed. His white lips moved, and all around him listened with breathless attention to catch, if possible, the words that fell from them: "*Ita Pater quoniam sic fuit placitum ante Te.*" It was his final act of acquiescence in that Father's Will which had decreed for him a *living* martyrdom, in the sacrifice of his life's one glorious dream, and in the suffering he was to endure for the cause for which he had vowed to give that life. Father Neville began to say the prayers of the agonizing, in which all present joined, and it was evident that Francis was fully conscious, and was uniting.

Father Neville paused a moment before commencing the recommendation of the soul that was apparently close to its departure, for Francis seemed as if he wished to speak. The Father bent down his ear.

"Pray for me, and pray that my sacrifice may be acceptable—for—for *them*," were the broken words that fell from his lips.

"We are all praying for you, my child, and your sacrifice *is* accepted. I am going now to give you the last Absolution and Plenary Indulgence."

Francis clasped his crucifix with that convulsive movement which is so certain a precursor of death, and then, a few moments after the words of Absolution had ceased, he whispered the concluding prayer of the Holy Sacrifice: "*Placeat tibi Sancta Trinitas: and grant that the sacrifice which I, unworthy, have offered up in the sight of Thy Majesty, may be acceptable to Thee, and through Thy mercy be a propitiation for me, and all those for whom I have offered it.*" The words came brokenly, for his breath was failing fast, but they were audible enough to those who stood around.

Shortly after, his eyes seemed to rest upon some object they had found. A deep sigh and a groan burst from his lips, followed by these three words, "*Ite Missa est*," and in another minute all was over. His face was turned towards the window, through which the last golden beams of the setting sun were softly streaming. He had crossed a wider and a deeper ocean now than that upon which his dying eyes had rested, and had traversed another path than that track of gold across the waves which had so often been to him the figure of the way leading to the Eternal Shore.

The *life's sacrifice* was over now. The *vow* had been

accomplished. The *Missioner* had at last departed—not to the scene of labour, but to the promised land of his reward. Truly he had " *sown in tears,*" but who could say the number of the sheaves which his apostolate of suffering and of sacrifice had garnered into the Harvest Home above!

Two hours later he lay upon his bier, in the grey twilight of that fair spring evening, and all the various members of the household, as they came to watch that night beside him, could not but observe the almost heavenly beauty that rested upon his countenance, whereon the holiness and the self-sacrifice of his sacerdotal and apostolic soul seemed to have left its impress.

A few days later, and many Priests were assembled at the Manor. They came to testify, in following his remains to the tomb, their appreciation of the devotedness of that young life, which no human feeling had been capable of checking in its noble enterprise for the salvation of the Heathen.

The little picturesque cemetery wherein the members of the Willington family were interred, was about half a quarter of a mile from the house, situated on a slope from whence could be seen the whole range of sea that lay in the distance. Upon the coffin, which was borne upon the shoulders of Priests who had requested to perform this office, was the biretta,—that emblem of the *kingship* of God's Priests,—the stole, and some exquisite exotics, white and red, brought by Philip as a last mark of his affection, and woven by Mary's skilful hand into a graceful wreath. Upon the coffin-plate were read these words:

Francis John De Britto Willington,

PRIEST OF THE FOREIGN MISSIONS,

Died May 5th, 18—,

In the 28th year of his age, and the 4th of his Priesthood.

R. I. P.

"Desiderium animæ ejus tribuisti ei et voluntate labiorum ejus non fraudasti eum."—Ps. xx.

A plain stone cross marks the spot where he lies, in the burial-place of his ancestors, instead of being laid in some distant land, as his life's dream so long had pictured to him, and which had seemed so nearly realized; but the inscription upon the cross, similar to that upon the coffin, which we have just recorded, is no less truthful than if he had actually crossed the seas and had died in the *visible* service of the souls for whom he thirsted.

"Truly," said Father Neville to the Colonel, as they stood one day at the foot of the grave over which the green grass was now waving; "truly he *was given his heart's desire,* even in this world, for if ever a vow was accepted, surely his was; and thus '*the will of his lips has not been withheld from him.*' If he has not died the *violent* death of a martyr, his martyrdom was no less real, and I believe that he has indeed won, by his devoted apostolate of suffering and self-sacrifice, the palm and the crown of a martyr."

"He has found his poor Heathen *là haut*, converted into *redeemed* souls," said the Colonel; "and, I doubt not, many and many among them will recognize him as that which he loved to call himself, and in effect *was*, the '*Father and Servant of the Blacks;*'" and then he added, his aged eyes filling with tears as he spoke, "I do not regret to have given him for such a cause."

"Neither, dear friend, will you regret it hereafter," replied Father Neville, earnestly; "*you* also will have *your* share in the good work for which he lived and died."

Seldom a day passed without the grave of Francis being visited by some of the family. Stanislaus' children brought fresh flowers to lay thereon, and Philip never failed to bring exotics of the kind Francis had loved best, whilst the faithful old man took wholly to himself the care of the shrubs and flowers planted around the grave.

What more remains to be said? Captain Warnford still remains in India, ever the same brave officer and true-hearted Catholic. Whenever he is able to render any service to European Missioners, he rejoices in doing so, and many have been the difficulties smoothed away for them in the course of their ministry by the influence and intervention of the courteous and zealous English officer, the report of whose many good actions in the interest of Priests, and in the conversion of the Pagans, has travelled back even to English circles. He has not ceased to correspond with the family at the Manor, and great was his grief on hearing of the death of Francis, whom he had hoped to meet in India as a Missioner. If he lives to return to England, he says he shall go and end his days near that spot where the happiest hours of his life had been spent.

John de Britto, Francis's little god-son, has trodden in the footsteps of his holy uncle. At an early age, he showed symptoms, such as Francis had done in his boyhood, of a future vocation for the Foreign Missions. The altar in the wood, and "*Sancian*," and other traces of Francis's early propensities were still kept up, and the apostolic seed cast into that young soul by his uncle seemed to have fallen upon fertile soil. He is now a youth of eighteen, in whom is fast developing a true vocation such as was his uncle's.

Miss Margaret no longer declaims against "*Priests leaving England,*" when the "*charity of Christ presses*" them to do so, for the salvation of their perishing brethren across the sea, and many of those who formerly shared in Miss Margaret's sentiments, have learnt to believe and acknowledge that when divine vocation calls men to labour for the Heathen, it is in vain to endeavour to keep them at home.

Many, too, at last begin to think that, as Christ died

for all, it matters not in what portion of the great vineyard we labour, so only we labour in the special portion that is allotted to us; and that, after all, the surest means of drawing down blessings upon our own dear country, is to be generous in contributing to break the Bread of Life to the millions of poor Heathen on far-off shores.

"THAT THEY MAY KNOW THEE, THE ONLY TRUE GOD, AND JESUS CHRIST, WHOM THOU HAST SENT." (S. John xvii. 3.)

THE MISSIONER'S SONG.

"*Ignem veni mittere in terram, et quid volo nisi ut accendatur?*"

Hark! the Heart of Jesus whispers
   Words It breathed in ages past!
"Fire I came on earth to kindle,—
   Fire o'er all the land to cast."

Hasten forth to tell the story
   Of the Heart that broke with love,
Of Its mystic life amongst us,
   Of Its pleading far above.

Let the watchword of Ignatius
   Burn into our very soul—
"*Ad majorem Dei gloriam,*"—
   Let it urge us to the goal.

With a Xavier's zeal all burning,
   Hasten to far distant lands:
Bear across the sea glad tidings,
   Bear it o'er the desert sands.

With a Claver's strong compassion
   For the black despiséd race,
Go ye forth with hearts as loving,
   And his blessed footsteps trace.

With the ardour of Spinola,
   Go and face the cruel stake :
Burning love will make you triumph
   Over death, for Jesus' sake.

In the forest, in the jungle,
   Where " the white man" scarce hath trod,
There a golden harvest waits you,—
   Harvest for the Heart of God.

Happy you to whom 'tis given
   First to raise on barbarous lands
Altars where the Mystic Victim
   Pleads and blesses by your hands.

You are they who " *on the mountains*
   Beautiful " to God appear ;
You are they whose noble mission
   Men and angels both revere.

See the light of knowledge dawning
   In the wild and savage eye,
As you name the *true* " *Great Spirit*,"
   Dwelling far above the sky.

See again the love light kindle
   In that now tear-moistened eye,
As you tell him of the Saviour
   Who, *for love of him*, would die.

The Missioner's Song.

Go, and with the Heart of Jesus,—
    With Its love for every race,
Win the souls for whom It thirsteth,
    Clasp them in that love's embrace.

Let no selfish interest chain you,—
    Love of native land, or home;
Let the thirst for God's dear glory,
    Lure you where He's yet unknown.

Carry far the wondrous story,
    To the souls who yearn for love;
Tell them of the love, all deathless,
    Of their God in heaven above.

Go then, forth, O Christ's apostles!
    Bearing light to Heathen lands,
Whilst by prayer with you united,
    We to Heaven will raise our hands.

Go and break the hateful boundaries
    Men have set to Jesus' reign;
Go and tell His Heart's own story,
    Preach it wide o'er sea and plain.

Human hearts will prove resistless
    'Gainst such love, where'er they be:
Thus the Sacred Heart shall triumph,
    And shall reign "from sea to sea."

St. Joseph's Society of the Sacred Heart

FOR

FOREIGN MISSIONS.

Try to realize to yourself—you who live in the possession of the Faith and of the Holy Sacraments—that there are at this present time upon the globe 600,000,000, some statisticians say 900,000,000, of Pagans and Infidels.

Of these nearly 200,000,000 are our fellow-subjects.

Every day 50,000 Pagans and Infidels pass into the presence of the awful tribunal of the Sovereign Judge. What instruction have any of them ever received at our hands on their duties to the Great God?—what knowledge has been carried to them of the Redemption by the Most Precious Blood—shed for them as for us?

What have you hitherto done to become a Messenger of Peace, an Angel of Salvation to these unhappy millions who pass their days and die in alienation of soul from their Supreme God?

We—the Catholics of this Empire—have a great responsibility before God. We are doubly bound—bound by the common law of Charity—bound by our national position and power—to carry the torch of Faith into the darkness of the heathen nations.

But for the personal zeal of some of the sons of S. Benedict and of S. Ignatius in years past, the old English Catholic tradition of zeal for propagating the Faith abroad might almost have died out amongst us. Thanks and honour to those who revived and kept alive the Apostolic spirit of your early ancestors! Before either England or Ireland had been fully converted, their Missioners were speeding into foreign lands. Faith and charity burn to communicate themselves.

You are now all invited—clergy and laity, young and old, poor and rich—all to help to educate Foreign Missioners.

All may become Members of St. Joseph's Foreign Missionary Society of the Sacred Heart.

The conditions are simple:—1st. To give an alms every year for the Education of the Missioners of the Society; 2nd. To be inscribed on the register of the Society (for this, send your name to the Very Rev. P. Benoit, St. Joseph's College, Mill Hill, London, N.W.)

St. Joseph's Society has sent out nearly thirty Missioners already to America and India; and thirty or forty more Students are now preparing in St. Joseph's College for the same Apostolic career. They leave Europe for life, to spend themselves and be spent in the salvation of the unevangelized races.

Your co-operation is invited in this Apostolic work. Funds are urgently needed to obtain firing, clothes, and food, for the Students in the College.

Funds are needed in order that a larger number of Students may be accepted.

MISSIONERS OF THE SACRED HEART!—Their name alone must touch the hearts of all who wish to spread the love and knowledge of their Lord through the distant regions of the earth, and who burn to atone and make reparation for the insults heaped upon Him in His Sacred Humanity.

Perhaps, to some of those who read these lines, the thought may come, "But what can I do?"

Be you rich or poor, you can each do something, deny yourself something, suffer something, offer up something, for the love of our dear Lord, and for the spreading of His truth among those who know it not. Away with the narrow-minded view that charity should not only begin at home but stop there. Are not all souls His? Whether under the polar sky or in the torrid zone, all have been bought by His Precious Blood. He is waiting to garner *all* into His fold; and He waits for us—for our co-operation—for our work—for our prayers and mortifications—above all, for our hearts—to win these souls to Him.

Our Holy Father has granted an Indulgence of 300 days to every contributor, whenever he shall say three Glorias with the invocations, "St. Joseph, pray for the Heathen." Also a Plenary Indulgence once a month, if, in his thanksgiving after Holy Communion, he shall pray for the conversion of the Heathen.

In support of the above appeal, and in confirmation of the truth of the evangelic word: "*Date et dabitur vobis,*" it will be permitted us to quote the following from "*Le Messager du Cœur de Jesus,*" for November, 1878:

"I must relate to you also a *trait* of the great faith and rare penetration of Cardinal Mathieu," writes Monseigneur Besson, the Bishop of Nîmes: "In the first years of his episcopate, at Besançon, he gave his Priests, not without repugnance, to the

Religious Congregations and to the Foreign Missions. It seemed to him that this was to despoil himself with too little foresight, and that it was necessary, before all, to secure for the future a sufficient clergy for his own diocese. After some years of trials, he changed his sentiment, and the diocese changed its aspect. The more departures for the Missions that he authorized, the more subjects God gave him for his Church. For one Missionary who had obtained permission to depart, two or three Seminarists were seen to come forth from the same village.

"*The great ecclesiastical prosperity of the diocese of Besançon dates from the day when its sons have directed themselves towards the distant Missions, in order to evangelize the peoples still buried in the shadows of death.* The document which you saw, and which is dated 1851, counts 45 Missionaries. The Ordo of 1878 counts 70, and this does not include the exact number of religious vocations which have sprung up in this beautiful diocese.

"Probably there are not less than 200 Priests,—Jesuits, Dominicans, Capuchins, Oblates, Marists, Brothers of Mary, Missionaries and Religious of all kinds and of all names, which belong to the diocese by birth and by education, and who are the flower of the country, the *élite* of the sacerdotal army, and, as said Pius IX., the most courageous, the most cheerful, the most enterprising, and the most fertile of apostles. *And despite this legion given to Foreign Missions, the diocese of Besançon is so rich, that it can lend to the other dioceses of France subjects full of merit. So true it is that the more we give to the Lord, the more the Lord delights in restoring to us!*

"It is in these sentiments that I have just blessed, however great may be my distress, the vocation of a young cleric who has quitted the diocese of Nîmes, in order to enter the Foreign Missions, and who will make at Paris the vow of his sub-diaconate, to carry into Cochin China the devotedness of his great soul. I have not retained him for my diocese, *persuaded that his sacrifice, which is so complete, will obtain for me recruits for all the altars of the native land.*"

May these noble sentiments find an echo in many a heart in our own dear country, awakening them to the cries of distress that come to us from across the seas, where the fields are white for the harvest, but where the labourers are so few, that *millions of souls* are perishing for whom the Heart of Jesus thirsts and pleads! Let us listen to Its voice, pleading with us from the silent Tabernacle,—pleading too, within our own souls,—pleading for our co-operation in His dearest interest, for which He prayed to His Eternal Father the night before His Passion, "that they may know Thee, the only true God, and Jesus Christ whom Thou hast sent," "*Ut cognoscant te, solum Deum verum, et quem misisti, Jesum Christum.*" (S. Joan. xvii. 3.) And for Priests, and alms, and prayers, and sacrifices that we shall have given for the evangelization of the poor Heathen, a hundred-fold will be shed into our own bosom. "*Date et dabitur vobis.*" Then will "*the desert places be built up*" again in our own loved land, and "*the land that was desolate shall be glad, and the wilderness shall rejoice and shall flourish like the lily.*" (Isa. xxxv. 1.)

WORKS RECENTLY ISSUED
BY
Thomas Richardson and Son,
LONDON AND DERBY.

THE PRIMACY OF S. PETER demonstrated from the Liturgy of the Greco-Russian Church. With an Appendix containing several Documents. By the REV. C. TONDINI DE QUARENGHI, Barnabite.
Demy 8vo, price 3s.

THE NUN OF THE ORDER OF THE VISITATION, by name, **Anne Madeleine de Remusat,** of Marseilles, called the Second Margaret Mary of the Sacred Heart. *Foolscap 8vo, price 3s. 6d.*

The **SACRAMENTALS** of the **HOLY CATHOLIC CHURCH**; being Instructions on the Prayers and Benedictions of the Church. By the Rev. W. J. BARRY. *Royal 32mo, price 1s. 6d.*

SPIRITUAL EXERCISES OF MARY. A Sequel to the "Path of Mary." *Royal 32mo, price 2s.*

THE PATH OF MARY. A New Edition, with Additions. Approved by the Bishop of Nottingham.
Royal 32mo, price 8d.; bound in cloth, 1s.

MIDDLEFORD HALL. A Tale for Children. Edited by the Authoress of "ELLERTON PRIORY," "CLAIRE MAITLAND," &c. A most entertaining and instructive volume. *Foolscap 8vo, price 3s.*

Shortly will be Ready, in one thick volume, demy 8vo.

THE LIFE OF DOM BARTHOLOMEW OF THE MARTYRS, Religious of the Order of St. Dominic, Archbishop of Braga, in Portugal. Translated from his Biographies, written in Portuguese, French, and Spanish, by five different Authors, of whom the first and most eminent was FATHER LEWIS OF GRENADA. By LADY HERBERT.

Richardson and Son's New Publications.

MINIATURE WORKS OF DEVOTIONAL AND PRACTICAL PIETY.

Demy 18mo, handsomely bound, price Sixpence each.

Comfort for Mourners. By S. Francis de Sales. From his Letters.

Stations of the Passion, as made in Jerusalem. And Devotions on the Passion, from the Prayers of S. Gertrude.

Holy Will of God: a short Rule of Perfection. By the Rev. Benedict Canfield, Capuchin Friar.

The Our Father: Meditations on the Lord's Prayer. By S. Teresa.

Quiet of the Soul. To which is added, Cure for Scruples.

NEW SHILLING SERIES OF
CATHOLIC TALES.

Foolscap 8vo. handsomely bound in cloth, with black printing on side, and lettered in gold.

Elsie Mc'Dermott, the Little Watercress Girl By M. A. Pennell.

Hilda's Victory; and Una's Repentance. By M. F. S.

Little Musicians who became Great Masters. FIRST SERIES. Translated by Mrs. Townsend.

Little Musicians who became Great Masters. SECOND SERIES. Together with the Flowers of Childhood. Translated by Mrs. Townsend.

Ellerton Priory. By the Author of "Claire Maitland."

Little Flower Basket. By Canon Schmid.

Search for Happiness, and other Tales for Young People.

Marie, the Fisherman's Daughter.

Godfrey, the Little Hermit. By Canon Schmid.

Forest Pony, Gipsy Boy, and other Tales. By Lady Elizabeth Douglas.

The Gift, containing three interesting Tales.

www.ingramcontent.com/pod-product-compliance
Lightning Source LLC
Chambersburg PA
CBHW020305240426
43673CB00039B/708